GW01271836

A Japanese Constellation Pedro Gadanho
Toyo Ito, Kazuyo Sejima, SANAA, Ryue Nishizawa, Sou Fujimoto,
Akihisa Hirata, Junya Ishigami

The Museum of Modern Art, New York

7 Foreword —Glenn D. Lowry

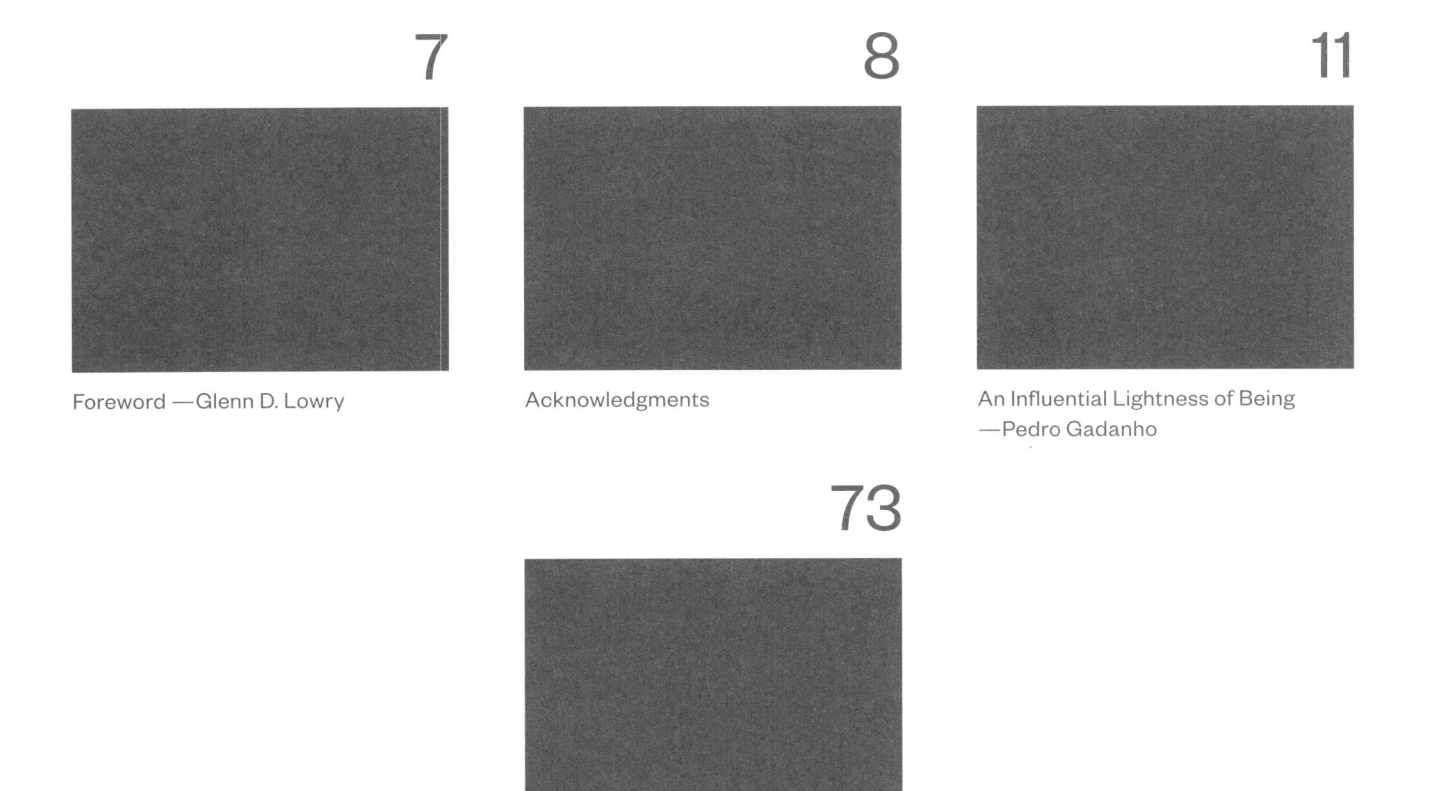

8 Acknowledgments

11 An Influential Lightness of Being —Pedro Gadanho

73 Magical Spatial Inversion —Terunobu Fujimori

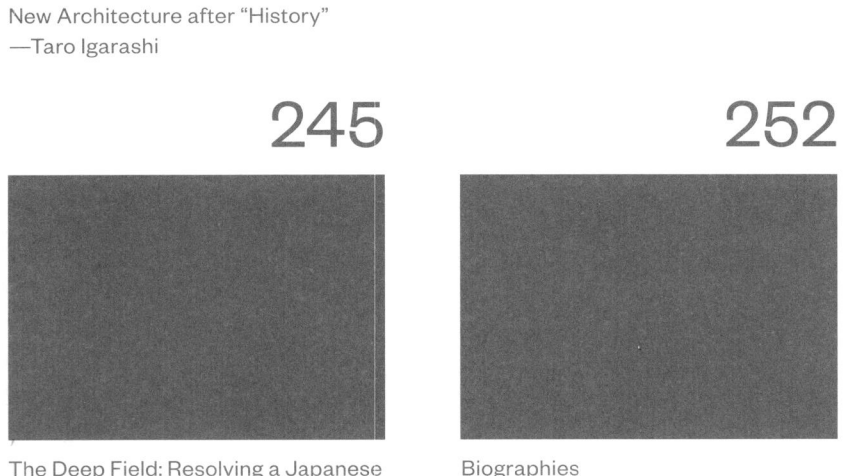

189 New Architecture after "History" —Taro Igarashi

245 The Deep Field: Resolving a Japanese Constellation —Julian Worrall

252 Biographies

Table of Contents

21 Toyo Ito

79 Kazuyo Sejima

105 SANAA

139 Ryue Nishizawa

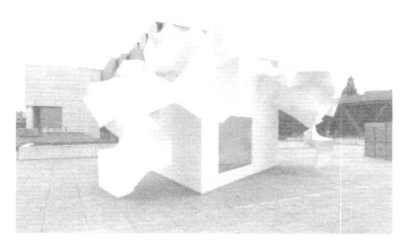

165 Sou Fujimoto

195 Akihisa Hirata

221 Junya Ishigami

Foreword

The Museum of Modern Art has interwoven Japanese architecture into its presentations from its inaugural architecture exhibition of 1932, *Modern Architecture: International Exhibition*, in which Mamoru Yamada's Tokyo Central Telegraph Office (1925) represented Japan's burgeoning modernism. In 1954, Junzo Yoshimura's full-scale post-and-beam demonstration house transformed the Museum's sculpture garden, bringing to its environs a modernism less familiar to New York audiences. The third and last of the House in the Garden series (1949–55), following projects by Marcel Breuer and Gregory Ain, Yoshimura's house combined seventeenth-century precedents with traditional *shoin* building techniques.

The very walls of the Museum are now the beneficiaries of this lineage in the graceful canopies of Yoshio Taniguchi's 2004 extension that frame the sculpture garden. Together with the collection's representation of the Japanese postwar turn to utopic, technoscientific schemes for cities, exemplified by Metabolist projects like Kisho Kurokawa's Helix City (1961) and Fumihiko Maki's proposed megastructures, as well as the imprint of Japanese influence in works from Frank Lloyd Wright to Rem Koolhaas, this history runs through the Museum's holdings. *A Japanese Constellation* introduces a contemporary chapter, turning to an architecture both in conversation with and responding to these earlier projects.

With *A Japanese Constellation*, one of the Museum's first exhibitions in ten years to focus on architecture from a particular country, and the first dedicated solely to Japanese practitioners, curator Pedro Gadanho focuses on a small cluster of contemporary Japanese architects working within the larger field, exploring their formal inventiveness and close professional relationships to frame a radical model of practice in the twenty-first century.

Unique in focus, *A Japanese Constellation*'s forty-four projects represent a diverse panorama of work from small domestic projects to museums. Presented in models, drawings, and projected slideshows, the work highlights the significant structural innovations and use of transparent and lightweight materials, while foregrounding the architects' refreshing commitment to the social lives of their buildings, reviving a social conscience that characterized earlier avant-gardes. Drawing on Japanese material traditions, the gallery design casts aside walls for soft partitions of semitranslucent fabric, which act as surfaces for multimedia and provide an immersive visual experience.

The luminous presentation in the gallery is complemented by the catalogue's generous color portfolios and critical essays by curators, architects, and scholars writing both from within and outside of Japan, which situate this architectural genealogy within a longer chronology of Japanese practice and, more broadly, a tangled inheritance of global modernity. *A Japanese Constellation* promises to be an indispensable resource for practitioners, students of architecture, and the general public.

I congratulate Pedro Gadanho, Director, Museum of Art, Architecture and Technology, Lisbon, for his engagement in theorizing new directions in contemporary architecture. Begun during his appointment as Curator of Contemporary Architecture at MoMA, *A Japanese Constellation* has been long in the making. His dedication and insight, together with the support of Phoebe Springstubb, Curatorial Assistant, Department of Architecture and Design, have brought this catalogue and exhibition to fruition. On behalf of the Trustees and staff of the Museum, I am grateful to the E. Rhodes and Leona B. Carpenter Foundation, The Japan Foundation, and Chris A. Wachenheim for major support in funding this endeavor. I deeply appreciate the generous funding provided by Obayashi Corporation, Kajima Corporation, Shimizu Corporation, Takenaka Corporation, the Graham Foundation for Advanced Studies in the Fine Arts, Kumagai Gumi, and The Obayashi Foundation. I extend sincere thanks for additional funding provided by MoMA's Annual Exhibition Fund and special thanks to Muji. The Dale S. And Norman Mills Leff Publication Fund provided essential support for this book.

Glenn D. Lowry
Director, The Museum of Modern Art

A Japanese Constellation highlights a luminous configuration of architects; the realization of this ambitious exhibition and catalogue would not have been possible without a corresponding group of collaborators who dedicated innumerable hours and expertise. At The Museum of Modern Art, we are grateful to the leadership and counsel of Glenn D. Lowry, Director; Ramona Bannayan, Senior Deputy Director for Exhibitions, Collections, and Programs; Todd Bishop, Senior Deputy Director, External Affairs; James Gara, Chief Operating Officer; Peter Reed, Senior Deputy Director for Curatorial Affairs; and Trish Jeffers, Director of Human Resources.

The exhibition has been the beneficiary of a generous group of supporters. We extend sincere thanks to the E. Rhodes and Leona B. Carpenter Foundation, the Japan Foundation, Chris A. Wachenheim, Obayashi Corporation, Kajima Corporation, Shimizu Corporation, Takenaka Corporation, the Graham Foundation for Advanced Studies in the Fine Arts, Kumagai Gumi, and the Obayashi Foundation for major support in funding *A Japanese Constellation*. In addition, we deeply appreciate the in-kind support from MUJI, which provided the materials for the exhibition's fabric walls and furniture.

The project is indebted to the group of architects featured in the exhibition. They were extremely generous and helpful hosts during trips to Tokyo, gave us unfettered access to their studios, entrusted us with their models and drawings, and accommodated the sometimes unpredictable process of putting together an exhibition. Together with Phoebe Springstubb, Curatorial Assistant, I extend warm thanks to the individuals at each office: Toyo Ito, Julia Li, Yuma Ota, and Maika Takagaki of Toyo Ito & Associates, Architects; Kazuyo Sejima, Ryue Nishizawa, Riccardo Cannatà, Tommy Haddock, Kenichi Fujisawa, and Shohei Yoshida of Kazuyo Sejima & Associates, Office of Ryue Nishizawa, and SANAA; Sou Fujimoto, Hugh Hsu, Nikki Minemura, and Masaki Iwata of Sou Fujimoto Architects; Akihisa Hirata, Hitomi Namiki, and Yuko Tonogi of Akihisa Hirata Architecture Office; Junya Ishigami, Haruka Shoji, and Wataru Shinji of Junya.Ishigami + Associates. We thank as well the individuals at each office, too many to enumerate here, whose efforts during the lead-up to this exhibition and before were no doubt essential. In addition, we are grateful to Reiko Sudo of NUNO, whose advice and expertise was instrumental in the early stages of planning the exhibition's fabric walls. We offer sincere thanks to lenders Waverly Lowell, Environmental Design Archives, College of Environmental Design, University of California, Berkeley; and Sharon and Bob Prince of Grace Farms, who generously supported the fabrication of a new model for the exhibition that has enriched it immensely.

The Department of Publications, led by Christopher Hudson, has been critical to the success of this catalogue. We thank Marc Sapir, Production Director, who both shepherded us toward meeting production deadlines and, with a sharp eye, attended to the many color images reproduced here. Charles Kim, Associate Publisher, kept us on budget, while David Frankel, Editorial Director, and Emily Hall, Editor, offered editorial counsel. We are especially grateful to Sarah Resnick, the catalogue's steadfast editor, who has been an incredibly attentive and patient critic, navigating essays composed in different languages and across time zones, juggling the many moving parts, and shaping the final content. Design work by Edwin van Gelder of Mainstudio brings the book together in a lucid and singular layout.

We would also like to thank dedicated colleagues around the Museum who have lent their time and expertise to the exhibition. We thank Kim Mitchell, Chief Communications Officer; Margaret Doyle, Director of Communications; and Paul Jackson, Communications Manager, for ensuring the exhibition's public presence and press. Lauren Stakias, Director, Exhibition and Program Funding; Bobby Kean, Assistant Director, Exhibition Funding; and their team have been instrumental in securing funding. We express sincere thanks to Rachel Kim, Associate Coordinator, Department of Exhibition Planning and Administration, for managing the exhibition's resources and budget. We are grateful to Caitlin Kelly, Senior Registrar Assistant, and Steven Wheeler, Associate Registrar, Collections, Department of Collection Management and Exhibition Registration, for expertly coordinating the logistics, transport, and care of models that traveled so far. We are beholden to Roger Griffith, Associate Sculpture Conservator, Department of Conservation, who went above and beyond in the complex conservation of the models, among other things, traveling across the Atlantic and advising on the purchase of live plants. Erika Mosier, Conservator, guided us in the care of the exhibition's delicate works on paper.

The Departments of Graphic Design and Exhibition Design and Production have found inventive ways to convey the exhibition's concept. We extend our appreciation to Matthew Cox, Assistant Production Manager, who oversaw the installation and engineered the intricate finishing and hanging details of its translucent fabric walls. Aaron Harrow, Design Manager, and Mike Gibbons, A/V Technician, were a superb A/V team, composing and expertly choreographing the exhibition's multimedia projections. In the Department of Graphic Design, Ingrid Chou, Associate Creative Director; Derek Flynn, Art Director; Claire Corey, Production Manager; and Danielle Hall, Designer, created an articulate and vivid graphic identity for the exhibition.

In the Department of Architecture and Design, we are deeply appreciative of the support and valuable feedback offered by the entire staff throughout the project. I am grateful to Barry Bergdoll, Curator, for enthusiastically welcoming and supporting this project upon my arrival in 2012 as the newly appointed Curator of Contemporary Architecture at MoMA. I want to express special gratitude to Phoebe Springstubb, Curatorial Assistant, who provided tireless and dedicated support during the four-year-long curatorial endeavor, including, among other things, authoring the descriptive project texts in this publication and acting as the critical link between the architects and collaborators in the production of both the catalogue and exhibition. Emma Presler, Department Manager; Paul Galloway, Collection Specialist; and Pamela Popeson, Collection Preparator, have offered invaluable assistance and advice. A dedicated group of interns made essential contributions at various points during the preparations: Aslihan Gunhan compiled core research informing the exhibition; Anna Sutherland translated texts and researched images; Anna Blair, stepping in as the project went into production, provided careful work on image permissions, proofing, and the organization of exhibition slideshows.

Additional colleagues across the Museum provided support. Pablo Helguera, Director, Adult and Academic Education; Jess Van Nostrand, Assistant Director, Exhibition Programs and Gallery Initiatives; and Sarah Kennedy, Associate Educator, Lab Programs, ably organized the exhibition's public program. Sara Bodinson, Director, Interpretation, Research, and Digital Learning, and Maria Marchenkova, Assistant Editor, Publications, were thoughtful readers and editorial guides on all exhibition text. Rebecca Stokes, Director, Digital Initiatives, and Gretchen Scott, Building Project Digital Marketing Manager, Department of Marketing, brought the project to the enthusiastic attention of the users of Instagram. Tunji Adeniji, Director of Facilities and Safety; Tyrone Wyllie, Director of Security; Rob Jung, Manager; Sarah Wood, Assistant Manager; and Tom Krueger, Assistant Manager, Art Handling and Preparation, have been indispensable to the management of operations, in-house transportation, installation, and security.

Lastly, we wish to acknowledge the thoughtful contributions of authors Terunobu Fujimori, Taro Igarashi, and Julian Worrall to this publication.

Pedro Gadanho
Director, Museum of Art, Architecture and Technology, Lisbon

An Influential Lightness of Being: Thoughts on a Constellation of Contemporary Japanese Architects
Pedro Gadanho

Prelude

As I was beginning work on this text in the spring of 2015, the Solomon R. Guggenheim Foundation announced the winners of a competition for a new museum in Helsinki with pomp and circumstance (fig. 1). According to a museum press release, the call attracted more entries than any of its kind in history, with 1,715 submissions from nearly eighty countries. Yet what captured my attention was the fact that the young French-Japanese firm awarded the commission, Moreau Kusunoki Architectes (est. 2011), is directed by disciples of Japan's SANAA (est. 1995), Kengo Kuma (born 1954), and Shigeru Ban (born 1957), whose architecture has been met with wide acclaim. This was, to my mind, yet another sign of the influence contemporary Japanese architects wield over the discipline worldwide. Moreover, their impact was escalating as the work of global architects began to be received with a new mood. As the vice chairman of the city of Helsinki's executive board said to the *New York Times* on the occasion, "It's not the fashion to create 'wow' architecture anymore,"[1] alluding to Frank Gehry's design for the Guggenheim Bilbao almost two decades before. Cast against the expressive flamboyancy of the American museum's first outpost, the submission by this virtually unknown duo of young architects was distinctly contextual, embracing local traditions and blending with the existing city. Mark Wigley, jury chair and professor and former dean of the Graduate School of Architecture, Planning and Preservation at Columbia University, told the *Times* that the proposal "kind of undoes the monumentality of most museums."[2] While the invariable, sometimes pharaonic styles of so-called starchitects—architects whose worldwide celebrity and acclaim have transformed them into idols of design—were gradually coming under attack, the subtle but influential sensitivity of some Japanese architects was emerging through the crevices of the previous establishment and flourishing.

Architecture for the Twenty-First Century

Society is undergoing shifts that are far more pragmatic and radical than we even imagine, so I harbor no frustrations concerning such a development, nor do I even think to despair over it. I have, therefore, but one interest: the question of whether architecture as architecture is feasible in such times.

—Toyo Ito[3]

As was the case across various fields in Japan during the early twentieth century, architects, too, had looked to Western culture to inspire change within the country's deeply ingrained traditions. As Terunobu Fujimori recounts elsewhere in this book (p. 73), in the first half of the twentieth century, a number of architects from Japan worked with some of Europe and the United States' most important modernists. Eventually, these Japanese apprentices would bring home innovative materials and a novel interest in functionalism, borrowings that would in part serve to fulfill ambitions of modernization across Japanese society. But the influence wasn't merely unidirectional: classical Japanese art and architecture had for some time generated considerable fascination among early modernists in the West. For those architects privileging both clarity of design and functionality over ornament—including masters such as Frank Lloyd Wright (1867–1959), Bruno Taut (1880–1938), and Walter Gropius (1883–1969)—traditional architecture from Japan offered a unique aesthetic, its undecorated geometric constructions and refined spatial qualities highly unusual. This mutual curiosity fomented a prolonged exchange between Japanese and Western architecture throughout the twentieth century.[4]

The resulting architectural cross-pollinations, the products of a fruitful give-and-take between two distinct conceptions of space, assumed different forms in the postwar period. During the 1960s, for instance, the Japanese Metabolists, as much as figures such as Kenzo Tange (1913–2005) or Arata Isozaki (born 1931), absorbed impulses from the Western avant-garde (fig. 2). They rose to prominence in Japanese society and eventually captured the interest of many forward-thinking architects elsewhere.[5] Two decades later, in the 1980s, the country's development of a local but significant variant of postmodernism not only aligned many Japanese architects with their Western counterparts; it also influenced architectural styles in the international arena.

In the 1990s, the circumstances were suited once again for Japanese architecture to become a reference for architects outside Japan. As an intensely metropolitan culture thrived in Tokyo and other major Japanese cities, the nation's architects found themselves immersed in a global culture as much as in an urban society fronting numerous trends that would come to mark the start of the twenty-first century— from the explosion of consumer culture to the omnipresence of information to the increasing erraticism and instability of national and global economic cycles.⁶ Japanese architecture anticipated and explored the ways in which the discipline could mirror the problems and aspirations of a new social condition.

As the twentieth century transitioned into the twenty-first, a new crop of Japanese architects found international acclaim. The elegant restraint and precise materiality of Tadao Ando's (born 1941) "critical regionalism"⁷ and the technical optimism and spatial innovation of Toyo Ito's (born 1941) conceptualism rendered Japanese architects influential once again in the global arena. Working at the crossroads of technological and social change, many of these architects intimated design languages that offered refuge from the frantic pace of urbanization; others, conversely, embraced the imaginative possibilities of "things to come." The subsequent generation of architects, among them Kuma, Kazuyo Sejima (born 1956), and Ban, respectively explored the renewal of tradition, of radical spatial possibilities, and of the innovative potential of sustainable design. The global recognition of Japan's architects skyrocketed; in no other national context would a group of architects achieve such high acclaim for their regional characteristics. Shortly after earlier masters Tange and Fumihiko Maki (born 1928, fig. 3) won the Pritzker Architecture Prize, each of the aforementioned architects became laureates of the profession's highest-ranking honor, with the exception of Kuma.⁸

Ito, in particular, was highly conscious of the socioeconomic transformations around him, and was keen to use this awareness to propel and sustain his architectural thinking. In the controversial yet essential manifesto quoted in this section's epigraph—authored, it is worth noting, in the wake of the country's 1980s asset-price bubble economy—Ito foresees the media frenzy that would increasingly mark the reception of high-end architecture. "Today, architecture is being constructed and consumed at a tremendous pace," Ito wrote. "Thus, we have no choice but to stand before the sea of consumption, immerse ourselves, and swim through it to discover what lies on the far shore."⁹ Taking a critical stance toward the previous wave of Japanese avant-garde architects, who achieved national and international acclaim only to abandon their utopian ideals,¹⁰ Ito urged his contemporaries to retain experimentation as an essential trait of what he called a "vibrant and stimulating" architecture that is "generated at the margins," and thus distinguishes itself from mass processes of production and consumption.¹¹

Embracing postmodernism's semiotic diversity rather than its style,¹² Ito's proposals for a nonspecific architecture driven by an avant-garde impetus and a quintessentially modern agenda would mold the interests of a constellation of Japanese architects extending more than three generations. The premise of this book, and the related exhibition at The Museum of Modern Art, is precisely that this lineage of architects both affirms and heightens the allure of Japanese architecture worldwide. Yet, the book also presents a set of architectural positions that may be considered an important model for the architecture of the twenty-first century—not least for this model's rearrangement of hierarchical relationships among architects themselves.

Reinstating the Architectural Avant-Garde

Architecture that is modern in style only no longer has the power to change society. Architecture that is recognized only by architects and not by the public has no future. I believe that an architecture that truly has the power to reform society today must channel its critical power into a different form of proposal.

—Toyo Ito¹³

The international influence of contemporary Japanese architecture in the 1990s followed on postmodernist debates that polarized around a regression of architecture to its more conservative stylistic roots and a contrasting desire to prolong the modernist project. Although in Europe and the United States postmodernist architects embraced either historicism or its nemesis, deconstructivist architecture,¹⁴ in Japan architects responded instead to the increasing omnipresence of popular urban culture. As architectural theorist Charles Jencks said of Ito and other Tokyo practitioners during this era, their embrace of the city as a "theatre of signs and symbols" reiterated the emergence of semiotics during the 1970s.¹⁵ In an interview conducted shortly after the turn of the century, Ito suggested that architecture must act as a "media suit," by which he means, in his own words, as a "figuration of [the] information vortex."¹⁶ Following Marshall McLuhan's theory that clothes and shelter act as an extension of our skin—that is, as a means to adjust to the natural environment—Ito claimed that contemporary architecture should serve as "a means to adjust ourselves to the information environment."¹⁷

Fig. 1: Moreau Kusunoki Architectes (France, est. 2011). Guggenheim Helsinki Museum. Proposal. 2015. View from the north square. Fig. 2: Arata Isozaki (Japanese, born 1931). Re-ruined Hiroshima, Hiroshima. Project. 1968. Perspective: ink and gouache with cut-and-pasted gelatin silver print on gelatin silver print, 13 7/8 × 36 7/8" (35.2 × 93.7 cm). The Museum of Modern Art, New York. Gift of The Howard Gilman Foundation. Fig. 3: Fumihiko Maki (Japanese, born 1928). Golgi Structures. Project. 1967. Plexiglass and acrylic, 5 3/4 × 12 3/4 × 10 7/8" (14.6 × 32.4 × 27.6 cm). The Museum of Modern Art, New York. Gift of the architect in honor of Philip Johnson. Fig. 4: Kazuyo Sejima (Japanese, born 1956). Saishunkan Seiyaku Women's Dormitory, Kumamoto City, Japan. 1990–91. Scale model 1:100. Acrylic resin, 3 1/2 × 27 5/8" (8.9 × 70.2 × 70.2 cm). The Museum of Modern Art, New York. Gift of the architect

fig. 3

fig. 4

12

What began as a spontaneous response to a fast-changing urban environment would soon prompt a return to avant-garde ideals in Japan, an updated version of the radicalism found in early twentieth-century modernism. To be sure, the transformation wasn't immediate. There was, for instance, a period in which these architects were attracted to the idea of "withdrawal" from urban intensity.[18] As Ito put it, "the act of carving out discrete points of space—beautifully untouched and devoid of inscribed meaning—in cities seemed very fresh at the time."[19] Projects such as Ito's White U, of 1976, in Tokyo (see fig. 2, p. 189), and even Sejima's much later Saishunkan Seiyaku Women's Dormitory, of 1991, in Kumamoto City (fig. 4), created an enclosed architectural universe that, following on the legacy of Kazuo Shinohara (1925–2006) and of the oil crisis of 1973, rejects the surrounding urban chaos. In a recent interview, Ito emphasized that these buildings—which, as he described them, "turned their backs to the city"—correspond to an "era of introspection," each an attempt to be "in touch with the changing circumstances of society."[20]

Nonetheless, he would soon recognize that "architecture's attempts at autonomy or artistry," while valid in the 1970s, were no longer justifiable.[21] Sejima, on the other hand, rejected the hierarchical thinking inherent in conventional approaches to architecture. Her Women's Dormitory reinvented the city "outside" in a living space that, as Yuko Hasegawa, chief curator at the Museum of Contemporary Art Tokyo, noted, destabilized the "idea of borders between private and public domains" and critically examined "concepts such as personal space, identity, society and public."[22]

Ito upheld as essential to his vision a critical stance he inherited from the modern avant-garde: that architecture should serve as a "rejection of the existing social system" and as a form of social critique. This belief could be seen as problematic when worldwide the architect's mission was increasingly recognized as the simple delivery of functional artifacts. Yet, following the reception of Ito's groundbreaking 2001 Sendai Mediatheque (fig. 5), a cultural resource center in Sendai, the architect confessed he felt heartened that his most radical proposal to date was also the one audiences met with the most delight. One of Ito's main objectives for the center, whose holdings include film, books, magazines, and visual art, was to do away with the "fixed barriers" that have traditionally divided various mediums, and to propose a model for "how cultural facilities should be from now on."[23] The building's ecstatic reception, both within the architectural milieu and among everyday users, affirmed that a transformative design concept can in fact influence social perceptions and that, as held by the early modernists, architecture's "critical spirit had the power to change society."[24]

This affirmation not only encouraged Ito to invent novel architectural languages with each new project but also yielded an intellectual context in which the generations that followed could chase their own radical visions. Thus, SANAA, a firm founded by Sejima and Ryue Nishizawa (born 1966), persistently reinvents avant-garde strategies. They employ abstract functional diagrams to create distinctive spatial experiences that, above all, privilege unexpected discovery and sensorial pleasure on the part of their users. Thus, Sou Fujimoto (born 1971), an architect of the following generation, aspires to "create a fundamental or new relationship between people"[25] by advancing architectural strategies with indeterminate conceptions of space. He dares to promote artistic statements that, despite invalidating architectural functionalism, captivate clients nonetheless, offering them a different kind of everyday life.[26] Thus, Akihisa Hirata (born 1971), who envisages transcending the limitations of late modern architecture in "an era without ethics," adopts radical formal and ecological strategies that privilege architecture's "interdependent relationship with its surroundings."[27] Thus, Junya Ishigami (born 1974) investigates the physical limits of architecture, artistically exploiting lightness, structure, and scale (fig. 6). His pursuit of "pure possibilities"[28] afforded his work the impetus of an avant-garde disconnected from the contingencies of an increasingly conservative environment.

Early in the twenty-first century, Toyo Ito, SANAA, and their younger affiliates thoroughly questioned every conceivable architectural rule and premise. Their architectural explorations resisted the shortcomings of neomodernist designs emerging elsewhere, while simultaneously remaining true to the destabilizing stances of the first modern avant-gardes. Moreover, these architects sought out exquisite, unexpected beauty, charging their work—and that of the Japanese architects they have influenced—with a mix of ethics and aesthetics that in other architectural contexts was slowly disappearing.

Aesthetic Statements and Social Commitment

As a philosopher I have approached architecture from the phenomenological viewpoint and have always argued that architectural experience entails a wide variety of factors and [cannot] exist without them. I felt that Ito too . . . [knew] that architecture is inseparable from the experiences of the people who live in it and that it cannot be understood solely in terms of visual styles.

—Koji Taki[29]

In a 2001 curatorial project, I examined the work of a group of contemporary Dutch architects and proposed that their approach, which relied heavily on functional diagrams, attempted to surpass the apparent randomness of aesthetic decisions in the architectural design process. These diagrams, which translate directly into architectural space, were presented by the architects as a rational and inescapable legitimation for design decisions in which aesthetic intuition, not to say dubious notions of beauty, no longer played a role.[30] After this broader, international diagrammatic turn—and the faux pragmatism that ensued from it—few architects would dare say they sought only to make beautiful buildings.

Yet, this is precisely how Ito has described some of his more important projects. Of the Sendai Mediatheque he has said that he wanted "to create tubes of light so blindingly beautiful it would be difficult to tell if they were structural."[31] Reemerging alongside Ito's own approach to diagrammatic design was a notion of architectural experience tied to aesthetic impact—to the tactile and, in Ito's words, the "enjoyable" reception of new kinds of space.[32] What for Ito had begun as a kind of withdrawal from the contemporary city, or an "ideological refusal of [its] obnoxious banality," as he has also called it, soon turned into a conceptual investigation of architecture that, while refusing formalism, celebrated "the discovery of a new urban reality" in aesthetic terms.[33]

In any case, an architecture that reflects changing urban contexts need rely on more than superficial effects. As Ito recognized early in his career, in a society decidedly "pre-packaged and hermetically sealed," architecture risks turning into a fiction, with architects "beautifully [visualizing] the wrapping rather than [attempting] to make the content look real."[34] Ito's radical aesthetic, common also to Sejima's early works, took inspiration from generic building types, such as the convenience store, whose hierarchical and uniform spaces he would then overturn, positing changed social organizations and novel perceptual experiences.[35] Ito married a dramatic sense of beauty with a commitment to respond to new social needs and modes of spatial consumption.

Remarkably, Ito's pledge to both aesthetics and ethics accompanied his return to core aspects of the architectural discipline. The centrality of structure to Ito's work following Sendai—be it in his use of exoskeletons to define a building's image or his interest in interiors derived from complex geometries[36]—was soon matched by Sejima's and later SANAA's profound questioning of established functionalist blueprints, their innovative organization of clients' needs, and their sophisticated use of materials such as glass and metal. Architecture in Japan would from then on leave behind languages based on signs and symbols, and with them, any simplistic version of architectural beauty. Although terms such as *kawaii* (cute) have been used in analyses of contemporary Japanese architecture,[37] such descriptions, as with characterizations founded on the structures' apparent simplicity, are profoundly misleading when considering the built achievements of SANAA.[38] The firm's aesthetic feats, beyond their defining lightness and effortlessness, have been described as "inclusive" and "democratic," owing to their innovative, nondeterministic spatial organizations.[39] Ito has offered that Sejima's conceptual freedom "liberated from social conventions and restrictions" gave her "greater insight into social realities."[40]

Architects such as Fujimoto and Ishigami have been similarly praised for their architectural commitment to both radical aesthetics and the production of social change. Fujimoto's work has been described as taking "the elements of architecture apart," only to reassemble them in a leisurely yet critical commentary on privacy in contemporary society.[41] And while Ishigami's architectural quests may seem obsessive and focused almost exclusively on abstract disciplinary issues, he counts on users and their experiential sense of wonder to render meaningful his artistic endeavors.

Ito has described his aesthetic pursuits as a search for "places that are free of institutional constraints." He has strived not only to probe "the meaning of public buildings" but also to interrogate "the excessive importance architects attach to expression." Convinced that local governments and architects conceived architecture "according to a manual and with little consideration of the people who use them," he realized that "the social significance of architecture [needed] to be reconsidered."[42] Ito displaced the discipline's emphasis on design, preferring instead to attend to audience reception—as he did with Sendai Mediatheque—thereby shifting the inflection of his work. Sendai was a manifesto against what Ito has called "ready-made ideas," but it was also indicative of the "struggle between the respect for a powerful idea and all technical constraints and legal regulations."[43] In parallel, while Ito's architectural ideas constituted the fundamental driving force in overcoming constraints and captivating people, his design approach increasingly relied on his discussions with residents, local communities, and clients—that is to say, on those who would in fact be using the buildings.[44]

The 2011 Great East Japan Earthquake only reinforced this changing attitude. In the wake of the disaster, architects in Japan developed a new consciousness, recognizing that their work must extend beyond the immediate urban context and support emergent social needs. As Ito described it, architecture should move "beyond delight," "refrain from criticism," and seek "self-effacement."[45] And yet, the 2012 Venice Biennale Golden Lion winning project, Home-for-All—in which Ito together with SANAA, Fujimoto, Hirata, and other architects created simple, lodge-like structures in rural areas, enabling residents of temporary housing to gather for meetings and social events—retained an experimental edge.[46] It pointed to contemporary Japanese architecture's ability to maintain an avant-garde attitude in face of everyday requirements,[47] and confirmed that in Japan's network of established and emerging architectural luminaries, shared core values superseded individual interests.

Fig. 5: Toyo Ito (Japanese, born 1941). Sendai Mediatheque, Miyagi, Japan. 1995–2001. Scale model 1:150: acrylic, 10 5/8 × 31 1/2 × 29 1/8" (27 × 80 × 74 cm). The Museum of Modern Art, New York. Gift of the architect in honor of Philip Johnson. Fig. 6: Junya Ishigami (Japanese, born 1974). Balloon. 2006–07. Aluminum truss, 24 × 42 × 46' (730 × 1,280 × 1,400 cm). Museum of Contemporary Art Tokyo. Fig. 7: Sou Fujimoto (Japanese, born 1971), Akihisa Hirata (Japanese, born 1971), Kumiko Inui (Japanese, born 1969), and Toyo Ito (Japanese, born 1941). Home-for-All, Rikuzentakata, Japan. Scale model 1:50. 2012. Polystyrene board, 8 11/16 × 7 1/2 × 6 11/16" (22 × 19 × 17 cm). Collection Akihisa Hirata Architecture Office

An Influential Lightness of Being: Thoughts on a Constellation of Contemporary Japanese Architects

Pedro Gadanho

Another Kind of Architectural Star System

To embody in architecture that which has never been architecture before—I wish to explore this possibility. The scales of space engendered by the natural environment. The liberating feeling of a landscape extending seemingly forever, the vastness of the sky, the lightness of the sky, the lightness of a cloud, the fineness of rain drops.

—Junya Ishigami[48]

In the early twentieth century, like-minded artists disposed to upset social conventions and produce radical critiques of the period's social transformations collectively formed avant-garde movements. The quest for personal artistic success came as an afterthought, if it emerged at all. By the end of the century, however, the art market, and the dramatically increased financial value of individual works of art, incentivized artists to pursue solo careers, and their concomitant rewards, and led to the appropriation of the formal accomplishments of successive avant-garde programs. In parallel, the artist's newfound creative autonomy from everyday needs buried art's commitment to social change.

In the world of architecture, which from the 1980s onward embraced neoconservative politics and the free-market economy, these developments converged in a newly formed "star system." The term, imported from the Hollywood studio system, refers to a group of globally praised professionals that replaced the avant-garde. And even if, much like the term "starchitect," the designation has many detractors—namely among those who meet the definition—the classification has become usual currency and, consequently, an effective tool to analyze contemporary architectural production.[49]

For one, the celebrity status of architects is not historically unprecedented. Also, contrary to the instant fame of many contemporary media celebrities, the recognition of today's internationally acclaimed architects emerged from concrete achievements. Most of those who are now called "starchitects" have, on account of hard-won technical aptitude, led long careers and made important contributions to their profession, often developing idiosyncratic and influential architectural visions. Their success is typically well-deserved; but, like a double-edged sword, it can also attract hasty attacks. Criticism of today's starchitects tends to reprimand their share of important international projects; condemn their supposed indifference to local values; or, as lately, outright blame them for the upsurge in distended skylines across contemporary metropolises.[50] More pointedly, one could say that any star system tends to trap its protagonists in formulaic and predictable responses to any given demand. Out of conviction for personal style, many starchitects repeat formal and technical models while remaining indifferent to the context in which they are intervening. And while they may celebrate distinctive individualism on a global scale, at home their popularity, and corresponding cultivation of an uncritical following, often contributes to a lack of architectural diversity and even hinders the flourishing of new talent.[51]

The constellation of architects that eventually diverged from mainstream architecture in Japan, and now gravitates around Ito and Sejima, testifies to a different scenario. Ito, in particular, exemplifies at once an ethic of public responsibility and an unparalleled virtuosity, having responded to diverse challenges with a variety of architectural languages, thereby opening the field to new positions. As the Pritzker Prize committee wrote of Ito on its website, "It is evident that while innovating and pushing the boundaries of architecture forward, he does not close the road behind him."[52] Of course, when Japan's star architects favor cross-fertilization and cross-generational mutual support that move beyond mere competition and self-aggrandizement, they are observing a Japanese tradition that maintains as essential mutual respect between master and disciple. Yet, it must be noted that, by returning to the avant-garde values described earlier, these architects have also reverted to a notion of collective endeavor in which the desire to impact society supersedes singular will. That these aspirations were reciprocally reinforced—as exemplified by prominent figures like Ito consistently praising younger colleagues and paving the way for their achievements[53]—surely allowed these architects to continue wedding vigorous aesthetic exploits with both a profound architectural integrity and a renewed sense of social responsibility.

The potential difference between a star system and a constellation is that in the latter major and emerging stars are tied by gravitational pulls that render their aggregation of interests recognizable, if partially imagined. In contrast to shooting stars, single entities doomed to fade spectacularly, constellations evoke a very different image: each individual star, of course, carries its own significance, but so too does the stars'

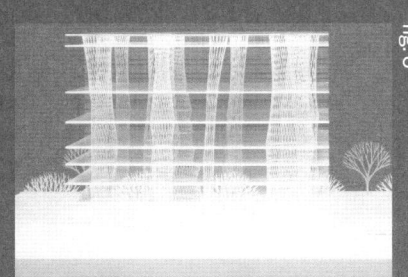

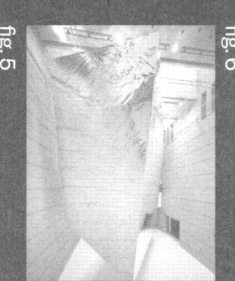

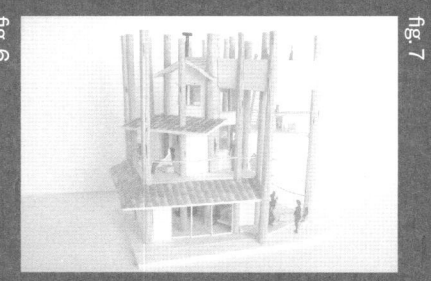

fig. 5

fig. 6

fig. 7

collective arrangement; their relative proximities and distances, and their combined brilliance, suggest more than a sum of parts. Since ancient times, constellations have offered direction to those looking to the skies for guidance.

One certainly hopes that the lightness celebrated in the work of this particular constellation of architects begets a legacy that surpasses its formal and material tropes.[54] The material transparency and elegant fluidity emanating from their work demands appreciation to be sure; but, even more so does the belief they uphold in architecture's ability to alter cultural perceptions and induce social change for the better.[55] This they do with what can only be deemed a graceful lightness of being as they avoid dogmatic manifestos and egotism. Amid the glimmer and incandescence of their aesthetic pursuits, this particular constellation of Japanese architects offers an ethical reference to the world of architecture at large. Beyond the fascination of appearances, this is why their work should remain influential.

Tokyo, July 2015

Notes

1. Osku Pajamaki quoted in Robin Pogrebin and Doreen Carvajal, "Guggenheim Helsinki Unveils Design," *New York Times*, June 24, 2015, http://www.nytimes.com/2015/06/24/arts/design/guggenheim-helsinki-unveils-design.html.
2. Ibid. As critic Anna Kats put it, while the Guggenheim had "typically opted for monumental, single buildings to house its global network of institutions," in this instance the architects offered "a complex that consists of fragmented structures that hold urbanism at its core." See Anna Kats, "Guggenheim Helsinki's Winning Design Reacts against Guggenheim's Past," *Blouin Artinfo*, June 23, 2015, http://www.blouinartinfo.com/news/story/1185096/guggenheim-helsinkis-winning-design-reacts-against.
3. Toyo Ito, "A New Architecture Is Possible Only in the Sea of Consumption," in *From Postwar to Postmodern, Art in Japan 1945–1989: Primary Documents*, ed. Doryun Chong, Michio Hayashi, Kenji Kajiya, and Fumihiko Sumitomo, trans. Maiko Behr (New York: Museum of Modern Art, 2012), 358. Essay first published in 1989 as "Shôni no umi ni hitarazu shite atarashii kenchiku wa nai," in *Shinkenchiku* 64, no. 11 (November 1989): 201–4.
4. For an account of such exchanges, see Evelyn Schulz, "Beyond Modernism," in *Future Living: Community Living in Japan*, ed. Claudia Hildner (Basel: Birkhäuser, 2013), 11–27.
5. Rem Koolhaas remarks that Japan was the first non-Western country to host an architectural avant-garde. For Koolhaas, Metabolism represented globalization's capacity to rearrange "architectural areas of initiative" and signaled "the end of the Western hegemony" as purveyor of the ideal city. See Rem Koolhaas, interview by Andrew Mackenzie, "Batik, Biennale and the Death of the Skyscraper: Interview with Rem Koolhaas," in *Architectural Review*, February 24, 2014, http://www.architectural-review.com/view/batik-biennale-and-the-death-of-the-skyscraper-interview-with-rem-koolhaas.
6. For an analysis of Ito's embrace of ephemerality as a response to Tokyo's "metropolitan non-contexts," see Andrea Maffei, "Toyo Ito, the Works," in *Toyo Ito: Works, Projects, Writings*, ed. Andrea Maffei (Milano: Electa, 2002), 9.
7. See for instance Kenneth Frampton, "Tadao Ando's Critical Modernism," in *Tadao Ando: Buildings, Projects, Writings* (New York: Rizzoli, 1984), 6–9.
8. Tange and Maki were awarded the Pritzker Architecture Prize in 1987 and 1993 respectively; Ando would follow soon after, in 1995. Between 2010 and 2014, four of the prize's laureates were Japanese: Sejima and Ryue Nishizawa (as SANAA), Ito, and Ban.
9. Ito, "A New Architecture Is Possible Only in the Sea of Consumption," 357. Ito continues, "The quick pace of society, or rather the sudden circulation of capital, has swept up almost every architect.... The issue has now become a question not of whether we can reject consumer society and still survive, but of whether we understand how completely we must break free of the idea that architecture alone can exist outside of consumption."
10. Although Ito studied under the influence of Metabolist architects Tange, Kiyonori Kikutake (born 1928), and Isozaki, he also recognizes his debt to Kazuo Shinohara's (born 1925) writings on "inner utopia." Ito confessed his disappointment with the Metabolists' contributions to the 1970 World Exposition in Osaka, noting how society often overtakes architecture's ideal visions of society. Toyo Ito, interview by Terunobu Fujimori, "In Pursuit of Truth under Changing Circumstances: Terunobu Fujimori and Toyo Ito," in Toyo Ito, *Toyo Ito 1971–2001*, trans. Hiroshi Watanabe (Tokyo: Toto, 2014), 15.
11. Ito, "A New Architecture Is Possible Only in the Sea of Consumption," 358.
12. See Charles Jencks, "Toyo Ito: Stealth Fighter for a Richer Post-Modernism," in *Toyo Ito*, Architectural Monographs 41 (London: Academy Editions, 1995).
13. Toyo Ito, interview by Toto Gallery staff members, "Sendai Mediatheque—Conversation with Toyo Ito," in Toyo Ito, *Toyo Ito 1971–2001*, trans. Hiroshi Watanabe (Tokyo: Toto, 2014), 265.
14. Philip Johnson and Mark Wigley, *Deconstructivist Architecture* (New York: Museum of Modern Art, 1988).
15. Jencks, "Toyo Ito: Stealth Fighter for a Richer Post-Modernism," 11.
16. Toyo Ito, "Toyo Ito: Designboom Interview," *Designboom*, March 25, 2013, interview conducted in 2001, http://www.designboom.com/architecture/toyo-ito-designboom-interview.
17. Ibid.
18. Ibid.
19. Ibid.
20. Toyo Ito, "Preface," in Toyo Ito, *Toyo Ito 1971–2001*, trans. Hiroshi Watanabe (Tokyo: Toto, 2014), 3.
21. Ito, "A New Architecture Is Possible Only in the Sea of Consumption," 358.
22. Yuko Hasegawa, "An Architecture of Awareness for the Twenty-First Century," in *Kazuyo Sejima + Ryue Nishizawa / SANAA*, ed. Yuko Hasegawa (Milan: Electa, 2005), 12.
23. Toyo Ito, "Mediatheque/Library," in Dana Buntrock, Taro Igarashi, Toyo Ito, Riken Yamamoto, *Toto Ito* (London: Phaidon, 2009), 133.
24. Ibid.
25. Sou Fujimoto, "In Conversation: Sou Fujimoto with Julia Peyton-Jones and Hans Ulrich Obrist," in *Sou Fujimoto: Serpentine Pavilion 2013*, ed. Sophie O'Brien (London: Walther König, 2013), 27.
26. Friedrich Meschede, "Reflections on Architecture, Space and Their Metaphors in the Work of Sou Fujimoto," in *Sou Fujimoto, Futurospective Architecture*, ed. Friedrich Meschede (Bielefeld: Kunsthalle Bielefeld / Koln: Walther König, 2012), 351.
27. Against a typically modern idea of "infinitely-expanding, homogeneous space," Hirata defends complexity and proposes "the need to consider the problem of architecture in light of the nature of the living world." See Akihisa Hirata, "Introduction," in *Akihisa Hirata: Tangling* (Tokyo: Inax, 2011), 9.
28. Taro Igarashi has suggested that Ishigami's initial interest in the domain of visual art emerged not only because young Japanese architects had difficulty finding work after the implosion of the 1980s asset-price bubble economy but also because Ishigami believes in an idea of architecture as utopia. As architectural commissions in Japan grew ever more conservative and less adventurous, Ishigami sought in temporary installations another type of architecture. Progressively, however, he was able to redirect his efforts toward concrete, permanent architectural designs. See Taro Igarashi, "A Few Things I Know about Junya Ishigami," in *Junya Ishigami—Another Scale of Architecture*, ed. Chinatsu Kuma (Kyoto: Seigensha Art Publishing, 2010), 270–89.
29. Koji Taki, "Architecture Is No Longer 'Architecture': Water Cube—Sendai Mediatheque and Beyond," in *Toyo Ito*, ed. Andrea Maffei (Milano: Electa, 2002), 19.
30. See Pedro Gadanho, "Hype(r)scapes," in *Post Rotterdam, Architecture and City after Tabula Rasa*, ed. Pedro Gadanho (Rotterdam: 010 Publishers, 2001), published on the occasion of an exhibition of the same name organized for the Porto 2001 European Capital of Culture, in Porto, Portugal.
31. Ito, "Sendai Mediatheque—Conversation with Toyo Ito," 265.

32 Ibid.
33 Ito, "A New Architecture Is Possible Only in the Sea of Consumption," 359.
34 Toyo Ito, "Architecture in a Simulated City," in *Toyo Ito*, Architectural Monographs 41 (London: Academy Editions, 1995), 9.
35 For Ito, the Sendai project departed radically from the conventional design of public buildings: its innovative spatial "uniformity" departed from the commonplace grid. As Ito pointed out, "the space can accommodate any activity anywhere, but places within that space are differentiated by the tubes." See Ito, "Sendai Mediatheque—Conversation with Toyo Ito," 263.
36 As Ito confesses, he became aware of structure with Sendai: "I began to feel that diverse things could be done with 'structure.' In addition, the memory capacity of computers became huge right around the time of Sendai, making it possible to computer analyse anything." See Toyo Ito, in conversation with Terunobu Fujimori, "The Power of Architecture," in *Toyo Ito 2002–2014*, trans. Hiroshi Watanabe (Tokyo: Toto, 2015), 13.
37 See Taro Igarashi, "Superflat Architecture and Japanese Subculture," in *Japan, towards Totalscape: Contemporary Japanese Architecture, Urban Planning and Landscape*, ed. Moriko Kira and Mariko Terada (Rotterdam: Nai Publishers, 2000), 98–101.
38 As the 2010 jury citation on the Pritzker Architecture Prize website states, "The buildings by Sejima and Nishizawa seem deceptively simple," but in fact "explore like few others the phenomenal properties of continuous space, lightness, transparency, and materiality to create a subtle synthesis." See http://www.pritzkerprize.com/2010/jury. Similarly, Hasegawa posits, "It is difficult to analyze the complexity, ambiguity and looseness concealed in the simplicity of SANAA's architecture. . . . To understand how they explore unknown fields liberated from conventional architectural concepts, it would be far more interesting to examine how their architectural works are used over a period of time." See Hasegawa, "An Architecture of Awareness for the Twenty-First Century," 7.
39 The 2010 Pritzker Prize jury citation remarks that the architects' "equivalence of spaces" gives way to the creation of "unpretentious, democratic buildings according to the task and budget at hand." See http://www.pritzkerprize.com/2010/jury.
40 Toyo Ito, quoted in Hasegawa, "An Architecture of Awareness for the Twenty-First Century," 7.
41 Niklas Maak, "On Sou Fujimoto," in *Sou Fujimoto: Serpentine Pavilion 2013*, ed. Sophie O'Brien (London: Walther König, 2013), 52.
42 Toyo Ito, interview by Toto Gallery staff members, "Home-for-All—Conversation with Toyo Ito," in Toyo Ito, *Toyo Ito 2002–2014*, trans. Hiroshi Watanabe (Tokyo: Toto, 2015), 321.
43 Ito, "Sendai Mediatheque—Conversation with Toyo Ito," 264.
44 Toyo Ito, interview by Designboom, "Interview with Architect Toyo Ito," *Designboom*, June 16, 2015, http://www.designboom.com/architecture/toyo-ito-interview-06-16-2015.
45 Even a project such as the Toyo Ito Museum of Architecture, Imabari, is born from a desire to educate, a role for which in Japan Ito is highly recognized, more than he is for self-aggrandizement. See Ito, "The Power of Architecture," 41.
46 Ito points out that the architects not only designed shared houses for local communities; they also rallied support to finance and build the projects. See Ito, "Interview with Architect Toyo Ito."
47 As Eve Blau, a professor of urban form and design at Harvard University, recalls of SANAA's 21st Century Museum of Contemporary Art, in Kanazawa, "When it opened, the [museum] was celebrated as a new kind of cultural institution in Japan in which high art and daily life mix." But Blau asserts that this synthesis has deep roots in traditional Japanese culture, one that no doubt forms a substantial part of the fascination Western audiences hold toward Japanese architecture. See Blau, "Inventing New Hierarchies," Kazuyo Sejima and Ryue Nishizawa, 2010 Laureates, on the Pritzker Prize for Architecture website, 2010, http://www.pritzkerprize.com/2010/essay.
48 See Ishigami, "Another Scale of Architecture," 4.
49 See, for example, Davide Ponzini and Michele Nastasi, *Starchitecture: Scenes, Actors and Spectacles in Contemporary Cities* (Turin and New York: Allemandi, 2011).
50 See Witold Rybczynski, "The Franchising of Architecture," *New York Times*, June 11, 2014, http://tmagazine.blogs.nytimes.com/2014/06/11/gehry-norman-foster-moshe-safdie-starchitects-locatects-franchising-of-architecture. See also the debate that followed: "Are the 'Star' Architects Ruining Cities?," with contributions by Allison Arieff, Vishaan Chakrabarti, and others, in the *New York Times*, July 28, 2014, http://www.nytimes.com/roomfordebate/2014/07/28are-the-star-architects-ruining-cities-9.
51 I have reflected on this subject previously when considering the influence of starchitect Álvaro Siza Vieira on his contemporaries. See Pedro Gadanho, "Under the Influence: From Volcano to Gene Pool," in *Kortárs portugál építészet / Contemporary Portuguese Architecture*, ed. Zorán Vukoszávlyev and Szentirmai Tamás (Budapest: TERC, 2010), 313–17.
52 As Lord Peter Palumbo, Alejandro Aravena, Juhani Pallasmaa, and others said of Ito in his Pritzker Prize citation, Ito's work contains a "spectrum of architectural languages." His idea that "different circumstances lead to different answers," as well as his lack of adherence to particular formal trends, reflect the openness in his approach. Ito, according to the committee, "is a pioneer and encourages others to benefit from his discoveries and for them to advance in their own directions as well. In that sense, he is a true master who produces oxygen rather than just consumes it." See, "Jury Citation," Toyo Ito, 2013 Laureate, Pritzker Prize for Architecture website, http://www.pritzkerprize.com/2013/jury-citation.
53 This attitude is one that Ito himself inherited from his masters. In an interview conducted by Toto Gallery staff members, the staff refer to Arata Isozaki (born 1931) as belonging to an older generation that "provides opportunities for work to younger architects" and praise this type of intergenerational relationship as one "that allows mutual criticism but also provides opportunities to help and to be helped." See Toyo Ito, interview by Toto Gallery staff members, "First Public Buildings—Conversation with Toyo Ito," in Toyo Ito, *Toyo Ito 1971–2001* (Tokyo: Toto, 2014), 177.
54 Deyan Sudjic has described the notion of lightness in the work of SANAA as standing "against the massive, and the rhetorical, in architecture." Much as Ito's interest in "lightweight ephemeral structures" is a response to social impermanence, SANAA's lightness is more a material characteristic. For Sudjic, this lightness filters "architecture of all its excess baggage, by reducing building to a distilled essence." See Sudjic, "The Lightness of Being," in *Kazuyo Sejima + Ryue Nishizawa / SANAA : The Zollverein School of Management and Design*, ed. Kristin Feireiss (Munich and London: Prestel, 2005), 50.
55 Writing on the work of Fujimoto and Japan's renewed belief in architecture's power to change society, Niklas Maak optimistically forecasts the end of a "depressing phase in architectural history—when architects justified their well-tempered unimaginativeness by claiming that architectural utopias had only brought misery to cities and their inhabitants." See Maak, "On Sou Fujimoto," 56.

To Create Architecture that Breathes

I prefer soft objects to hard, curved lines to straight, ambiguity to clarity, spatial diversity to functionalism, and naturalness to artificiality. Humans came out of caves or climbed down from trees and created architecture using geometry. It was considered a human virtue to create geometric order in a naturally chaotic world. Ever since, architecture has been received and appreciated as distinct from nature. The same is true of the body. Humans believe that the beautiful body is separate from nature, a perfectly proportional form to be inscribed in circles and squares. The body, however, is connected to nature through the eyes, ears, nose, and mouth. Humans used to live by rivers and absorb their taintless water as if part of a stemming stream branch. Humans were part of nature. Ecology and sustainability are gaining importance today. It is evident that architecture must be part of nature, not separate from it. Most modern architecture is composed of euclidean geometry, although there is no perpendicular grid in the natural world. Branched trees display angles of varying degrees, for example, but no branch intersects precisely at a perpendicular. Trees merely repeat a simple rule of branching, and yet they are able to produce complicated forms that fit comfortably within the natural environment. Today we are able to create architecture based on the rules in the natural world by using computer technologies. However, we should use these rules not to make forms that imitate nature but instead to create architecture that breathes and is congruous with the environment.
Toyo Ito

Sendai, a sleek, cubic structure, combines a multimedia hub, library, and information-services center for the audiovisually impaired. Interior walls are eliminated to allow for a fluid space that departs from the typical uniformity of the flat-slab-and-column construction of modern architecture. Thirteen tube-like columns support a stack of lean 538-square-foot (50-square-meter) steel floor plates. Each structural tube is an open latticework of steel that is torqued to resist building stresses and changes in cross section between floors. The dissolution of the structural columns into reticulated, lightweight forms allows each, in addition to providing support, either to carry air-conditioning and power conduits; serve as a

Toyo Ito
Sendai Mediatheque
Sendai, Japan
1995–2001

light well; or hold vertical circulation. The facade's double layer of glass acts as a mediated surface: by day, it fluctuates between reflection and translucency; by night, it dissolves against the illuminated building. Envisioned during the early design phase as a pliable structure of "soft tubes that wav[e] slowly under water" and "rubber tubes filled with fluid,"[1] the building's remarkable transparency is, in the architect's words, encountered "like a Japanese garden, where space comes into being as the sum total of the sequences experienced by a person walking through it."[2] —Phoebe Springstubb

Previous spread: South facade from Jozenji-dori
Above: Detail of the south facade

1. Toyo Ito, "Three Transparencies," in *Toyo Ito: Works, Projects, Writings*, ed. Andrea Maffei (Milan: Electa, 2002), 346. First published in Toyo Ito, *Suké Suké*, trans. Alfred Birnbaum (Tokyo: Nuno Nuno Books, 1997). 2. Toyo Ito, interview by Toto Gallery staff members, "Sendai Mediatheque—Conversation with Toyo Ito," in Toyo Ito, *Toyo Ito 1971–2001*, trans. Hiroshi Watanabe (Tokyo: Toto, 2014), 180.

Toyo Ito
Sendai Mediatheque
Sendai, Japan
1995–2001

Aerial view of the southeast corner

25

From top: View upward into a tube. Second-floor newspaper- and magazine-browsing area

Toyo Ito
Sendai Mediatheque
Sendai, Japan
1995–2001

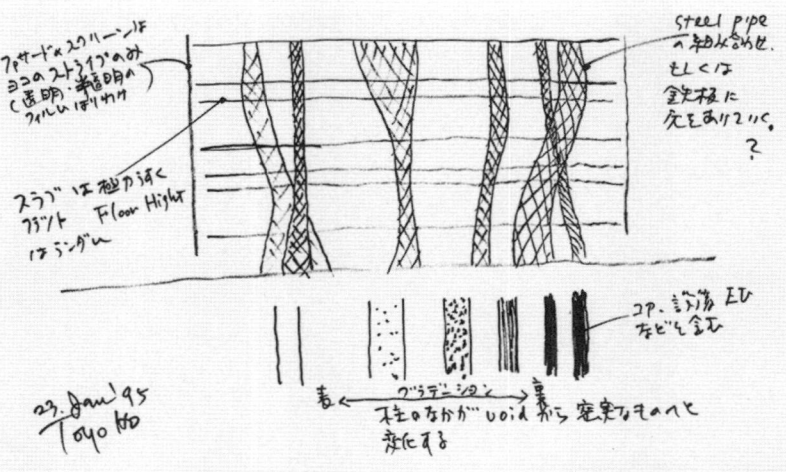

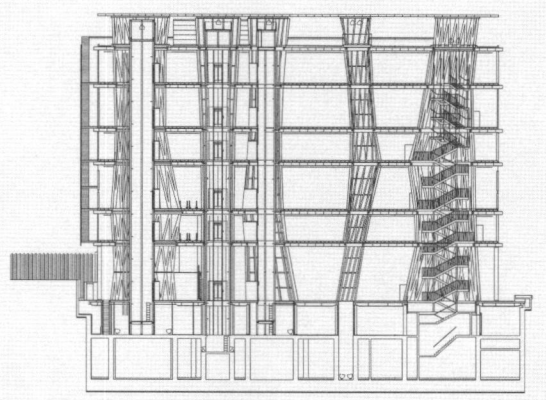

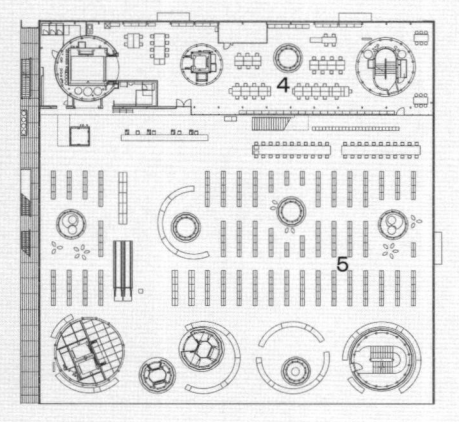

Floor 3

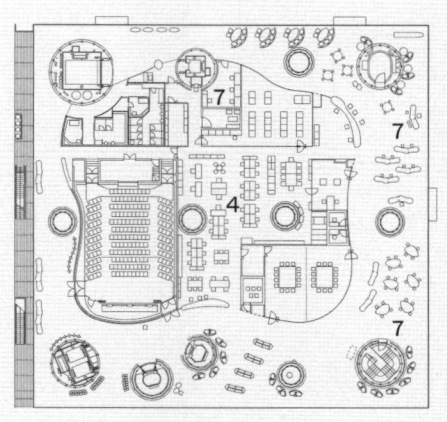

Floor 7

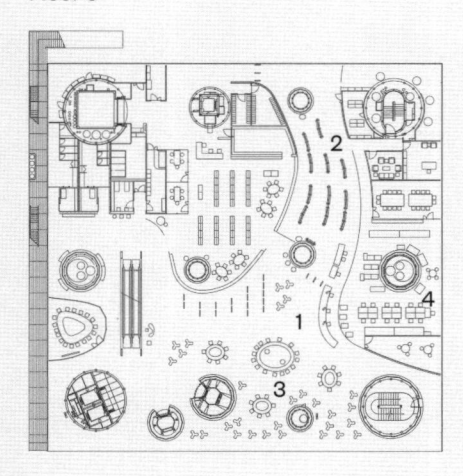

Floor 2

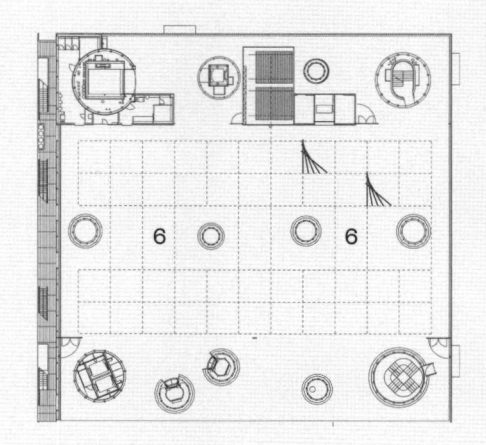

Floor 6

From top: Initial sketch proposing composition of structural tubes, 1995. East-west section. Plans of the second, third, sixth, and seventh floors with information center (1), audiovisual library (2), browsing (3), offices (4), library (5), gallery (6), and studio (7)

This contemporary folly was commissioned as a temporary project to commemorate the European Union's designation of Brugge as the 2002 European "capital of culture." The pavilion straddled an archaeological site containing the ruins of a medieval cathedral in the city's historic center. Lifted above a circular reflecting pool designed to protect the ruins, the pavilion's walls and roof were made of a lightweight aluminum panel folded over a sheet of polycarbonate that served as a bridge. The honeycomb pattern, insufficiently rigid on its own, was structurally reinforced by the application of large, flat ellipses that evoke the cutouts of Belgian lace. Taking an essentially decorative pattern as its generative motif, the

Toyo Ito
Brugge Pavilion
Brugge, Belgium
2000–2002

pavilion transformed the pattern through scale and material, forming a facade that was both structural and, with its filigreed aluminum, transparent—presence without mass. The open, honeycomb-shaped tessellations of the aluminum created a shifting perceptual experience that hid and revealed the cityscape in fragments as visitors passed through the pavilion. Reflective and ephemeral, the pavilion was a playful counterpoint to the surrounding masonry buildings. The light appearance mandated by the preservation of the historic site placed it in conversation with the existing architecture. Intended as a temporary project, the pavilion was disassembled in 2013.—PS

Previous spread: Interior view toward Burg Square
From top: Exterior. Detail of surface panels at the interior

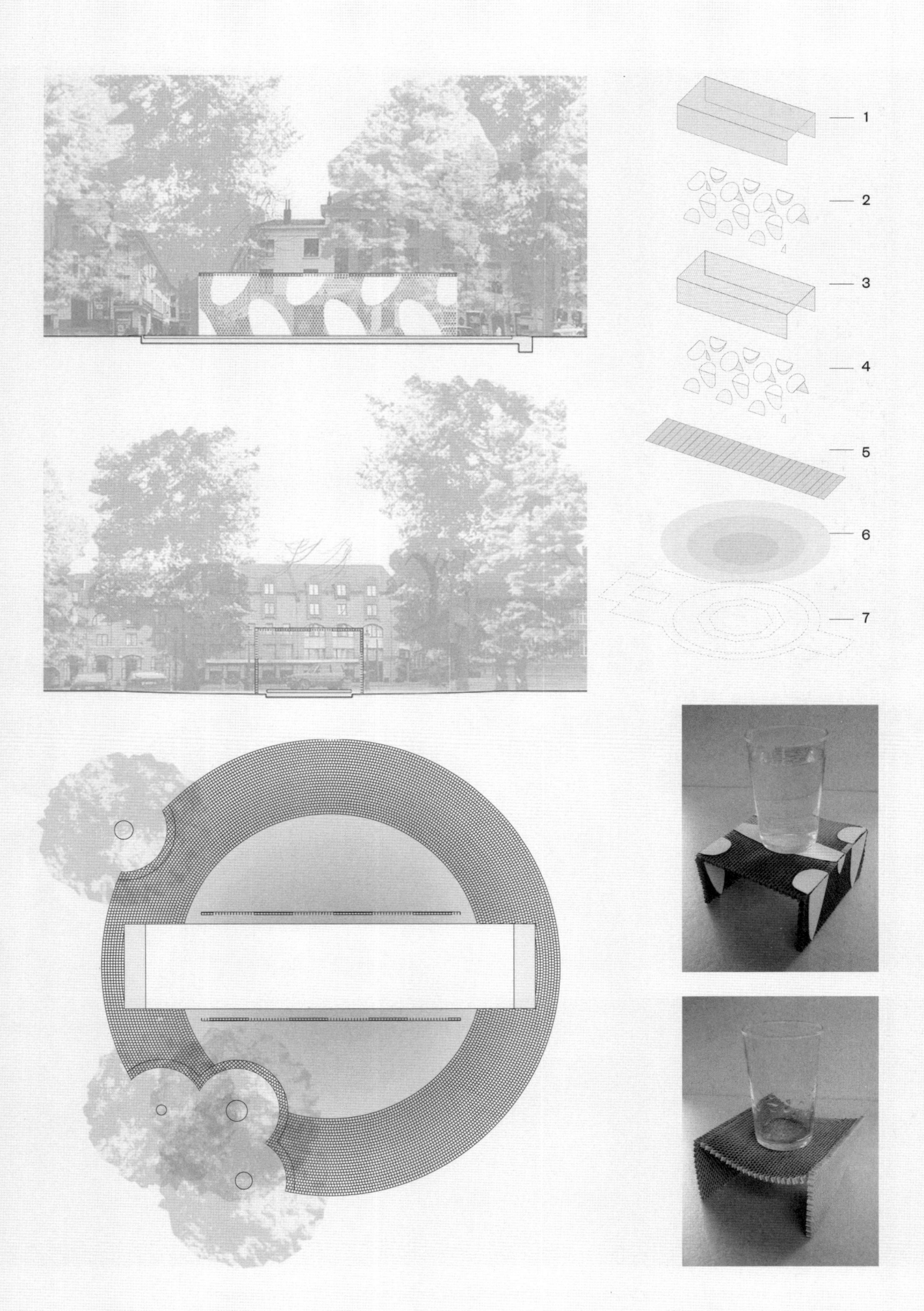

Toyo Ito
Brugge Pavilion
Brugge, Belgium
2000–2002

Clockwise from top right: Pavilion components: polycarbonate (1), aluminum plate (2), aluminum honeycomb (3), aluminum plate (4), floating bridge (5), pond (6), cathedral foundations (7). Aluminum honeycomb structure reinforced with surface panels. Plan. Sections

This dynamic structure is one of a series of temporary summer pavilions commissioned by the Serpentine Gallery since 2000 for Kensington Gardens. Developed in collaboration with the structural engineer Cecil Balmond, the design used an algorithm to distort an orthogonal grid, rotating and scaling a number of squares inscribed in a spiral to generate an unexpected, fractured form. The mathematical pattern flirted with the appearance of instability—a chaotic network of intersecting lines circumscribed by the box's perimeter forms the building envelope. Each line was translated into an element of the steel frame—intersections creating structural equilibrium. Fabricated out of a series of welded panels that

Toyo Ito

Serpentine Gallery Pavilion

London

2002

were bolted together on-site, the asymmetrical lattice of trapezoidal and triangular openings was fitted with alternating glass and aluminum panels and hosted a café along with event spaces for lectures and parties. With no discrete architectural components—columns, windows, or doors—the planes of walls, floor, and ceiling were identical patterned surfaces that boldly combined structure and figuration.—PS

Previous spread: South facade with Serpentine Gallery
From top: Café at interior. Detail of structural panels

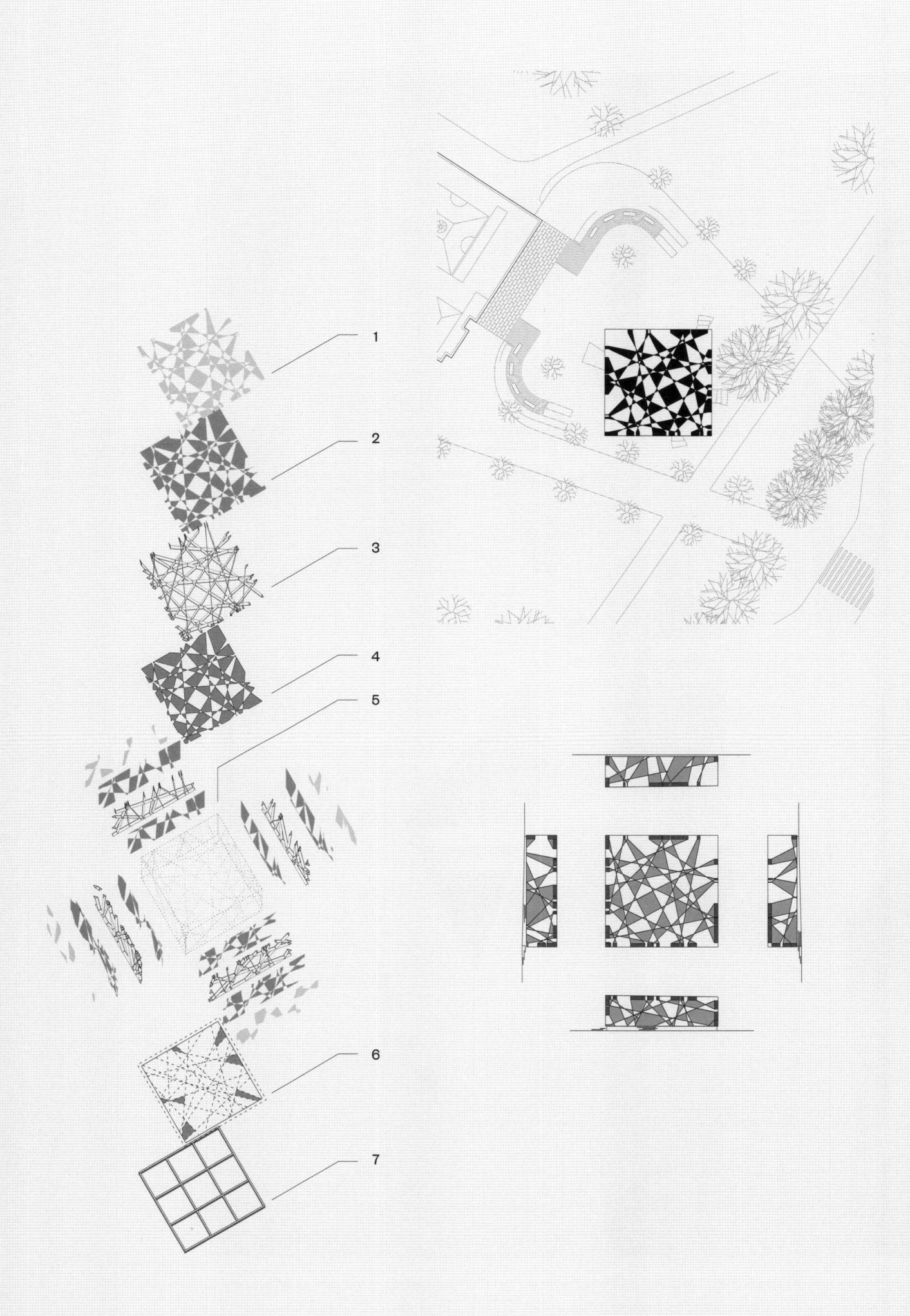

Toyo Ito
Serpentine Gallery Pavilion
London
2002

Clockwise from top right: Site plan. Reflected ceiling plan and sections. Pavilion components: glass (1), aluminum plates (2), grillage of flat steel bars (3), aluminum plates (4), café and event space (5), plywood floor (6), steel grillage and wooden joists (7)

35

This flagship store for shoe and handbag retailer Tod's is located on Omotesando, an avenue of luxury retailers that has evolved into a showcase for high-profile architecture since the early 2000s. To give continuity to the L-shaped site, which has only a narrow front on the commercial avenue, the building's facade was conceived as a continuous screen of interlocked concrete piers that evoke the neighborhood's allées of ornamental zelkova trees. The design merges a highly abstracted, graphic interpretation of nature with the logic of its structural system—bifurcated branches thicken to trunk-like piers according to the downward flow of forces acting on the building. The robust, approximately

Toyo Ito
Tod's Omotesando Building
Tokyo, 2002–04

twelve-inch- (thirty-centimeter-) thick piers, broad at ground level, taper to intricate grillwork at the top of the seven-story building. By concentrating the load bearing in the facade, the shop interiors are freed of columns with retail spaces spanning thirty-three to forty-nine feet (ten to fifteen meters). Asymmetrical openings in frameless glass offer expansive street-level displays and multiple smaller openings for the offices at the upper floors. The exploration of nonlinear geometries creates an iconic structure compelled by what Ito has described as "a constant tension generated between the building's symbolic concreteness and its abstractness."[1] —PS

Previous spread from left: Detail of the facade's branching concrete piers. Aerial view.
Clockwise from top left: Night view from Omotesando Avenue. Staircase inside the shop. Sixth-floor interior

Toyo Ito

Tod's Omotesando Building

Tokyo

2002–04

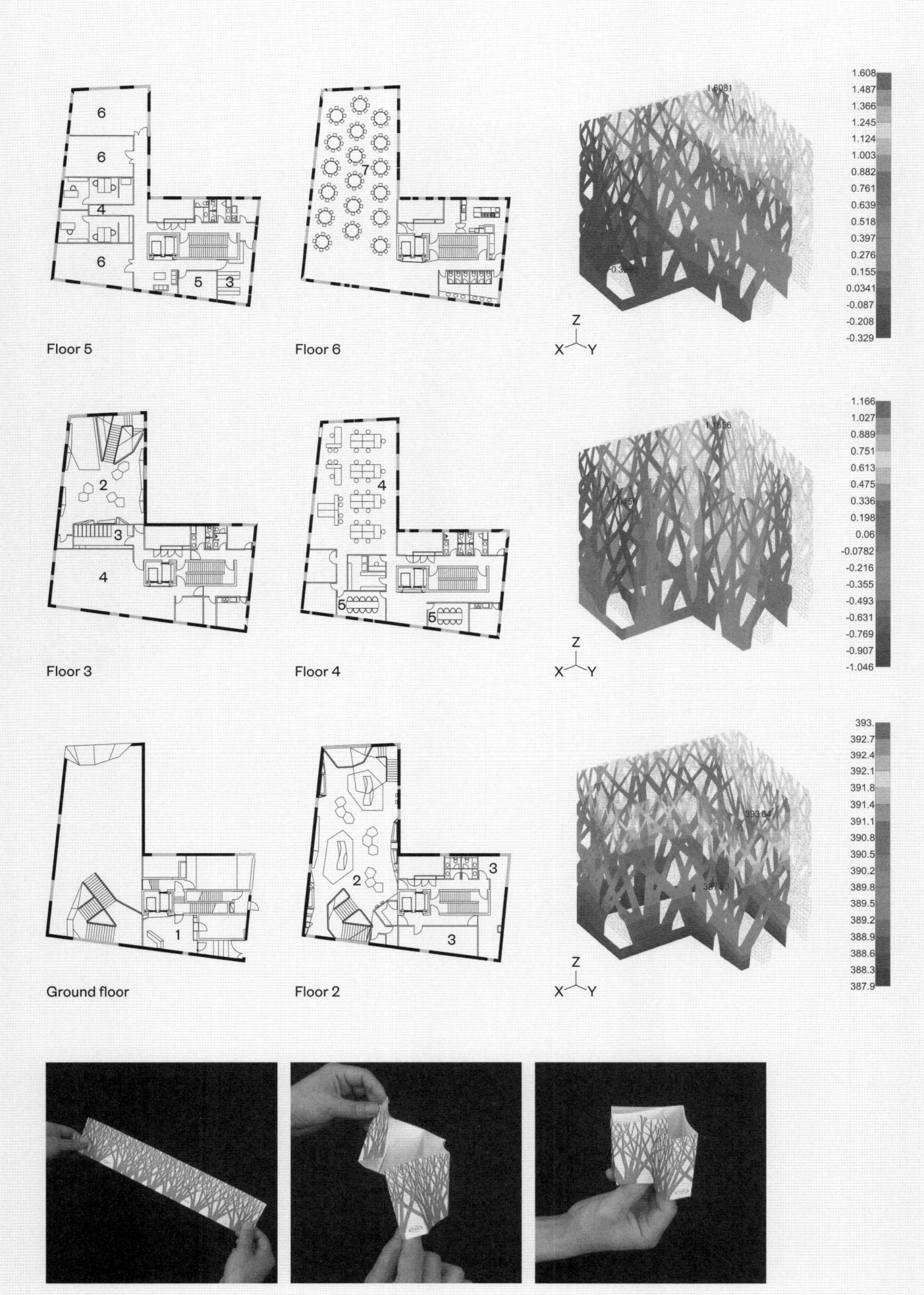

39

Floor 5

Floor 6

Floor 3

Floor 4

Ground floor

Floor 2

Clockwise from top right: Structural analysis of seismic loading. Abstraction of the silhouettes of zelkova trees to create the structure. Plans of the ground through sixth floors with office entrance (1), shop (2), stock room (3), offices (4), meeting room (5), showroom (6), and party room (7)

Set amidst the hills of Kakamigahara on the edge of a small artificial lake, the funeral hall Meiso no Mori (Forest of meditation) is cloaked in an undulating roof of white concrete that gives the building the appearance of suspended motion—a cloud afloat or a bird in flight. The fluid canopy is a reinforced-concrete shell that extends over more than 21,500 square feet (2,000 square meters). At a dozen points, the surface puckers and stretches to the ground to form columns that are continuous with the roof and act as structure as well as rainwater conduits. Designed to replace an older crematorium, the enclosure is set back from the roofline and includes a mix of ceremonial and back-of-house spaces

Toyo Ito

Meiso no Mori Municipal Funeral Hall
Kakamigahara, Japan 2004–06

organized between the columns in top-lit rooms framed in travertine. To accommodate the operational requirements of the crematorium, Meiso no Mori buries the massive machinery of the furnace into the bulk of the hill at the southwest of the site, opening the interiors to funerary rituals and serving as a meditation on form. In this way, the soft curves of the roof become a nuanced ceiling with varied heights that meet the range of funerary functions and respond to practical needs with a bold spatial and structural experiment. —PS

Previous spread: View across the reinforced concrete roof
Clockwise from top: North facade from the pond. Waiting-room interior facing the pond. View from the cemetery

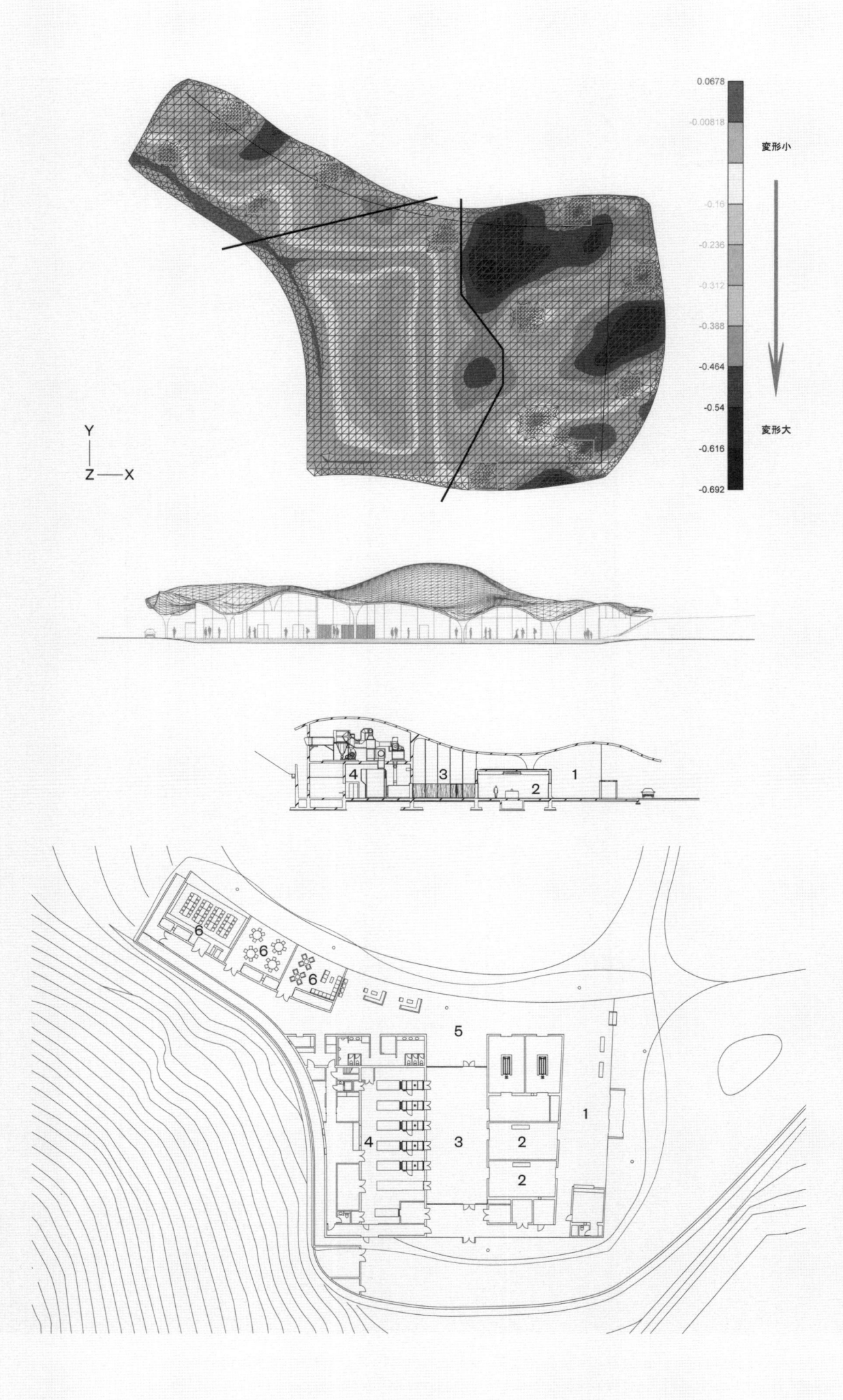

Toyo Ito   Meiso no Mori Municipal Funeral Hall   Kakamigahara, Japan   2004–06

変形小
変形大

From top: Structural-displacement diagram of the roof. North elevation. North-south section. Ground-floor plan with entrance hall (1), valedictory room (2), ceremonial hall (3), crematorium (4), lobby (5), and waiting room (6)

43

Tama Art University Library is located on the university's graduate campus in Hachioji, a southeastern suburb of Tokyo. The upper floor hosts reading stacks and study spaces, while the ground level, which is pitched three degrees to the site's slope, holds offices and communal spaces, including a café, gallery, and multimedia center. Illuminated by night, the library reveals a vaulted interior of tapered columns and exposed concrete that retains the feeling of a subterranean grotto. The sculpted interior, developed in an initial scheme that placed the library belowground, contrasts with a streamlined glass exterior that shears the vaults, revealing their angularity and emphasizing their semicircular sections at the building's

Toyo Ito
Tama Art University Library, Hachioji Campus
Tokyo
2004–07

acute corners. Referencing classical arched structures, the columns are unusually attenuated and linear, with cruciform profiles that are generated by the intersection of two planes and minimized by a core of reinforcing steel. The spans of the arches vary, with the largest fifty-three feet (sixteen meters). They are regulated by a structural grid of curved lines that creates sinuous colonnades organically extending across the interior. Weaving through the arches, book stacks follow their own curved logic, creating labyrinthine reading spaces that are experienced entropically. —PS

Previous spread: Corner of the east facade
Clockwise from top: Second-floor open stacks and reading area. North facade with main entrance. Staircase leading to the second floor

Toyo Ito

Tama Art University Library, Hachioji Campus

Tokyo

2004–07

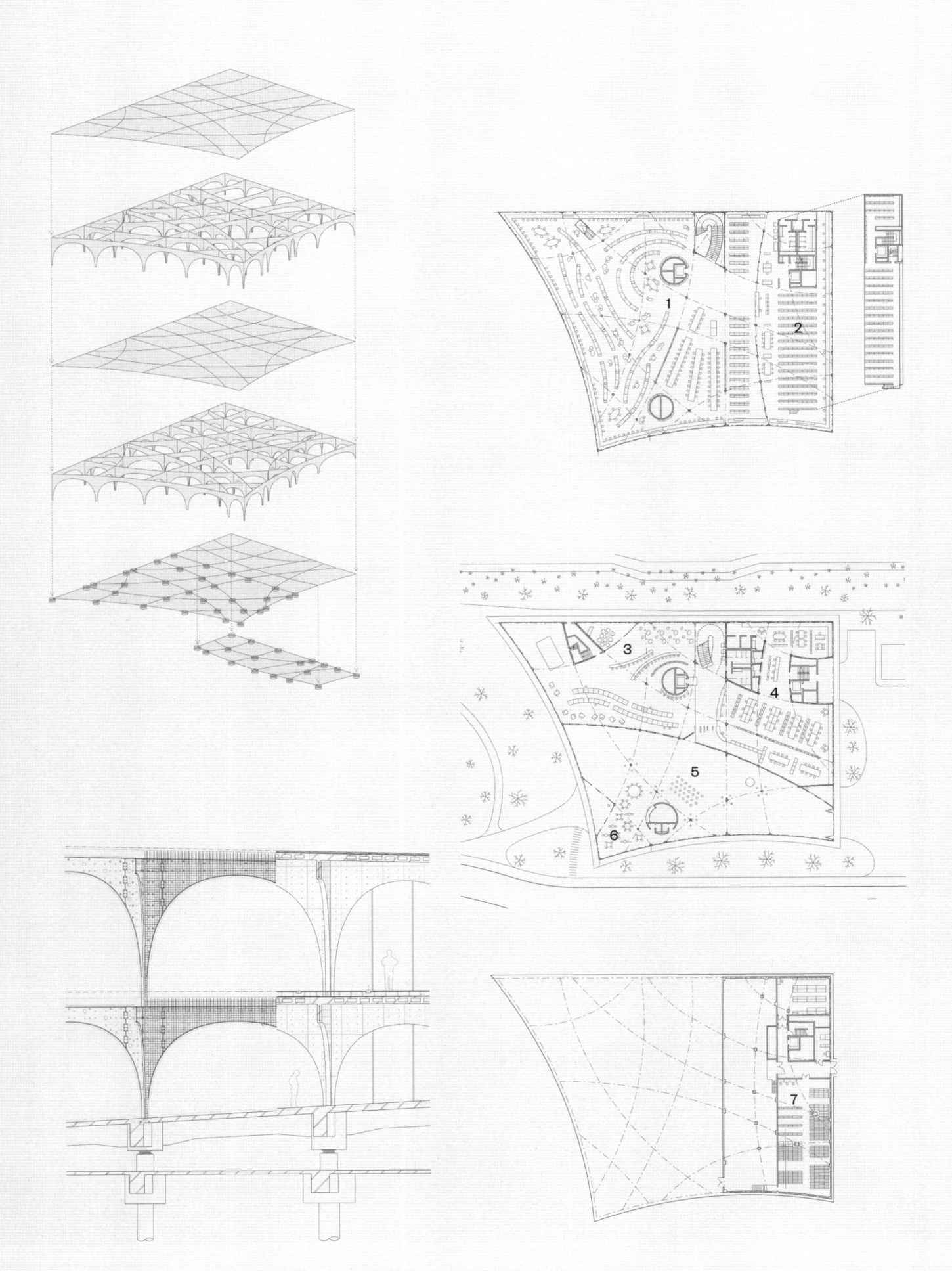

Clockwise from top left: Diagram of arched structural system of steel and concrete. Plans of the second, ground, and basement floors with open-stack reading room (1), closed stacks (2), multimedia center (3), offices (4), arcade gallery (5), café (6), and compact and valuable stacks (7). Section detailing stages of arch construction

Nestled in a compact residential neighborhood across from one of Tokyo's elevated rail lines in the western part of the city, ZA-KOENJI is a six-story, mixed-use theater. The main theater and café are located aboveground, while the bulk of the building is recessed below, including a second theater, a hall for the choreographed dance festival Awa Odori, and rehearsal, film, and music-editing rooms. The theaters are vertically stacked to accommodate the small site; to maintain acoustic conditions, Ito devised a structural system that individually insulates each floor. The building's roof was fabricated with thin, black steel plates that define peaked and scalloped surfaces. Its expressionistic forms were generated by carving

Toyo Ito

ZA-KOENJI Public Theatre

Tokyo

2005–08

platonic solids—cones and cylinders—from a cube, creating a geometrically complex shape that could be unrolled into planar surfaces for construction. These forms give the theater a bold, asymmetrical profile that inserts an animated presence among the flat and ninety-degree planes of the surrounding buildings. Inside this unusual volume, circular light wells, made out of frosted glass inset in the steel, create an atmospheric constellation of indirect light within the deep red interiors.—PS

Previous spread: View from the northwest toward elevated railway
Clockwise from top left: Staircase. Ground-floor entrance foyer. Aerial view of the west facade

Toyo Ito
ZA-KOENJI Public Theatre
Tokyo
2005–08

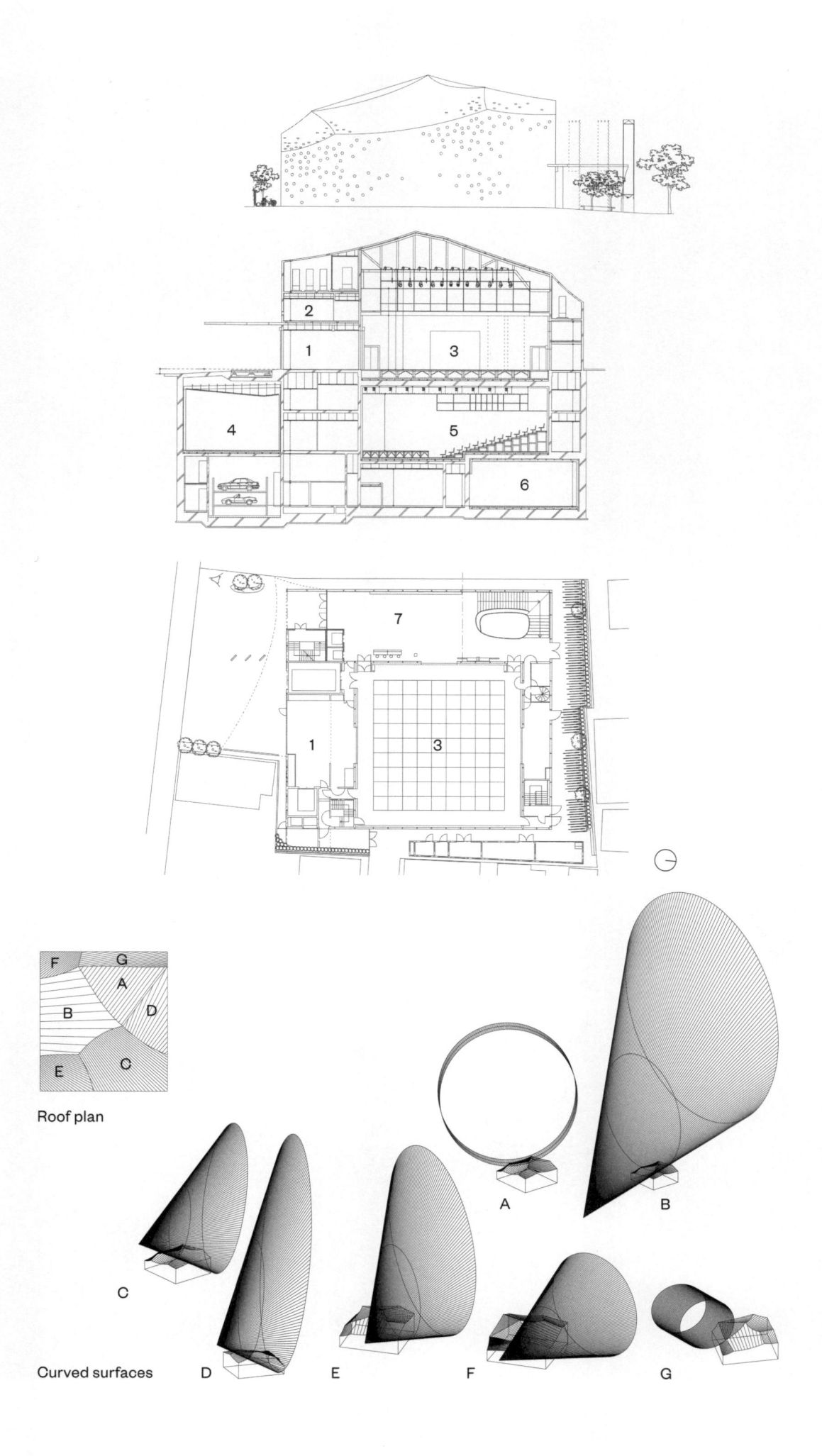

Roof plan

Curved surfaces

Clockwise from top left: Section with loading bay (1), administration (2), ZA-KOENJI One (3), Awa Odori Hall (4), ZA-KOENJI Two (5), and rehearsal room (6). West elevation. Study for the curved surface geometry of the roof. Ground-floor plan with foyer (7)

In this unrealized proposal to replace an existing brutalist building by Mario Ciampi, a grid of contoured white forms sheathed in glass combines an art museum and a film archive. Located on the southeastern edge of the University of California, Berkeley, campus, where the university meets the city, the proposed three-story structure holds exhibition spaces and research facilities accessible to students, faculty, and the public. The upper two floors house galleries, while the lower floor holds a theater, black box, and restaurant. The design was generated through a series of transformations to an orthogonal grid. Each ninety-degree corner is gently warped to become a radiused curve. Where the wall meets the floor

Toyo Ito
University of California, Berkeley Art Museum and Pacific Film Archive
Berkeley, California. Project 2006–10

or two walls intersect, a softened threshold is introduced by folding the plane seamlessly into the adjoining space. The sculptural walls offer a blended sequence of rooms, with the removal of the edge creating a psychological and visual experience of continuity, even as the plan retains traces of the grid's ordered quadrants. Encasing a thin layer of concrete between two steel plates creates the tautly curved surfaces. With its design period coinciding with the 2008 financial collapse, the project was never realized due to budget reasons. —PS

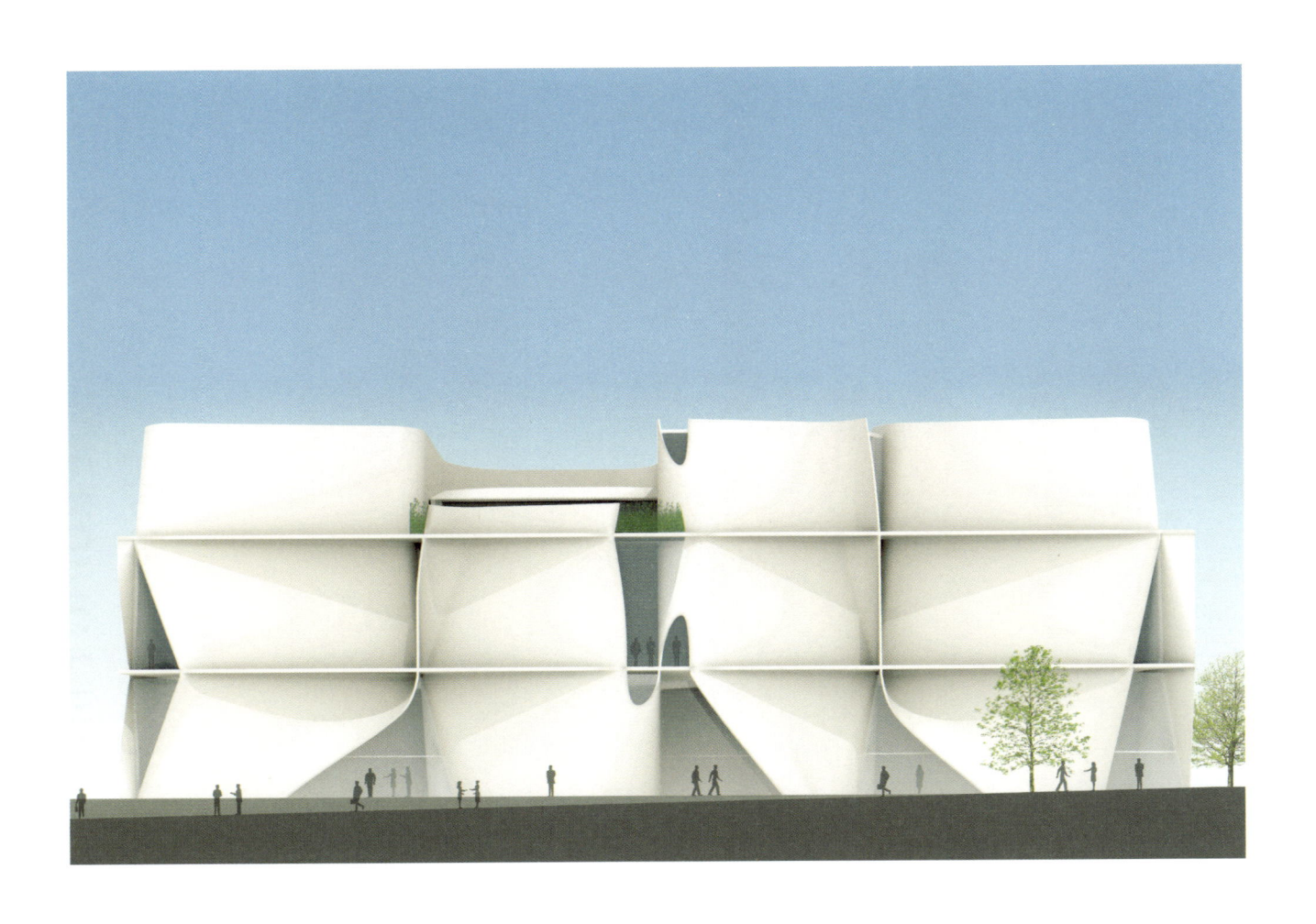

Previous spread: Perspective of the southeast corner looking toward the city
From top: South elevation. Perspective of the south facade from Center Street

Toyo Ito
University of California, Berkeley Art Museum and Pacific Film Archive
Berkeley, California. Project 2006–10

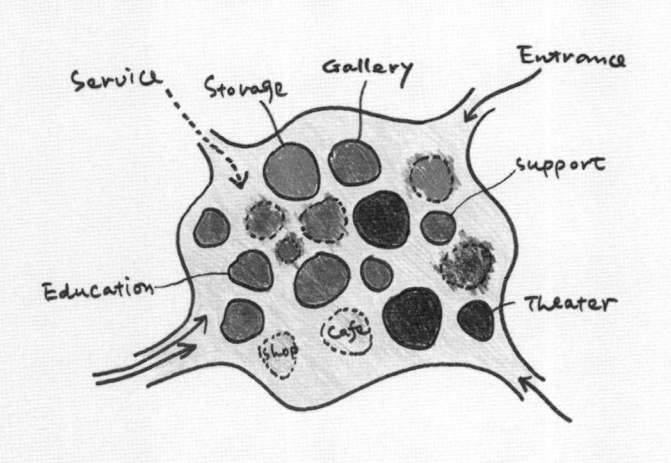

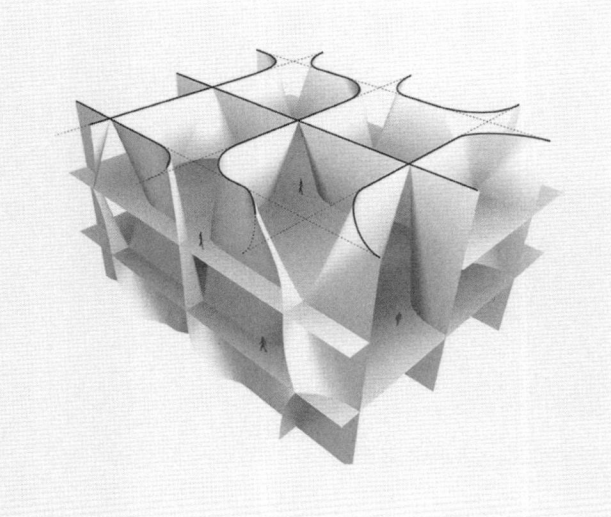

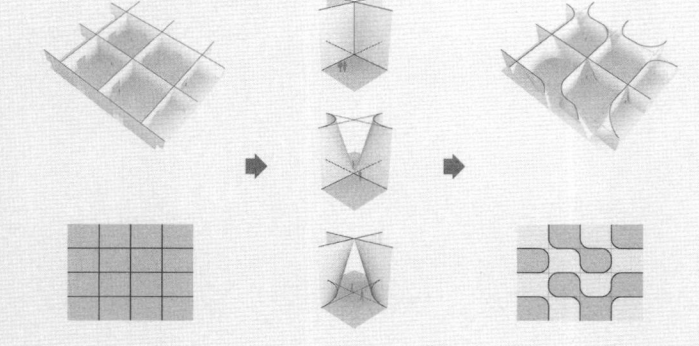

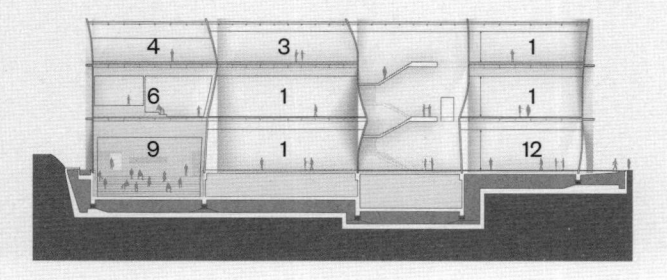

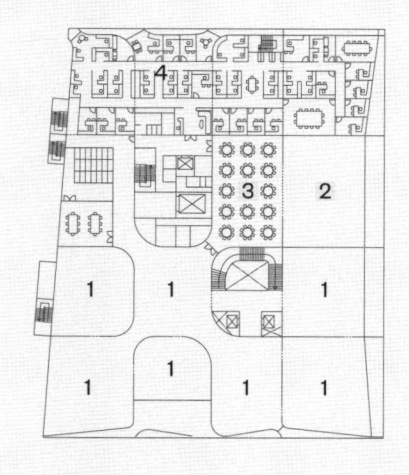

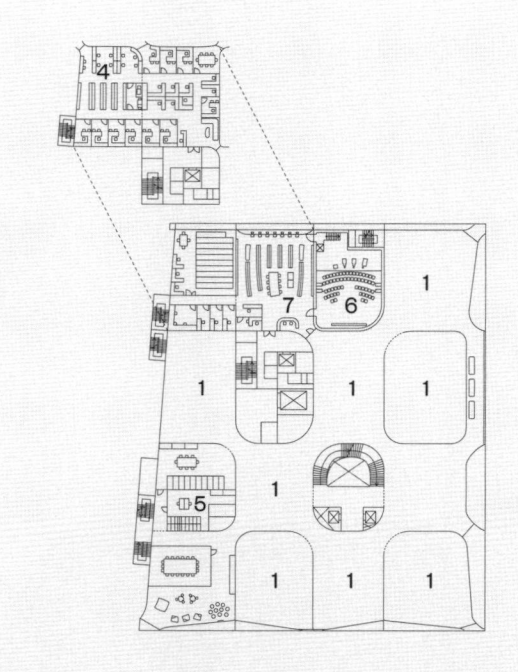

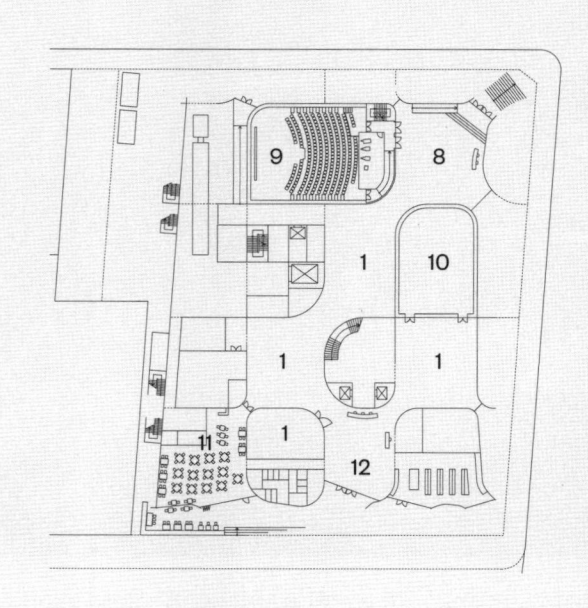

Clockwise from top right: Plans of the third, second, and ground floors with gallery (1), terrace (2), event space (3), offices (4), study center (5), screening room (6), art and film library (7), theater lobby (8), theater (9), black box (10), restaurant (11), and main entrance (12). West-east section. Distortion of the orthogonal grid to create curved walls and continuous spaces. Diagram of curved gallery walls. Conceptual sketch of interconnected functions

Located on a hillside of Omishima, a small island on the Seto Inland Sea, Toyo Ito Museum of Architecture, Imabari, is composed of Steel Hut, an exhibition space for Ito's work, and Silver Hut, an educational workshop and research center. The two buildings are in close proximity, linked by landscaping and a winding path. Steel Hut is a series of polyhedral modules, each with ten-foot (three-meter) sides that link together to create exhibition galleries. Fabricated out of steel painted black, the geometric forms stand apart from the landscape and give the building the appearance of an oversized molecular structure—an effect experienced on the interior as well, where gallery walls angle according to the number of sides.

Toyo Ito

Toyo Ito Museum of Architecture
Imabari, Japan 2008–11

Three stacked modules form a Brancusi-like tower for hosting lectures and roundtables. Nearby, Silver Hut recostructs, virtually unaltered, Ito's pavilion-like Tokyo home design from 1984. Seven vaulted roofs made out of lightweight steel span concrete posts set at approximately 12-foot (3.6-meter) distances. Vaults extended over two bays create larger courtyard spaces. The use of translucent materials references traditional Japanese domestic architecture while reprising Ito's early experiments with lightweight, provisional designs that privileged spare, prefabricated elements over form. —PS

Previous spread: Steel Hut looking west toward Seto Inland Sea
Clockwise from top: Silver Hut looking west. Aerial view of the site. Interior of a workshop in Silver Hut

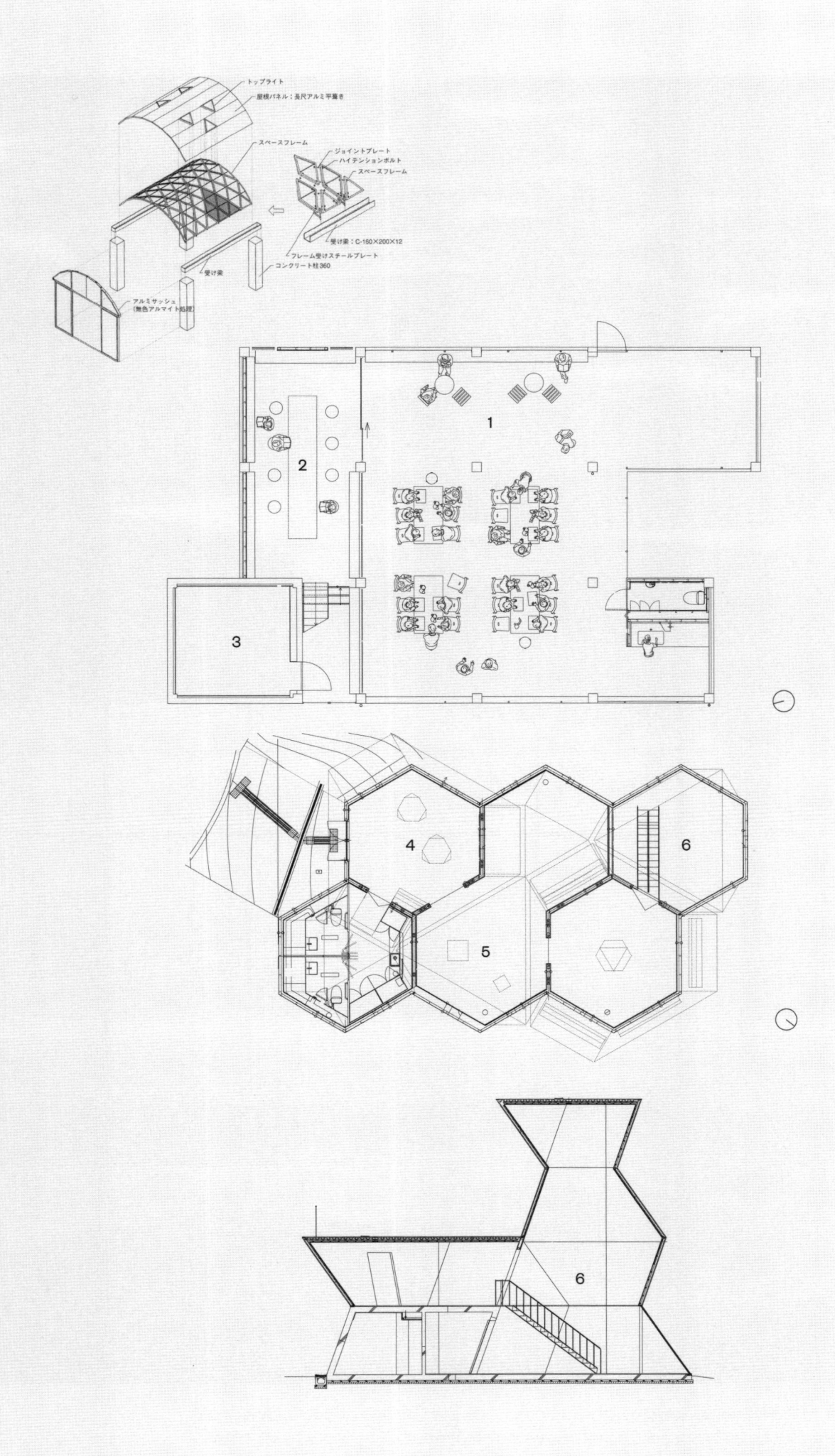

Toyo Ito

Toyo Ito Museum of Architecture
Imabari, Japan   2008–11

Clockwise from top: Diagram of Silver Hut components. Silver Hut plan with outdoor workshop (1), archive (2), and storage (3). Steel Hut ground-floor plan with entrance hall (4), gallery (5), and salon (6). Steel Hut section

Located toward the northern part of the National Taiwan University campus, the College of Social Sciences is comprised of two buildings: a single-story library and, rising above, an elongated eight-story block holding classrooms, conference rooms, and research laboratories. The beaux-arts style campus, established by the Japanese colonial government in the 1920s as Taihoku Imperial University, is dominated by a central axis along which the main university buildings are symmetrically organized. The college follows this general alignment while subtly introducing geometry inspired by patterns found in nature. The facade of the taller teaching wing is a regular concrete frame that extends beyond the line of the glass to become shade

Toyo Ito
National Taiwan University, College of Social Sciences
Taipei, Taiwan
2006–13

balconies and eaves; interspersed within this grid, two- and three-story voids introduce gardens, light, and air across the building. The library's open-stack reading area is composed around a grove-like cluster of columns. The locations and orientations of the columns were determined algorithmically; each slender, tubular support unfurls at the top into an irregular ellipse. Gathered together, these differently sized capitals leave gaps and crevices between, illuminating the library from above by dappled natural light. The reading room's geometry carries through both to the roof, where the elliptical planes hold an artificial lawn, and the surrounding plaza, where the forms are transformed into ovoid greens among winding walkways. —PS

Previous spread: Library reading room at night
Clockwise from top: Open stacks in the reading room. View of the library with the classroom and research block behind.
Reading room

Toyo Ito

National Taiwan University, College of Social Sciences

Taipei, Taiwan

2006–13

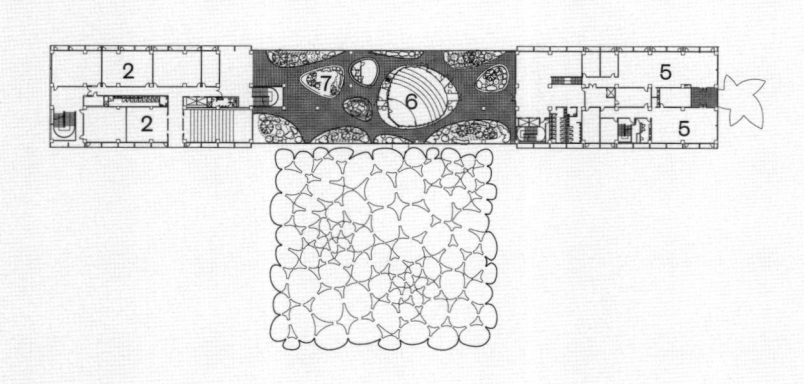

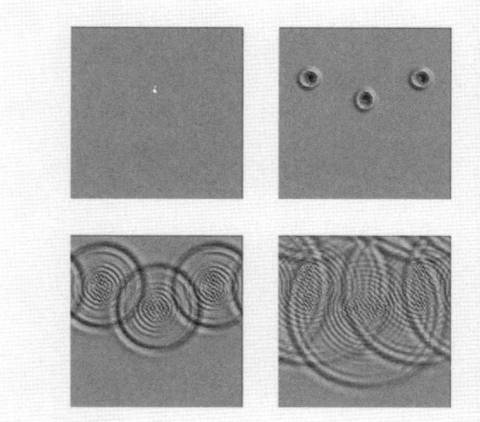

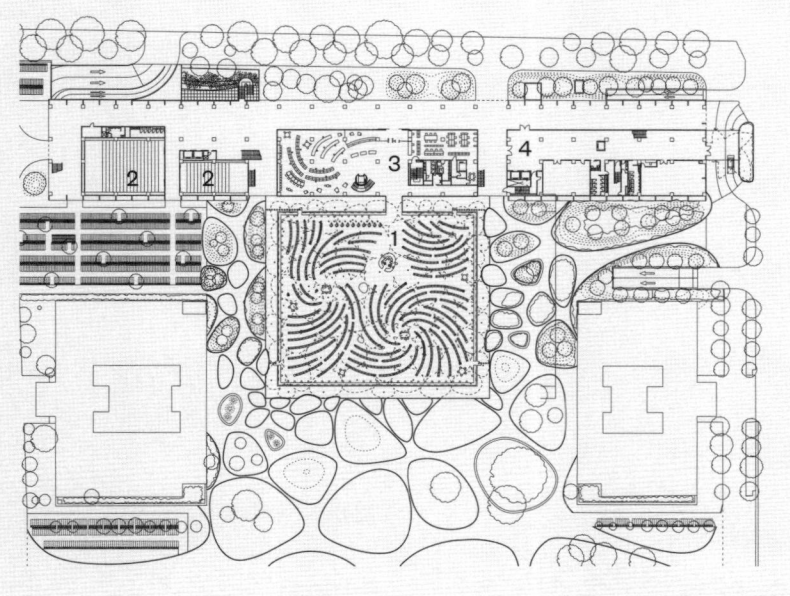

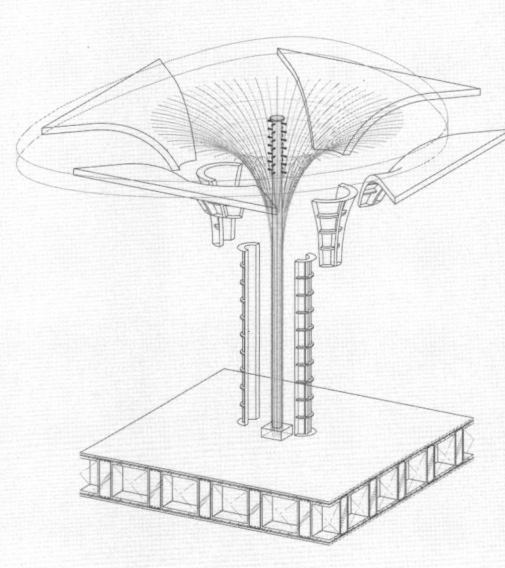

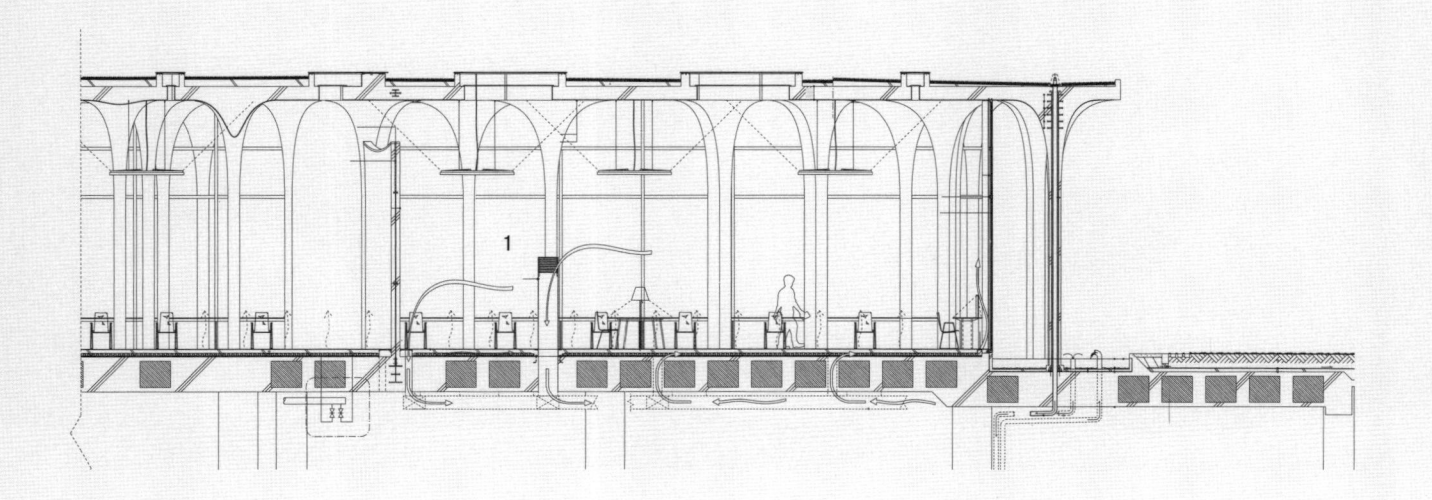

63

Clockwise from top right: Radial pattern of a water droplet. Diagram of the fiber-reinforced plastic framework used to construct the reading-room columns. Section detail of the ground-floor reading room. Plans of the ground and third floors with open-shelf reading room (1), classroom (2), library entrance (3), exhibition space (4), offices (5), conference hall (6), and garden (7)

Minna no Mori Gifu Media Cosmos, a two-story library, multimedia, and community center located in downtown Gifu, began with the idea of enclosing many homes under one roof. This idea is most explicitly explored in the second-floor reading room, with a series of suspended "globes"—as Ito calls them—creating intimate reading cupolas within the larger space of the library. Fabricated out of sheer polyester fabric stretched over rings, each globe shelters a space for a specific reading audience and is bounded by radially arranged book stacks. These individualized spaces for reading, play, and study are brought together beneath a majestic, gently rolling roof of laminated Japanese cypress. A diagonal grid of thin

Toyo Ito
Minna no Mori Gifu Media Cosmos
Gifu, Japan
2011–15

strips interlaced twenty-one-layers deep provides sufficient rigidity without additional structural steel. The fragrant cypress adds a less tangible, atmospheric dimension to the space, while the latticework allows in natural light. At the ground level, a series of volumes clad in different materials—a community theater, a gallery, an information center, and closed book stacks—give the impression of a loose composition of individual buildings along a public street. The project represents a shift in Ito's practice toward more ecologically sustainable, community-oriented design, which has had particular resonance following the 2011 Great East Japan Earthquake. —PS

Previous spread: Browsing "globe"
Clockwise from top: Second-floor reading room. Kinkazan terrace. Aerial view at night

Toyo Ito

Minna no Mori Gifu Media Cosmos

Gifu, Japan

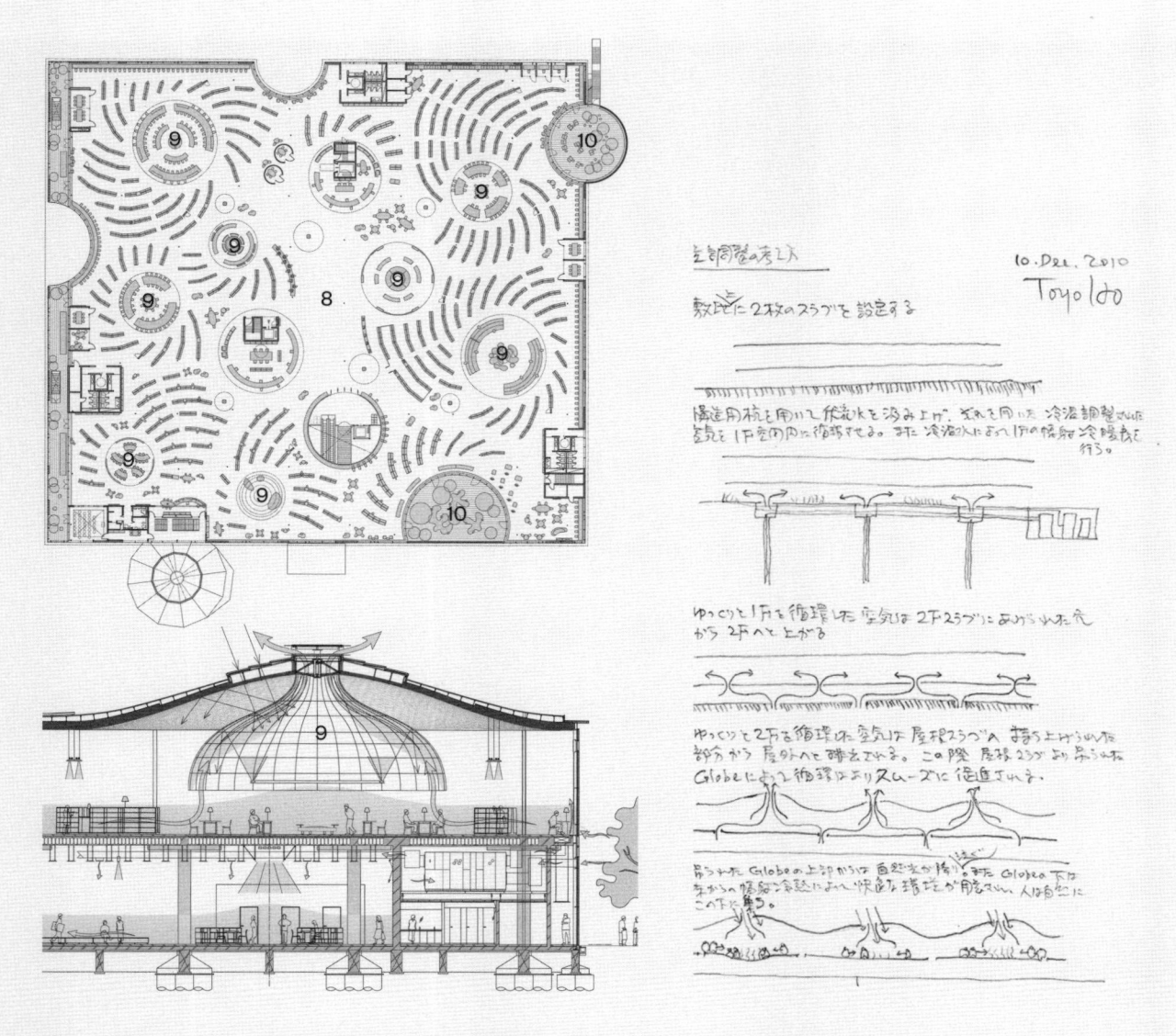

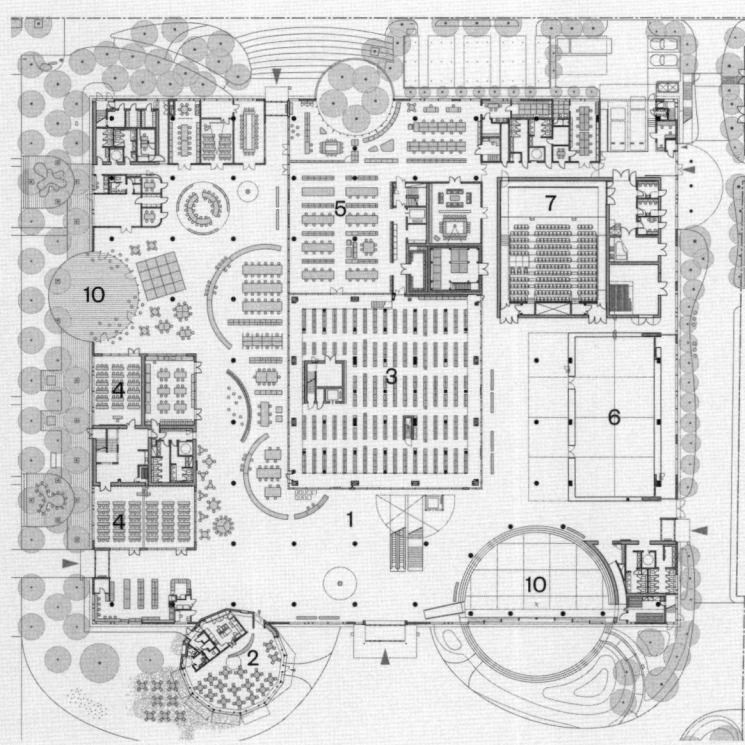

2011–15

67

Clockwise from top right: Initial sketch of the circulation of air and light through reading "globes," 2010. Ground-floor plan with entrance hall (1), restaurant (2), book stacks (3), lecture hall (4), offices (5), community gallery (6), and theater (7). Section detail at a reading "globe." Second-floor plan with open stacks (8), reading "globes" (9), and terrace (10)

National Taichung Theater, located in a redevelopment zone near the center of the Taiwanese city, holds three opera theaters—the Grand Theater boasts seating for up to two thousand people—along with retail shops and restaurants that open onto a landscaped plaza at the lower floors. The building's porous structure, described as a sound cave, is the result of a fluid topological grid in which three-dimensional curved shapes soften and distort the divisions between horizontal and vertical planes. Individually bent vertical truss walls form the catenary curves of the halls, skinned in metal mesh and given supple surface through sprayed and poured concrete. The concave spaces bear horizontal floors to accommodate

Toyo Ito

National Taichung Theater
Taichung, Taiwan

2005–ongoing

seating and theater stages. National Taichung Theater realizes a longstanding theme in Ito's work, in which the grid is modified and transformed to produce sensory-rich spaces that are as variable as those of the natural world. At the opera house, this connection to the environment is realized by merging interior and exterior in cambered forms that resemble the digestive organs that in Ito's words "are in some ways inside and in some ways outside the body."[1]—PS

Previous spread: View toward the city
From top: Southeast facade from the plaza. Main entrance at the southeast facade

1. Toyo Ito, interview by Terunobu Fujimori, "In Pursuit of Truth under Changing Circumstances," in Toyo Ito, *Toyo Ito 1971–2001*, trans. Hiroshi Watanabe (Tokyo: Toto, 2014), 29.

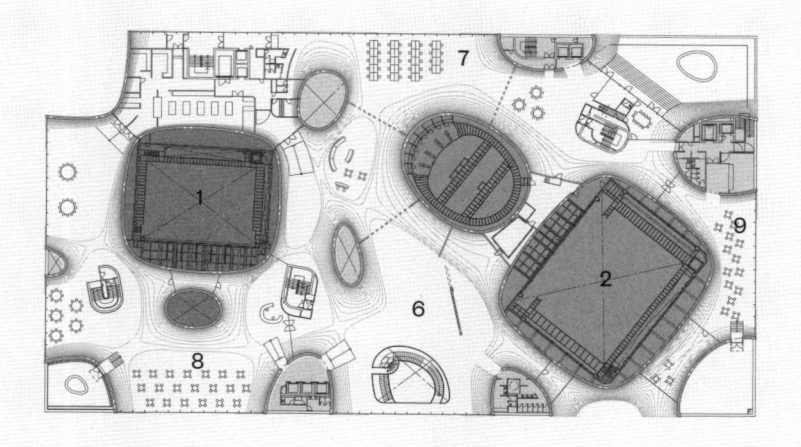

Floor 5

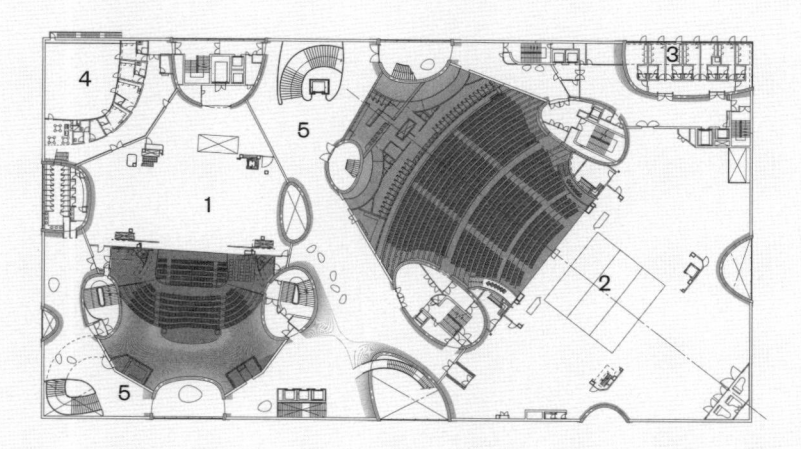

Floor 2

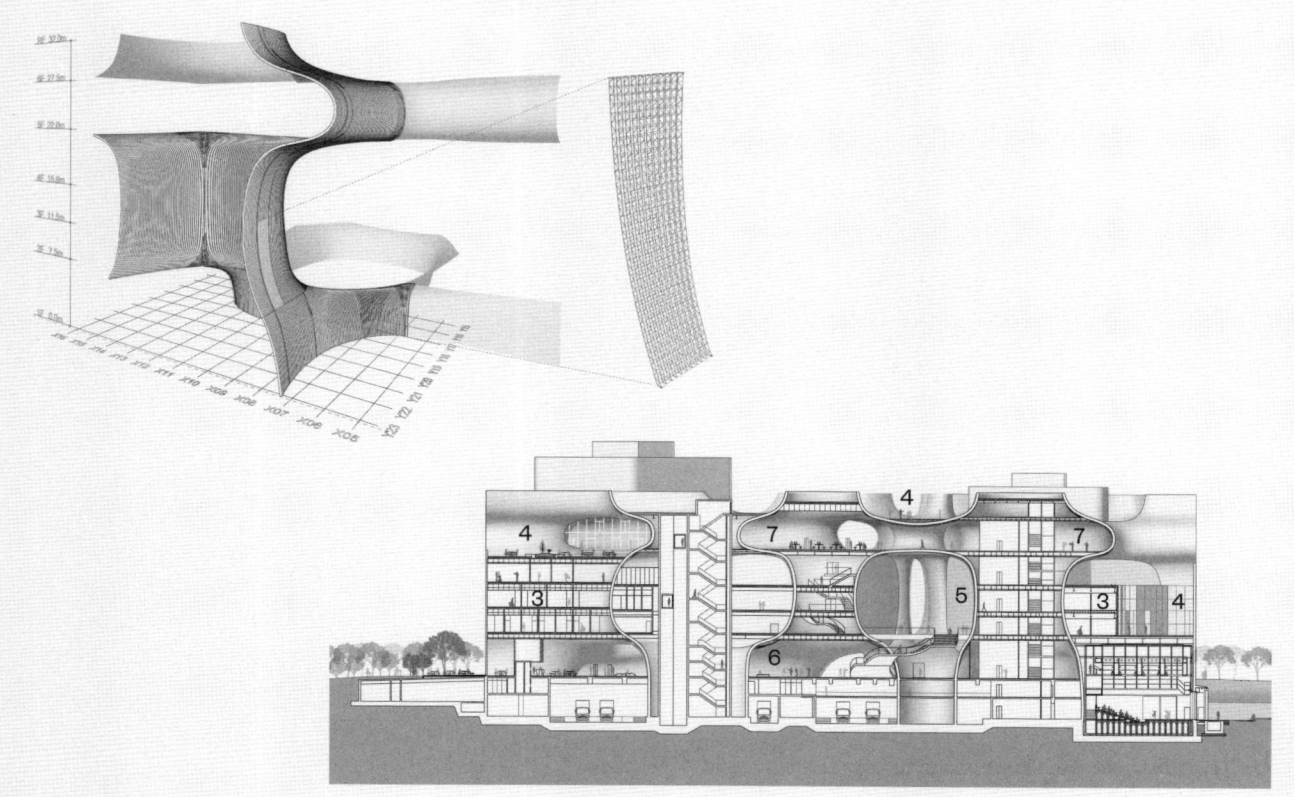

From top: Plans of the fifth and second floors with playhouse (1), grand theater (2), dressing room (3), terrace (4), foyer (5), event space (6), offices (7), restaurant (8), and green room (9). Catenoid construction unit made up of truss walls. North-south section

Toyo Ito

National Taichung Theater
Taichung, Taiwan

2005–ongoing

71

Magical Spatial Inversion

Terunobu Fujimori

By the end of the nineteenth century, the influence of historicism in architecture had reached its limits and was beginning to wane, making way for the sinuous outlines and stylized natural forms belonging to Art Nouveau. Within thirty years, Art Nouveau itself was succeeded by a new architectural approach emerging at the Bauhaus school in Weimar, Germany; founded in 1919 by architect Walter Gropius, the school's craft-based curriculum sought unity between art and design. Today we describe the most representative Bauhaus designs with terms such as "functionalism," "internationalism," and "modernism"—terms synonymous with twentieth-century architectural expression.

This is the usual way of explaining the events leading up to modernism. But architects and architectural historians seem to have forgotten an important harbinger: the year 1885, the year in which Friedrich Nietzsche published *Thus Spoke Zarathustra*, the year our gods died. Throughout Europe, for years to come, influential movements in the spheres of art, philosophy, literature, music, and architecture deeply mourned this loss.

Certainly since the time of Ancient Egypt, architecture has taken as its principal theme the existence of God (or of several gods). Of course, during the Renaissance era, architects trained as humanists, such as Leon Battista Alberti, attempted to design buildings that would appeal to both emotion and reason; but, even so, structures devoted to religious worship comprised by far the era's most important architecture. And although it is true that during the Industrial Revolution vulgar architectures flourished, they were often clothed in the borrowed raiment of religious structures.

Then God died, laying the foundations for twentieth-century architecture. Galvanizing the cultural and social spheres was not God's power to create but rather humankind's. A shift that began with Art Nouveau resolved itself thirty years later with steel, reinforced concrete, towering glass panes, pure white boxes, and dynamism. The resulting architecture evidenced the gifts wrought by twentieth-century science and technology. Functionalism, rationalism, internationalism—these were also the attributes of science and technology.

Meanwhile, in Japan, following a long history of timber construction, the year 1858 saw the start of an eighty-year enthusiasm for European Eclecticism, an architecture fashioned in brick and tile that mixed elements from previous historical periods with early modern styles. Japanese architects like Setsu Watanabe and Togo Murano studied Europe and America with care. In time they felt their work matched that of fine Western architects such as the prominent American architectural firm McKim, Mead & White, responsible, for instance, for New York's original Pennsylvania Station building (now demolished), considered a masterpiece of the beaux-arts style. But by 1935 at the latest, Eclecticism had given way to the influences of the Bauhaus.

Japanese connections to the German design school materialized with surprising speed. Takehiko Mizutani, a professor of architecture at the University of Tokyo, was in 1927 the school's first Japanese student. A few years later, in 1930, the husband-and-wife designers Iwao and Michiko Yamawaki, both of whom would go on to be educators, enrolled in the prestigious school. The same year, Bunzo Yamaguchi, who would go on to build several modernist structures in the Tokyo area, joined Walter Gropius's firm—this was shortly after Gropius left his position as head of the Bauhaus—and remained there until 1932.

The change was swift. In the 1930s, across the country, the government's Ministry of Communications (now the Ministry of Internal Affairs and Communications) outfitted its postal and telegraph offices in the style of the Bauhaus. The capital's elementary schools, too, were uniformly rendered in Bauhaus-inspired design.

As the Bauhaus took root in Japan, other Western influences also proliferated. In 1928, Kunio Maekawa, who would go on to become a key figure of modern Japanese architecture, traveled to France to apprentice in the office of Le Corbusier; he was soon followed by Junzo Sakakura. When eventually the two Japanese architects returned home, they actively sought to realize the ideals of their master. The architect Antonin Raymond, an American born in what is now the Czech Republic, came to Japan in 1919 to work for Frank Lloyd Wright; inspired by Auguste Perret's and Le Corbusier's expressive reinforced concrete, Raymond created structures distinct from those exhibiting the influence of the Bauhaus.

In the 1930s, both in Japan and worldwide, the ideas of Le Corbusier and the Bauhaus were often understood to share much in common, rejecting ornamentation and privileging, for instance, functional, open floor plans. The first to recognize and articulate the architects' differences was Kenzo Tange, then a young practitioner working in the office of Maekawa. In 1939, at age twenty-six, he published the critical essay

fig. 1

fig. 2

"A Eulogy to Michelangelo: A Preliminary Study of Le Corbusier."[1] Tange, who had studied Renaissance architecture, drew on Heidegger's 1937 essay "Hölderlin and the Essence of Poetry," only just translated into Japanese in 1938, quoting the philosopher's appraisal of the present as "the time of the gods that have fled and of the god that is coming."[2] Grouping together Filippo Brunelleschi, pioneer of early Renaissance architecture in Italy, and Gropius as architects enslaved to the frozen orthodoxy of geometry, Tange compared their work unfavorably to that of Michelangelo, Le Corbusier, and the three Grecian temples at Paestum, Italy, all of which, according to Tange, suggest uncontrived artistry. Michelangelo, he wrote in the essay, walked "along his own unique and tranquil path"[3] and took "on his shoulders the weight of the whole of history,"[4] while Le Corbusier was, at the time, "opening up a vista on the infinite."[5] The architectural expression of Brunelleschi and Gropius was dead; that of Michelangelo and Le Corbusier was alive.

The Bauhaus that Tange hated was, foremost, the Japanese version. Its leader was Mamoru Yamada, an architect in the Ministry of Communications, and the only Japanese designer to have a building included in The Museum of Modern Art's 1932 International Style showcase, *Modern Architecture: An International Exhibition*. Tange spoke disparagingly of Yamada's work as "sanitary wares."[6] Tange, by splitting Japanese modernists into two groups—those influenced by the Bauhaus and those influenced by Le Corbusier—discerned early on what other scholars and architects would conclude only much later.

—

The Bauhaus style was perfectly expressed though the school's own buildings: facades organized in tight geometric configurations driven by mathematical principles; large panes of glass set into white walls, slender and dazzling, the steel and glass technology seeming to promise invisibility. Bauhaus designs proffered a secular shrine to the twentieth century, the architecture simultaneously concrete and abstract. Let us call the Bauhaus school the "White School."

And what were the properties of the Corbusian school? Tange found in Le Corbusier's 1933 Swiss Pavilion (fig. 1), a dormitory built to house Swiss students at the Cité internationale universitaire in Paris, as with other works by the French architect, a "mysterious union of clarity and shade, of sadness and sublimity."[7] The pathos expressed in the pavilion's front-facing curved walls of natural stone and unfinished concrete fomented Tange's ideas in "A Eulogy to Michelangelo." Following the Swiss Pavilion, Le Corbusier's buildings set curved surfaces and lines against orthogonal geometries to achieve dynamic compositional effects. The French architect favored the sensual materiality of unfinished concrete and stone. Raymond, whose own expressive use of raw concrete anticipated that of Le Corbusier's, saw the gravel, cement, and sand mixture as a kind of natural stone for the twentieth century. Yet whether concrete, stone, or boulder, each holds a trait in common: each is of the earth. Let us call Le Corbusier's school the "Red School."

Mathematical, abstract, scientific, technical—these are the fundamental properties of the White School. Material, existential, carnal, earthy—this is the Red School. Mathematics versus materiality. One is a hidden world unavailable to the senses, controlled instead by calculations. The other is a world of what the eye sees, what the hand feels.

Of course if one were to ask which approach better reflects the fundamental qualities of the twentieth century, the answer is the White School. However, no matter how abstract, architecture ultimately must be built in relation to the earth—it should be experienced physically by those who pass through it. As long as this is the case, the architecture of the twentieth century cannot be separated from the reality of its materiality.

As a result, in our secular twentieth-century architecture, where mathematics is one with abstraction, and materiality one with the existential, these two schools stand like two magnetic poles. Architecture is in reality destined to exist somewhere between abstraction and materiality.

In this light, Japanese modernism has a sensibility that is decidedly distinct from its Western counterpart. Among the ranks of the White School architects before World War II were Yamada, as previously mentioned; Sutemi Horiguchi, who would become an expert on residential dwellings; and Kameki Tsuchiura, who embraced the standardization and efficiency of the International Style. After the war emerged Japan's first architects influenced by German architect Ludwig Mies van der Rohe: Kiyoshi Seike, a specialist in residential architecture; Fumihiko Maki, a modernist combining Eastern and Western influences into structures made of steel, glass, and concrete, and widely considered one of Japan's most distinguished living architects; Kazuo Shinohara, a mathematician turned architect who investigated architecture's fundamental dualities, such as privacy and publicness, openness and enclosure; Yoshio Taniguchi, architect of The Museum of Modern Art's redesigned building; and Hiroshi Hara, designer of the famous Umeda Sky Building in Osaka.

As for the Red School, Raymond, Maekawa, and Sakakura, each of whom I discuss above, were responsible for its debut before World War II. Immediately following the war, between 1950 and 1952, Takamasa Yoshizaka, too, would study under Le Corbusier, and would bring to Japan elements of the French architect's brutalism. And then our chief protagonist, Tange, would represent the Red School, followed by a few younger architects who were drawn to his ideas: Arata

Isozaki, whose early buildings mixed a new brutalism with Metabolism; as well as Kiyonori Kikutake and Kisho Kurokawa, both of whom were instrumental in founding the Metabolist group. The Japanese Red School's masterpiece is unmistakably Tange's Yoyogi National Gymnasium (fig. 2) in Tokyo's Yoyogi Park, built to host the swimming and diving events in the 1964 Summer Olympics, and whose dramatically sweeping curves and suspended roof are today iconic.

The White School and the Red School each realized its own moment of glory. Sometimes the two schools stood in strict opposition to one another; other times they conspired. But each was always strongly aware of its counterpart, and throughout the twentieth century, the two coexisted.

—

In the 1970s and 1980s, emboldened by the ingenuity of Tange's Gymnasium, Toyo Ito and Tadao Ando emerged as the leading lights of their generation, their path cleared by the architects who came before them. The overseas influence that so transformed the work of their progenitors was experienced only indirectly by Ito and Ando's generation; instead their architectural masters were almost singularly Japanese. But neither Ito nor Ando fit neatly into either one of the Red or White Schools.

I first made this distinction between the Red and White Schools of architecture in 1990, when I began to notice that Ando was somehow parting company with convention. If I had to say why, it was because I felt he was working in a Miesian, White School fashion compositionally, but using the raw, Corbusian concrete of the Red School. He was "pinkish."

Ito, from the first, strove for structures that were delicate, thin, and slender; in short, for the abstract. I placed him firmly in the White School, and Ito, too, acknowledged as much. But this would change throughout the progression of his career. Eventually Ito would decide to leave it to Kazuyo Sejima, a preeminent architect in the subsequent generation, to lead the White School. Instead, he declared his desire to follow after Gaudí and to make, in his golden years, a richly sculptural architecture like that of Le Corbusier.

Considering the White School's work from the 1990s with greater care: again, abstraction is a key feature, but the buildings were more than mere boxes. Curved lines and surfaces contributed an appealing dynamism. As the White School matured alongside the Red, the two schools did not harden their opposition, but in fact began to fuse. Ando and Ito were the first to achieve this fusion, and went on to inspire a new generation of architects in Japan. Their many followers include Sejima who, together with collaborator Ryue Nishizawa, founded the award-winning Tokyo-based studio SANAA, designer of the 21st Century Museum of Contemporary Art, of 2004, in Kanazawa, Japan (p. 106), and the Glass Pavilion at the Toledo Museum of Art, of 2006, in Ohio (p. 112); Akihisa Hirata, known for his geometric architecture inspired by his observations of the natural world, including his Tree-ness House, begun in 2009 (p. 214); and Junya Ishigami, whose work expresses his interests in the relationship between architecture, design, and geography, and blends the scientific with the poetic, as it does in the Port of Kinmen Passenger Service Center, begun in 2014 (p. 236).

—

The relationship between wall and space has always been central to architecture. Throughout most of architectural history, walls performed a function: to divide space into inside and outside. But in the twentieth century, modernist architects began using walls to harbor large panes of glass. Architecture, suddenly, was no longer merely about severing a series of rooms, one from the next. In these glass-paneled structures, space flowed uninterrupted between interior and exterior, drawing the two into an architectural relationship. This newfound continuity between inside and outside, as renowned architectural historian Vincent Scully points out, is a fundamental characteristic of modernism.

Ito, however, is less interested in the spatial continuity between inside and outside than he is in rendering the distinction ambiguous. In the summer of 2013, he told me in conversation, "If you set a straight wall on a flat slab, the space to each side of the wall, right and left, is the same. But with the slightest inflection in the wall, you create, to one side, a protected interior and, to the other, something without. And if, once more, you again inflect the wall, but now in the opposite direction, then what was interior is instantly transformed to the exterior. Likewise, what was outside is changed to the inside. I'm attracted to this spatial inversion."

Imagine a squishy rubber ball with a tiny hole in its surface. By reaching in and drawing out part of the rubber wall through the little hole,

fig. 3

fig. 4

outside becomes inside, and what was inside propels outside. Ito was likely the first to pursue this idea.

Two buildings of Ito's in particular—the 1976 White U (fig. 3) in Tokyo, a U-shaped house built of concrete, and his 1993 Shimosuwa Municipal Museum (fig. 4), an irregular-shaped concrete and steel-frame arc—prompted my identification of this phenomenon. Both buildings hold strong familial ties for Ito: White U served as a home for his grieving sister, while the museum paid tribute to the history and culture of Shimosuwa, the hometown of Ito's father and a place where Ito spent part of his childhood. The two buildings also have richly verdant surroundings. Comparing them against each other, I realized that if you turned White U inside out, you'd have something like the Municipal Museum.

To understand this, one might compare Sendai Mediatheque (fig. 5) to Le Corbusier's Maison Dom-Ino, of 1914 (fig. 6): Le Corbusier's columns become Ito's latticed tubes. The spatial consequences, however, are quite different. For example, when examining Maison Dom-Ino from the outside, one sees only internal space. When outside Sendai Mediatheque, however, one can see two distinct "insides": the interior of the building itself, and beyond that, the interior space of the tubes. Usually, in tubular structures, what falls outside the tube falls outside the architecture; whereas, in this case, what falls outside the tubes falls within the architecture.

Ito has conceived a new kind of space, one that can't be called inside or outside, a phenomenon one can only really imagine, one that, in part because outside air flows through the internal tubular columns, inverts the inside and outside of Maison Dom-Ino's columnar structure. What should one call a space within a space? Ito used his magic to complicate what was once a simple distinction—inside and outside—ushering in a new approach to space that evokes both at once.

But this raises an unavoidable problem. If there is no difference between inside and outside, how does one render the exterior? One could enclose the whole thing in a box, in four walls of glass; but Ito has said he wants his buildings to look as if there is no glass. How far can the erasure between inside and outside extend?

I'd like to take a moment before ending to explain myself. I'm an architectural historian, a specialist on Japan's modern era; Ito and I are, simply put, men of the same generation—and also of the same place. From a young age, I've been paying close attention to his progress. Especially after, at the age of forty-five, I too began designing buildings, I prudently made it a point to set my course directly opposite the one Ito took in his own designs. Even now I follow the same strategy. As a result I have also become a very close watcher of Ito and those influenced by him.

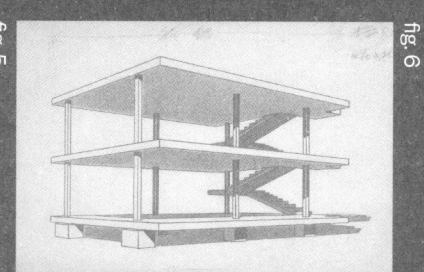

I can say, therefore, that many young architects who came of age just as Ito reversed the distinction between inside and outside in Sendai Mediatheque have each in their own way engaged passionately with this problem, coming up with their own various results. And that's my perspective: how I see Toyo Ito and his "children."

Fig. 5: Toyo Ito. Sendai Mediatheque, Miyagi, Japan, 1995–2001. South façade. Fig. 6: Le Corbusier. Perspective of a Dom-Ino module, 1915. Ink, pencil, and colored pencil on paper, 18 1/2 × 22 1/2" (47 × 57 cm). Fondation Le Corbusier, Paris.

fig. 5

fig. 6

Notes

1. First published as Kenzo Tange, "Michelangelo shō: Le Corbusier ron e no josetsu to shite," *Gendai kenchiku*, 1939, vol. 7. Reprinted in "A Eulogy to Michelangelo: A Preliminary Study of Le Corbusier," trans. Robin Thompson, *Art in Translation* 4 (2012): 391–405.
2. Martin Heidegger quoted in Tange, "A Eulogy to Michelangelo," 397. Original quote from "Hölderlin and the Essence of Poetry," trans. Douglas Scott, in *Heidegger, Existence and Being*, intro. Werner Brock (London: Vision Press, 1968), 313–14.
3. Tange, "A Eulogy to Michelangelo," 400.
4. Ibid., 403.
5. Ibid., 404.
6. Kenzo Tange and Terunobu Fujimori, *Kenzo Tange* (Tokyo: Shinkenchiku-sha, 2002), 60–61.

Space as Communication

As an architect, I feel it is part of our profession to use space as a medium to express our thoughts—space becomes a means of communication. Building is a conversation with the user, the client, the landscape, or the intended function itself. The job of the architect now is to understand and appreciate diversity and to create spaces where those differences can coexist. We need transparency that is not visual but experiential—that exists because the public can understand a building's organization by moving through it and, moreover, how to touch it or relate to it physically. Of course, this is not always possible, at least not immediately; but sometimes the relationship between a building and a body can be understood in a gradual way. The environment around a building should also always be understood through the atmosphere created by time.*

Kazuyo Sejima

On a corner plot in a residential neighborhood, this three-story white house is home to three generations: a couple, their two children, and a grandmother. The family asked to preserve as much of the small site as possible to replant plum trees; in response, Sejima devised a concise structure based on four quadrants divided into many smaller rooms. Departing from typical residential layouts that feature large shared living spaces and a bedroom for each inhabitant, House in a Plum Grove creates variable spaces for changing daily routines. To connect the spaces, the interior walls, which form the house's primary structural element, are kept very thin, prefabricated out of steel plate eleven-sixteenths of an inch (sixteen

Kazuyo Sejima   House in a Plum Grove   Tokyo   1999–2004

millimeters) thick. Different size apertures, left as stark openings unfinished by frames or glass, punctuate the walls. Each room is experienced in visual and audio synchrony with the rest of the house; the cut-outs transform activity in adjacent rooms into pictorial scenes framed against unadorned white walls and stripped of depth. Central to the house's conception is the idea that it will evolve with the life of its inhabitants. As Sejima describes, "All buildings support everyday use, but houses do that in a special way because they are spaces that are very close to the body."[1] Over time, through use, the spaces will be reinvented, generating "a softer sense of privacy [. . .] a little different from what we knew before."[2] —PS

Previous spread: Northeast and northwest facades during two different seasons
Clockwise from top left: Third-floor meditation room. Ground-floor bedroom. Ground-floor dining room viewed from bedroom

* Excerpt from "A Conversation with Kazuyo Sejima and Ryue Nishizawa," trans. Jamie Benyai, Liliana C. Obal, and Albert Fuentes, in "Sistemas de Continuidad/Continuity Systems: SANAA 2011-2015," special issue, *El Croquis* 179/180. Reprinted with modifications and permission by the architects. 1. "A Conversation with Kazuyo Sejima and Ryue Nishizawa," trans. Jamie Benyai, Liliana C. Obal, and Albert Fuentes, in "Sistemas de Continuidad/Continuity Systems: SANAA 2011-2015," special issue, *El Croquis* 179/180: 23. 2. Kazuyo Sejima, "House in a Plum Grove," *GA Houses* 70: 12.

Kazuyo Sejima   House in a Plum Grove   Tokyo   1999–2004   83

From top: Elevations. Plans of the ground and second floors with dining room (1), kitchen (2), tatami room (3), bedroom (4), library (5), and study (6)

A composition of three single-story buildings, Multipurpose Facility is located at the center of a large green in a semirural town northwest of Tokyo. Its shallow rooflines echo the surrounding residential architecture while pedestrian paths loop between the facility and the town. The initial competition brief called for an "indoor plaza"[1] and the completed structure retains this ambiguous hybrid of interior and exterior space through its use of glass and geometry. A multipurpose hall, sports center, and smaller administrative area wrap around one another in amoebic curves, sinking the gym and auditorium belowground. Between the main halls, the buildings stretch into narrow, glass-lined passages that round into

Kazuyo Sejima Multipurpose Facility Onishi, Japan 2003–05

bulb-like foyers and entrances. These attenuated spans carry the facility across the extent of the site, linking the different spaces while minimizing the building's mass. In contrast to the remarkably plastic forms of the plan, at ground level, the building's physical presence is muted by the play of reflection and transparency on the glass surfaces. These surfaces transform the facility into a lens through which to view the town, while also opening communication between the different halls and adjacent spaces. —PS

Previous spread: View from the multipurpose hall toward the sports hall
Clockwise from top: Aerial view of passage between sports hall and foyer. South facade. Sports hall interior

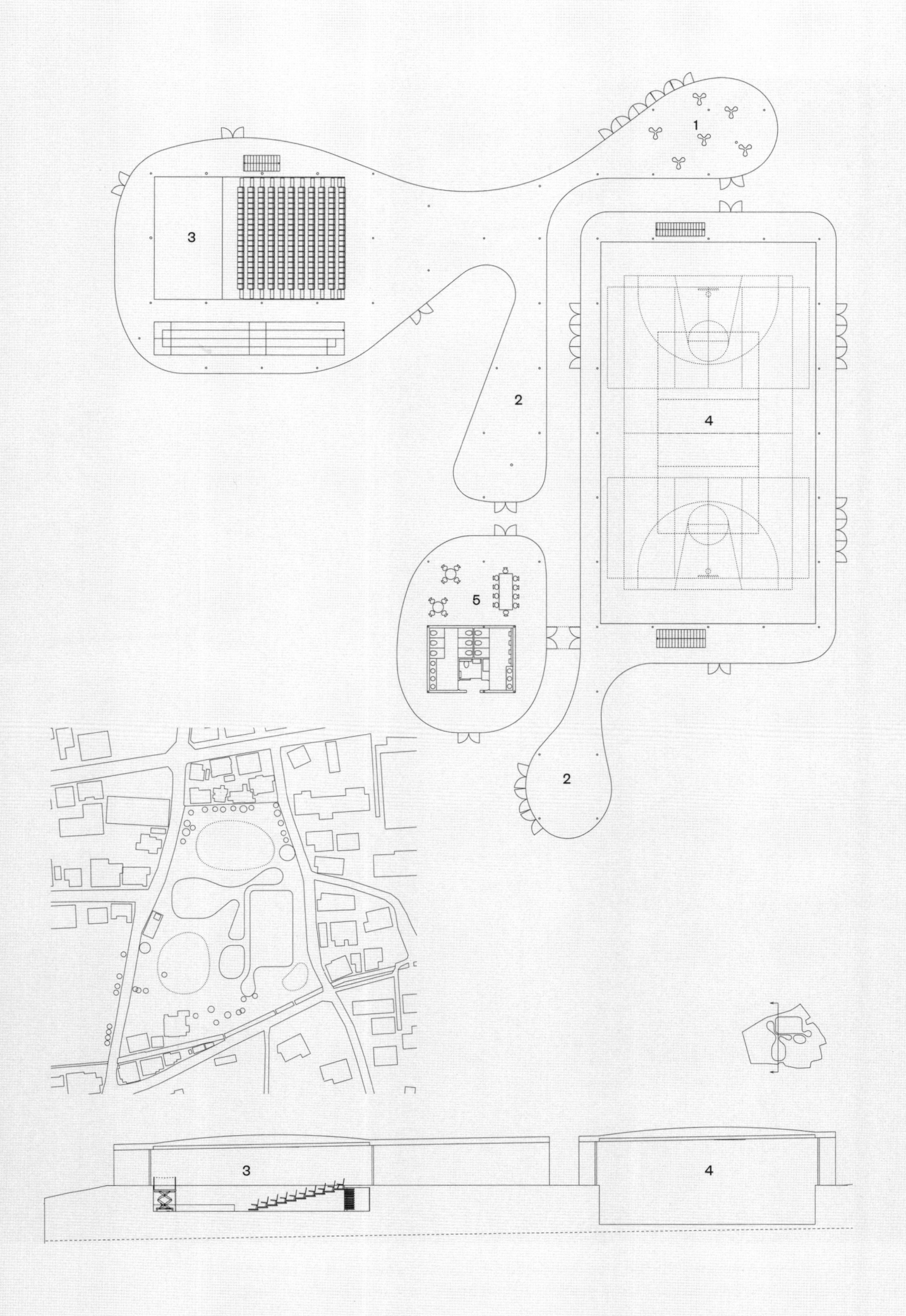

Kazuyo Sejima Multipurpose Facility
Onishi, Japan 2003–05

From top: Ground-floor plan with foyer (1), entrance (2), multipurpose hall (3), sports hall (4), and office (5). Site plan. Section through multipurpose hall and sports hall

87

Inujima Art House Project is five pavilions for the display of art and one rest area scattered among the domestic buildings of a village on a hilly harbor site on the Seto Inland Sea. One in a series of contemporary art and architecture projects funded by the Fukutake Foundation and Benesse Holdings, Art House Project is located on the postindustrial Inujima island, now home to a tiny, aging population. The pavilions, Nakanotani Gazebo and galleries labeled F-, S-, I-, A-, and C-Art House, mix materials used in residential architecture—stone and wood—with transparent acrylic and mirrored aluminum. Both new constructions and renovations, the pavilions are small in scale and embedded within the landscape, combining

Kazuyo Sejima   Inujima Art House Project   Inujima, Japan   2008–10

familiar features with surprising details. An essential part of the design is the promenade: encountered on foot—the island is without cars—the aluminum disc of Nakanotani Gazebo is discovered cresting a hill, while S-Art House's transparent channel offers an altered passage between two traditional wood frame houses. Introducing unexpected, abstract forms to Inujima's landscape, the architecture is in turn transformed by weather; the clear acrylic panels of A-Art House, for instance, are rendered translucent by fog. Sejima describes her initial concept as "treating the village itself as an art museum,"[1] and the project creates a scenery intimately scaled to Inujima's environment, subtly altering everyday experience.—PS

Previous spread: Aerial view of A-Art House with Haruka Kojin's *reflectwo*, 2013
From top: Passage between S-Art House and A-Art House with Haruka Kojin's *contact lens*, 2013. Interior of C-Art House with old timber frame supported by new pillars

1. Kazuyo Sejima, "Architecture Scaled to Its Environment," *Insular Insight: Where Art and Architecture Conspire with Nature*, ed. Lars Müller and Akiko Miki (Baden, Germany: Lars Müller Publishers, 2011), 428.

Kazuyo Sejima   Inujima Art House Project
Inujima, Japan

2008–10

91

Nakanotani Gazebo from the road to the south

From top: C-Art House. Garden gallery of F-Art House

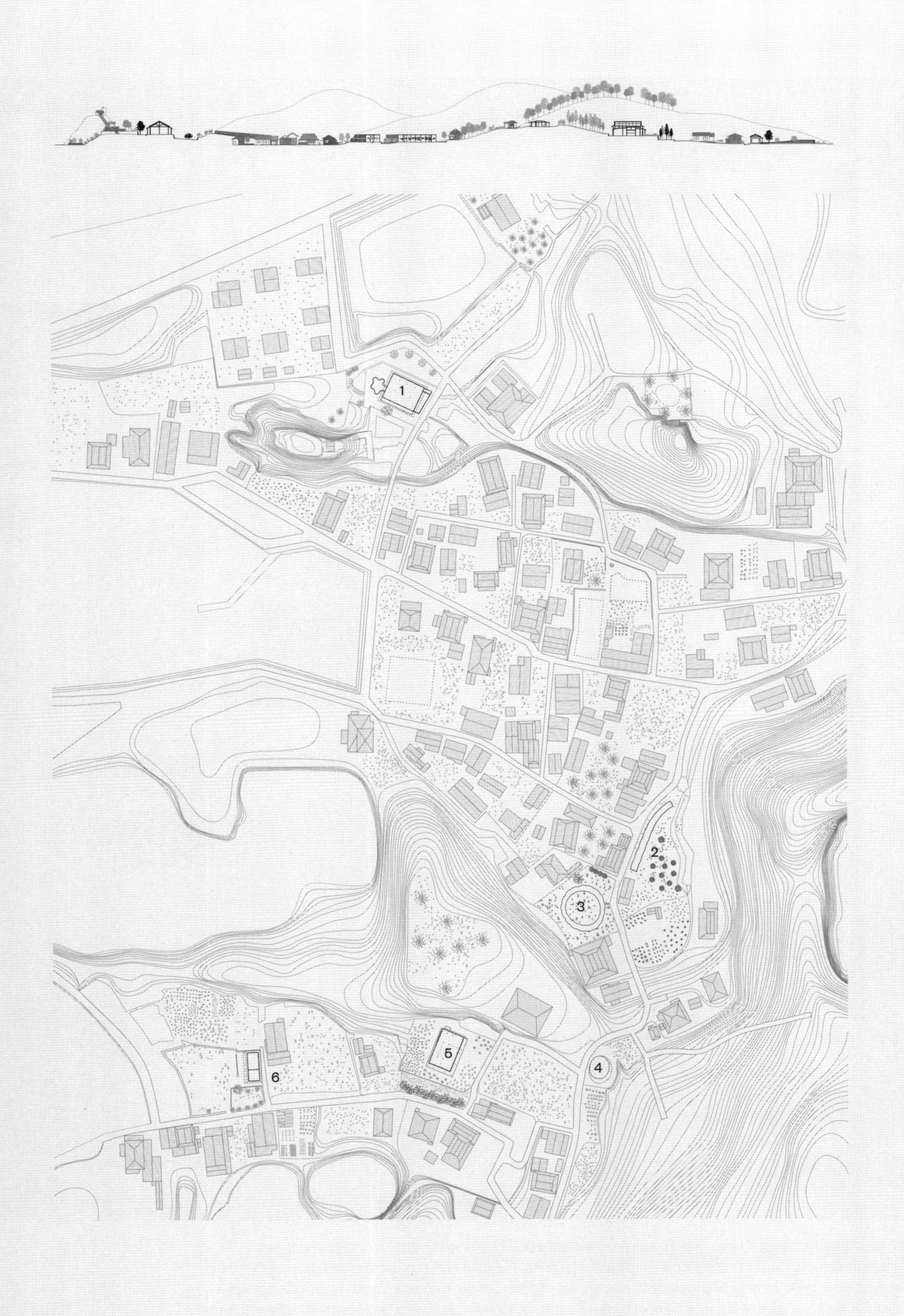

Kazuyo Sejima   Inujima Art House Project   Inujima, Japan   2008–10   93

From top: Site section. Site plan with locations of F-Art House (1), S-Art House (2), A-Art House (3), Nakanotani Gazebo (4), C-Art House (5), and I-Art House (6)

In a residential neighborhood of Kyoto, within view of Mount Hiei, Nishinoyama House clusters ten apartment units below a canopy of tilted and overlapping roofs. Responding to local building restrictions meant to preserve the city's historic urban fabric by regulating the angle, material, and color of residential roofs, the units are given pitched roofs of corrugated metal and kept at a modest scale in reference to the character of the surrounding architecture. To create a sense of community and accommodate density within the rectangular plot, the twenty-one roofs are inclined at different degrees and varied in height and direction; each shelters multiple rooms connecting neighboring apartments below shared

Kazuyo Sejima   Nishinoyama House   Kyoto, Japan   2010–13

planes. The roof angles and their misalignments create clerestories that bring daylight deep into the plan. The individual units, based on a grid and varying in size from 592 to 1076 square feet (55 to 100 square meters), offset the kitchen, living room, and bedrooms to create pathways, shared spaces, and gardens between the interlocked apartments. Inside, glass walls and sliding doors open directly onto courtyard gardens while solid partitions maintain privacy between units. With its semblance of a village, Nishinoyama creates an intricate balance between private and public life. —PS

Previous spread: Aerial view of overlapping roofs
Clockwise from top: Courtyard. Kitchen. View from study toward dining room

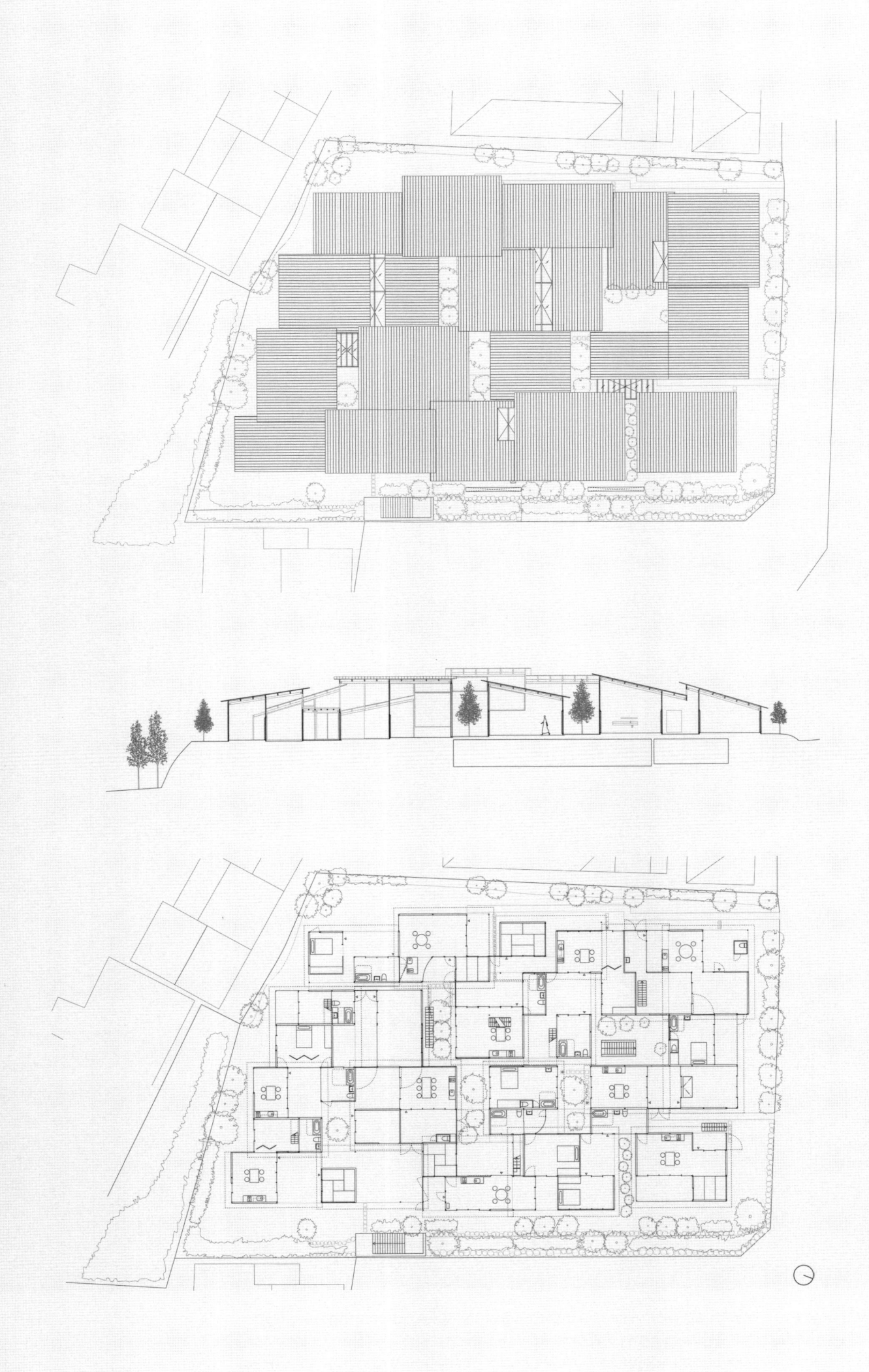

Kazuyo Sejima Nishinoyama House Kyoto, Japan 2010–13

From top: Roof plan indicating slope and angle. Section. Ground-floor plan of the ten-unit apartment complex distributed among twenty-one rooms

A community center and library are enclosed within seven canted, gently splayed volumes knitted together by an exterior of expanded metal mesh. The syncopated volumes establish different size spaces that are independent yet linked to support community gatherings and information exchange, the formal arrangement reflecting the social nature of Nakamachi Terrace. At ground level, separate enclosures host a cooking studio, café, and reception area. As the building rises, the forms lean in, merging into a larger, continuous space holding the library reading rooms at the upper two floors. This is expressed structurally at the ground floor where oblique steel frames, angled to converge at the second floor, create outdoor,

Kazuyo Sejima
Nakamachi Terrace Community Center and Library
Tokyo
2010–14

triangular passageways beneath the building. Passing through these corridors renders the building a visually fractured, expressionistic composition of steel and trapezoidal glass panels that reveals the different activities within. The internal complexity contrasts with the clear massing of the building when viewed from the street. At night, lit from behind, the facade of porous metal mesh illuminates the building's linked floorplates and ascension to a shared library. —PS

Previous spread: South facade from the street
Clockwise from top: Reception area. Third-floor library reading area. Ground-floor café

Kazuyo Sejima Nakamachi Terrace Community Center and Library Tokyo 2010–14

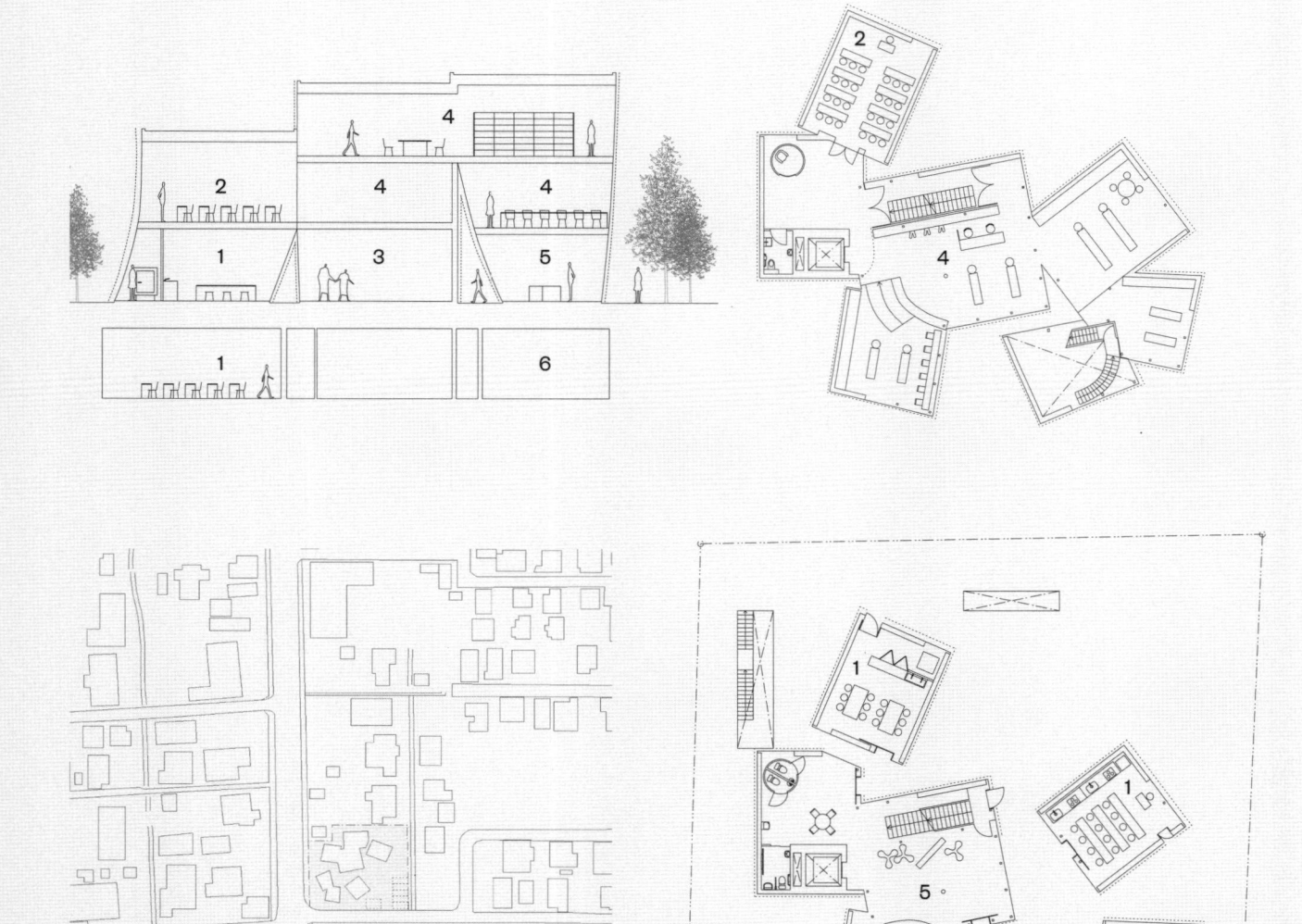

Clockwise from top left: Section with studio (1), lecture hall (2), entrance hall (3), reading lounge (4), reception (5), and office (6).
Plans of the second and ground floors. Site plan

Open Architecture

Our works of architecture are generally open in character. We make them open because we want to build relationships. Once a relationship is established, it motivates various creative developments. This is true of the relationship between outside and inside, as well as, to some extent, the relationship between two places. We are interested in thinking about architecture as being like furniture, or like landscape, or like a city. But, we also want to think about space as a means of communication. Architecture acts as a catalyst. Thinking about spatial structure is, for us, one of the most important steps in creating new relationships and bringing about new experiences. To achieve this, each partner has a different instrument and plays a different song, and, together, we create something new.[*]

SANAA

Suspended in a white, disc-shaped roof, nineteen exhibition galleries of varying shapes project at different heights like objects in a still-life tableau. With a permanent collection that includes commissioned works by Anish Kapoor and James Turrell, the 21st Century Museum combines galleries with community-oriented spaces, including a children's studio, a library, and lecture halls along the perimeter. Three hundred and sixty feet (one hundred and ten meters) in diameter, a band of curved glass encloses the museum, superimposing reflections of the city on views of the interior in a three-hundred-and-sixty-degree panorama. Without a formal front or back, the museum's structure is strikingly nonhierarchical: contained within a single

SANAA
21st Century Museum of Contemporary Art
Kanazawa, Japan
1999–2004

floor, a matrix of public corridors with a continuous ceiling height connects the galleries; visitors dictate their experience and sequence. The galleries, with different lighting conditions and proportions, range in height from thirteen feet (four meters) to thirty-nine feet (twelve meters) and have built-in flexibility: an exhibition can be contained within a single room or expanded across several and linked to the corridors, which also act as display spaces. Regularly transformed by artist projects, the museum's loose arrangement of galleries and luminous internal courtyards exemplifies SANAA's belief that in architecture "use is not limited to function. It is also a very powerful creative tool."[1]—PS

Previous spread: Aerial view from the west
Above: Interior view toward courtyard with Leandro Erlich's permanent installation, *Swimming Pool*, 2004, concrete, glass, 9' 3/16" × 13' 3/16" × 22 13/16" (280 × 402 × 697 cm)

* Excerpts from "SANAA 2008–2011: Kazuyo Sejima and Ryue Nishizawa," *El Croquis* 155; and Ryue Nishizawa, "On Relationships," trans. Lisa Tani, in "Kazuyo Sejima and Ryue Nishizawa, 2006–2011," special issue, *GA Architect* 20. Reprinted with modifications and permission by the architects. 1. "A Conversation with Kazuyo Sejima and Ryue Nishizawa," trans. Janie Benyai, Liliana C. Obal, and Albert Fuentes, in "Sistemas de Continuidad/Continuity Systems: SANAA 2011–2015," special issue, *El Croquis* 179/180: 23.

SANAA

21st Century Museum of Contemporary Art
Kanazawa, Japan
1999–2004

From top: Exterior from the northeast. View of foyer

From top: Interior with Katsuhiko Hibino's yearlong project, *Home and Away System*, of 2007, from his series Asatte Asagao Project 21, of 2006–08. Temporary exhibition gallery

SANAA

21st Century Museum of Contemporary Art
Kanazawa, Japan
1999–2004

From top: Plan with gallery (1), Turrell Room (2), Kapoor Room (3), People's Gallery (4), courtyard (5), theater (6), kids' studio (7), lecture hall (8), foyer (9), café (10), offices (11) and library (12). Sections. Site plan

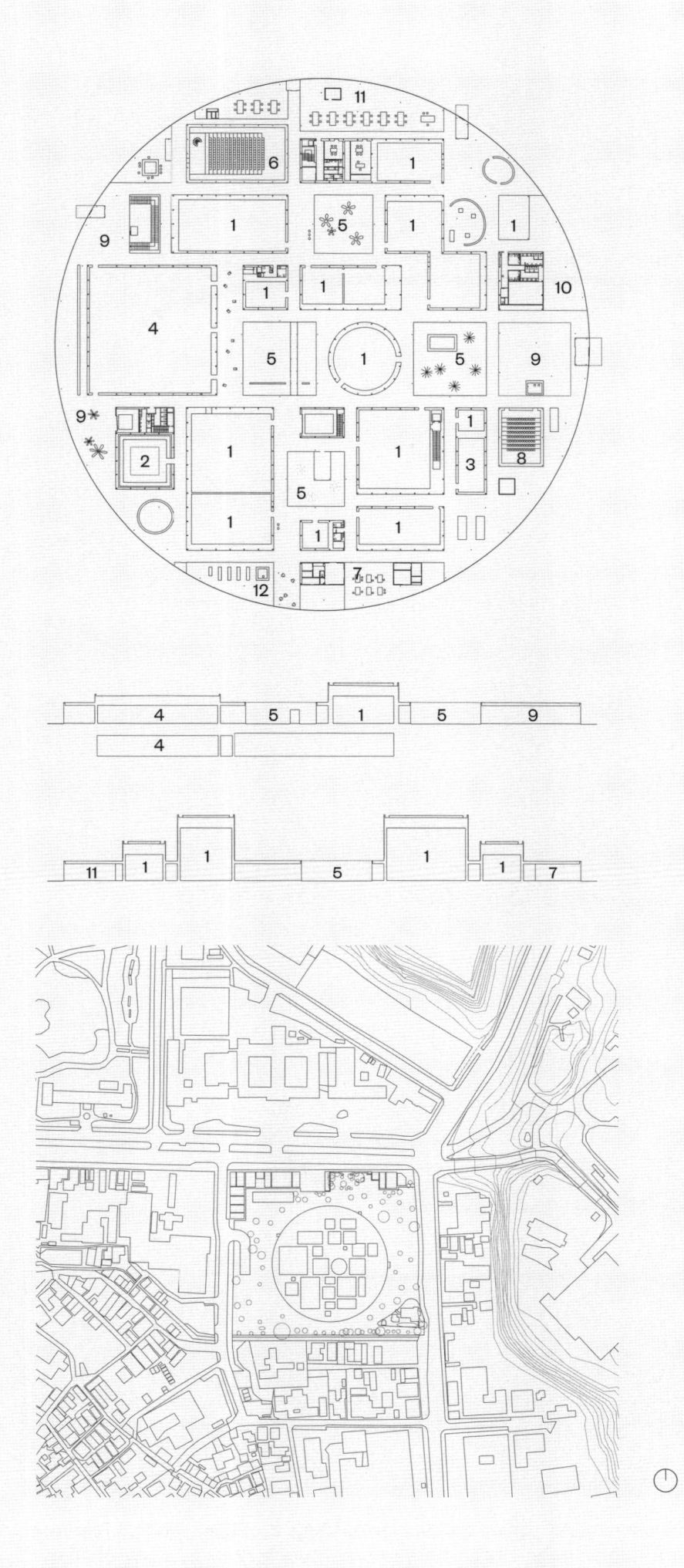

A single-story annex to the Toledo Museum of Art's main beaux-arts building, the Glass Pavilion features the museum's large glass collection, a legacy of the city's nineteenth-century history as a center of industrial and craft glass production. Radiused walls of glass enclose exhibition galleries, an active glass-making workshop with a demonstration area, and studios, while courtyards brighten the interiors and frame views of the sky. To foreground the transparency of the walls, the loading dock and mechanical systems are hidden belowground. Each room, rather than sharing a wall with an adjoining space, is enclosed by its own elliptical ribbon of glass, creating interstitial cavities between the hotshop, galleries,

SANAA

Glass Pavilion, Toledo Museum of Art
Toledo, Ohio   2001–06

113

and exterior, that regulate temperature and humidity and provide acoustic insulation. The layering of glass is both a functional solution to accommodate the museum's different activities and an exuberant sensorial experience: the glass is rarely transparent; its supple, curved surfaces mediate a play of shifting reflections and anamorphic distortions that fluctuate in accordance to changes in light, visitor movement, and the outside environment. The art is experienced in an atmosphere not delimited by walls but in continuum with an expansive visual panorama.—PS

Previous spread from left: Interior view toward courtyard two. Cavity space between courtyard one and rest area
From top: Exhibition galleries. Southeast facade with entrance

SANAA

Glass Pavilion, Toledo Museum of Art
Toledo, Ohio   2001–06

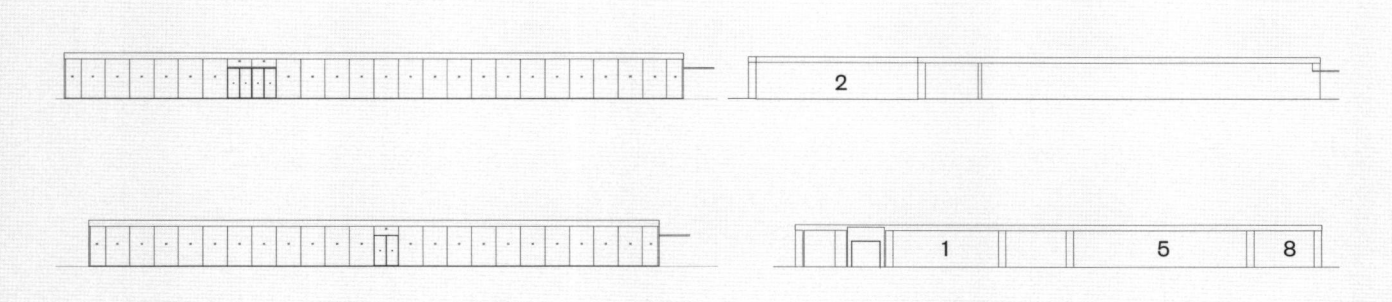

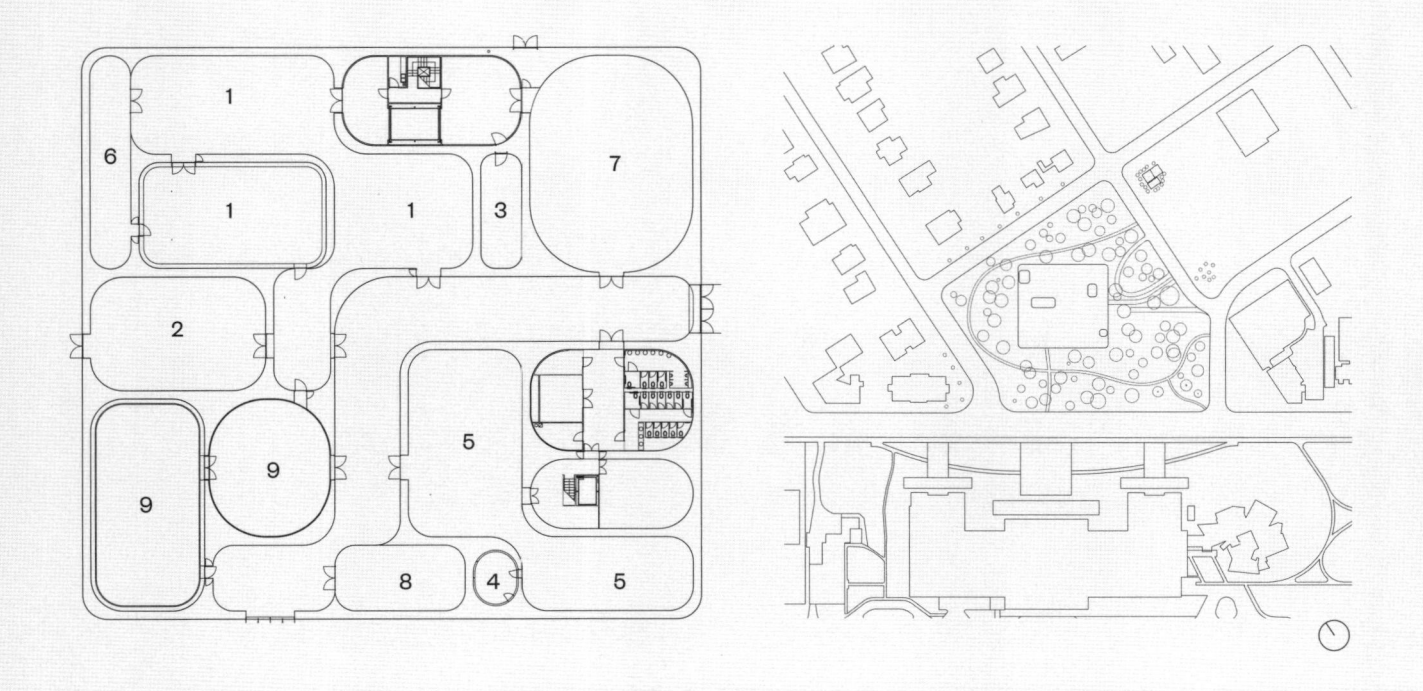

115

Clockwise from top left: Southeast and northwest elevations. Sections. Site plan. Ground-floor plan with gallery (1), courtyard one (2), courtyard two (3), courtyard three (4), hotshop (5), rest area (6), multipurpose area (7), café (8), and storage (9)

This school of management and design, is located in Germany's Ruhr region on the edge of the former Zollverein Coal Mine, a defunct industrial complex built in the nineteenth century and given modernist revision during the interwar years. SANAA's precise 377-square-foot (35-square-meter) cube stands out against the postindustrial landscape of pit baths, shafts, and coking plants. Of a monumental scale, its regular geometry is stippled with an asymmetrical pattern of cutouts placed irregularly in relation to the building's floors, achieving an abstraction not easily related to a conventional building type. At the interior, five floors linked by three cores hold studios, a library, and offices. Each level is a different

SANAA
Zollverein School of Management and Design
Essen, Germany
2003–06

height; the second floor is an open, discursive space nearly thirty-three feet (ten meters) high, while the uppermost floor holds a partially enclosed roof garden. From within, the building's apparent solidity dissolves into a screen of framed views onto the landscape. The building's contemporary interpretation of the industrial landscape is also functional: the thinness of the load-bearing exterior walls of reinforced concrete is enabled by redirecting warm water from the former mine shafts to act as active insulation for the school.—PS

Previous spread: Walter Niedermayr, *Bildraum S 130*, 2006, digital pigment print, two panels, 40' 15/16" x 8' 8 5/16" (104 x 265 cm).
Courtesy the artist and Galerie Nordenhake Berlin/Stockholm. © Walter Niedermayr
From top: Second-floor studio. Roof garden

SANAA

Zollverein School of Management and Design
Essen, Germany
2003–06

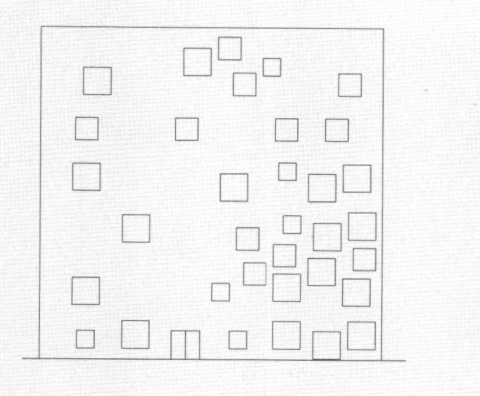

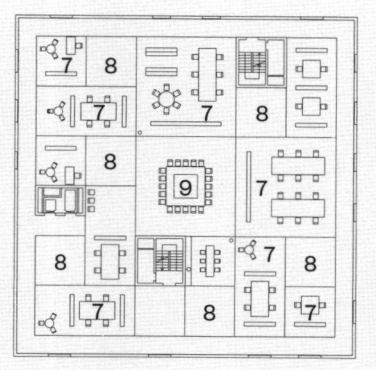

Floor 4

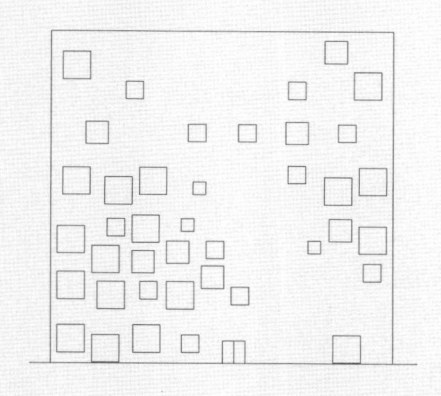

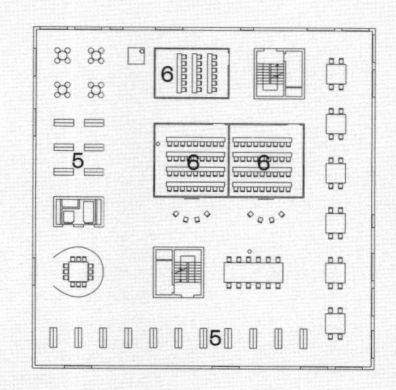

Floor 3

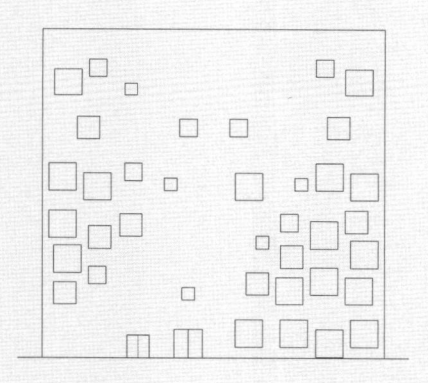

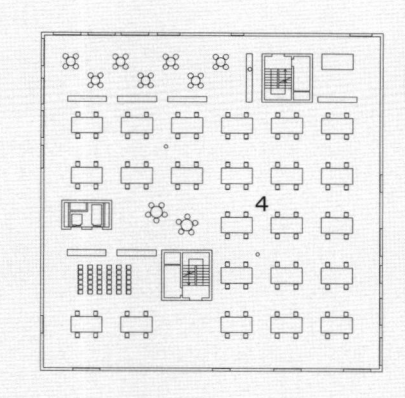

Floor 2

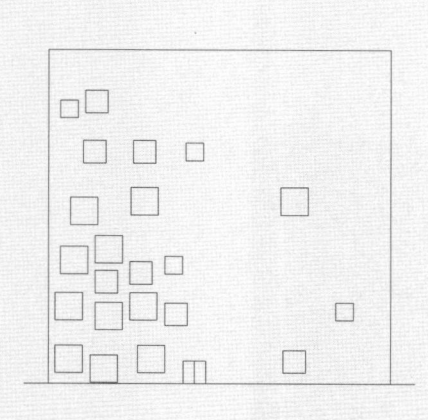

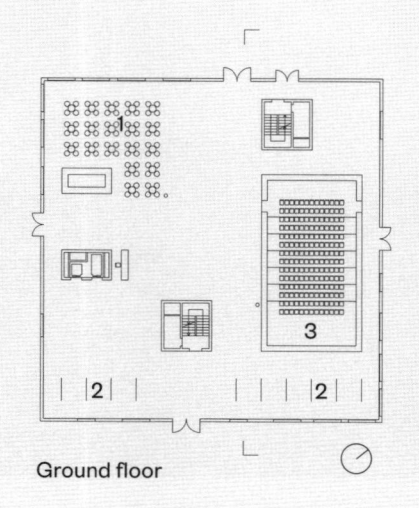

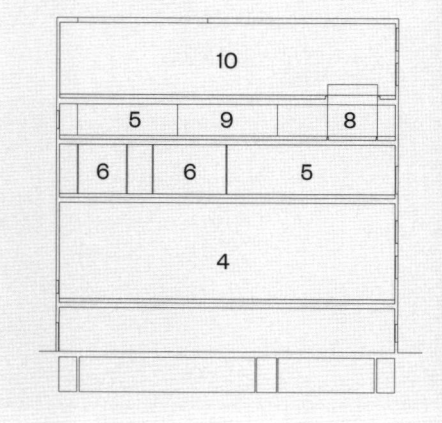

Ground floor

Left to right columns: Elevations. Plans of the ground, second, third, and fourth floors with cafeteria (1), gallery (2), auditorium (3), studio (4), bookshelf (5), seminar room (6), office (7), patio (8), conference room (9), and roof garden (10). Section

119

Located on the Bowery, this concise tower stacks six boxes, each rhythmically off-center from the volume above or below. Housing the New Museum, an organization founded in the 1970s for artists and artworks underrepresented in mainstream institutions, the building's staggered stories creatively respond to the required setbacks of the city zoning envelope. The offsets double as elongated skylights within the galleries and terraces of the upper floors, offering panoramic views north to the Chrysler Building and south to the Brooklyn Bridge. The first floor is floor-to-ceiling glass and opens directly onto the city street, while the second, third, and fourth floors are spare, clear-span galleries that maximize

SANAA

New Museum of Contemporary Art
New York
2003–07

display possibilities. A series of eccentric spaces—an unusually narrow staircase linking the third and fourth floors, for instance—and subtly differing ceiling heights accentuate the understated galleries. A silver, burnished scrim of anodized expanded metal mesh wraps the exterior and gives the facade an unusual combination of blankness and softness; against the facades of the neighboring buildings, it appears almost stripped of materiality, reading alternately as a cipher for the urban context and an opaque mass. Up close, the perforated mesh, installed in front of corrugated-aluminum panels, has depth and visual effect that varies depending on vantage point.—PS

Previous spread from left: Aerial view from the west. Bowery facade from Prince Street
From top: Ground-floor lobby. Seventh-floor Sky Room

SANAA   New Museum of Contemporary Art   New York   2003–07   123

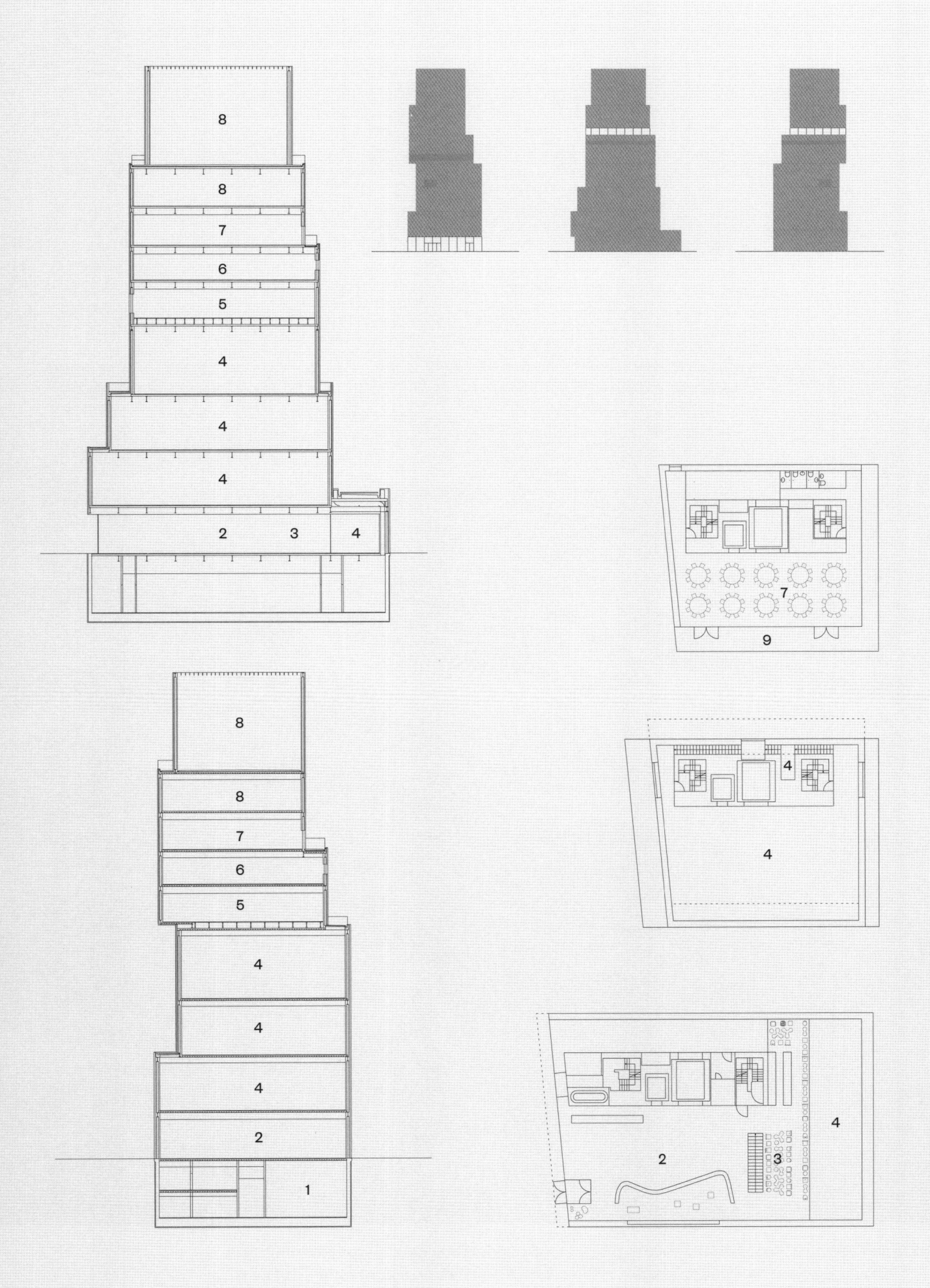

Clockwise from top right: West, south, and east elevations. Plans of the seventh, fourth, and ground floors. West-east and south-north sections with theater (1), lobby (2), café (3), gallery (4), education center (5), offices (6), Sky Room (7), mechanical roof (8), and terrace (9)

Extending over 215,000 square feet (20,000 square meters), this undulating single-story learning hub encloses a library, a multipurpose hall, study spaces, offices, and a café within a continuous space. Located on the campus of the École polytechnique fédérale de Lausanne, a school of engineering and physical sciences, a sculpted foundation slab of reinforced concrete combining a load-bearing shell with a series of arches creates the building's rippled form. Students crisscross below the smooth, arched underbelly to enter the main hall near the center of the structure. At the interior, the contoured floor creates a topography of mounds, slopes, and valleys, transforming movement across the building into a

SANAA

Rolex Learning Center, École polytechnique fédérale de Lausanne

Switzerland   2005–10

heightened physical experience of shifting horizons. The different activities are loosely arranged within this parklike setting, intermingling different functions and setting the stage for unexpected exchanges. Along the steeper surfaces, which incline as much as thirty degrees, an armature of horizontal platforms, ramps, and steps provides an even ground for furniture. Large circular holes create internal light wells and cast sun spots on outdoor spaces below. The curvature synchronizes the building to the surrounding environment: from elevated points within, Lake Geneva and the Alps are visible, while declivities return visitors to campus level. —PS

Previous spread: Aerial view of the campus with Lake Geneva
From top: Detail of the south facade. Interior

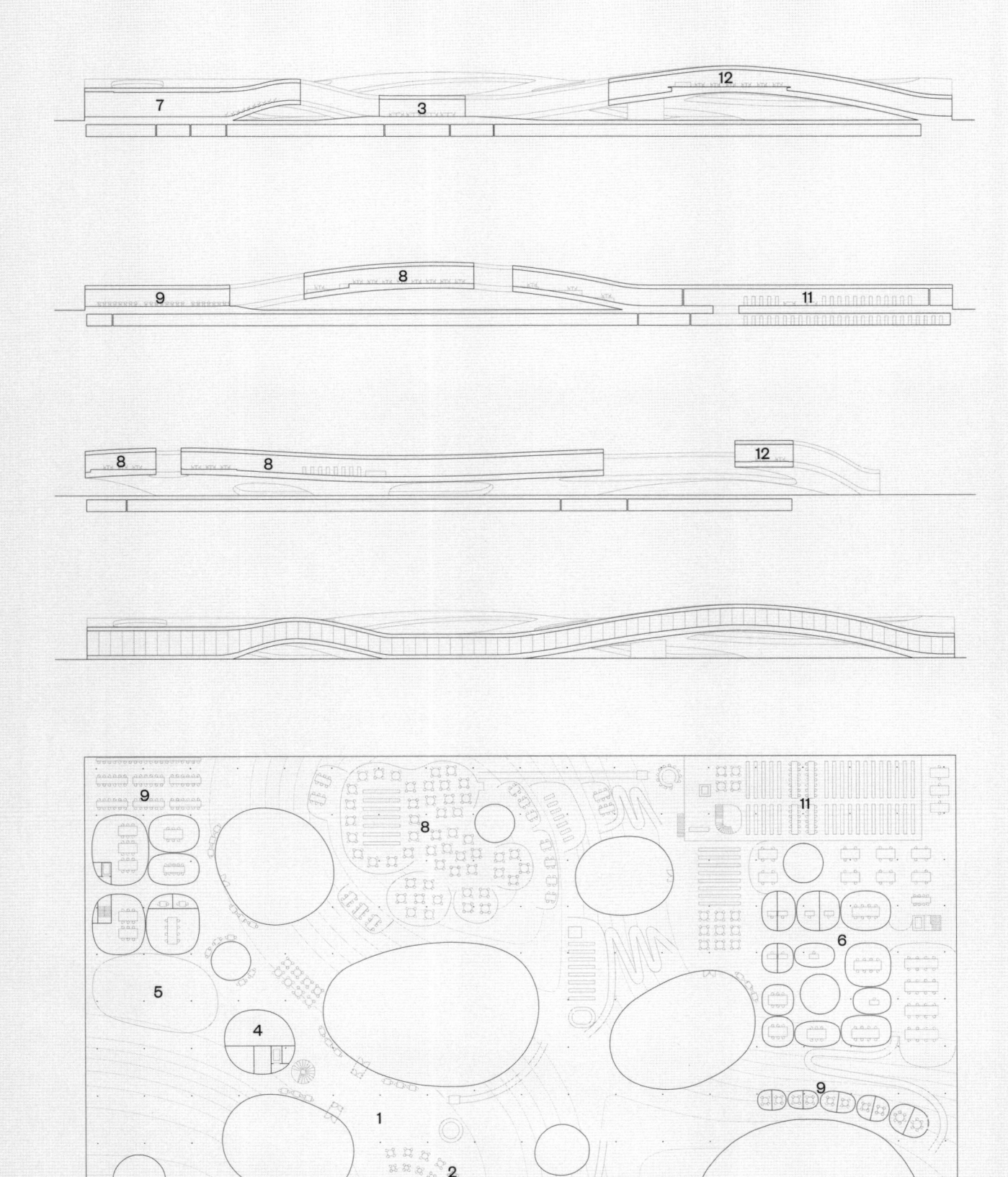

SANAA Rolex Learning Center, École polytechnique fédérale de Lausanne Switzerland 2005-10

From top: Sections. South elevation. Plan with main entrance (1), café (2), food court (3), bank (4), bookshop (5), offices (6), multipurpose hall (7), library (8), work area (9), ancient-books collection (10), research collection (11), and restaurant (12)

Winding across a landscape of wetlands and former farmland, this timber-frame structure encloses a library, sanctuary, common area, media lab, and gymnasium below the eaves of a single sinuous roof. A home for Grace Farms Foundation, a private nonprofit dedicated to justice, arts, and faith-based initiatives, the design's undulations extend the building across the landscape, setting it in close relationship to its seventy-five-acre site, which features trails and commissioned site-specific artwork. The floor dips below grade at two points to accommodate a recreational field for a gym and amphitheater-style seating for a seven-hundred-person sanctuary. Below the roof—a 1400-foot-long pergola floating on slender

SANAA

Grace Farms
New Canaan, Connecticut   2012–15

columns—wrappers of curved glass separate the different activities while establishing stretches of sheltered semi-outdoor space in between. These indeterminate areas provide a threshold for landscape observation and informal social interaction, adapting the *hisashi* spaces—peripheral veranda-like areas below overhanging roofs—characteristic of traditional Japanese architecture. Nishizawa describes the intent to "amplify the experience of the transition from outside to inside in order to integrate these two areas as much as possible."[1] Nicknamed "the river" for its smooth, glinting surface, Grace Farms' roof collects diverse elements within a single form while minimizing its trespass on the land.—PS

Previous spread: Aerial view from the northeast
From top: Exterior of the sanctuary. View from below the pergola

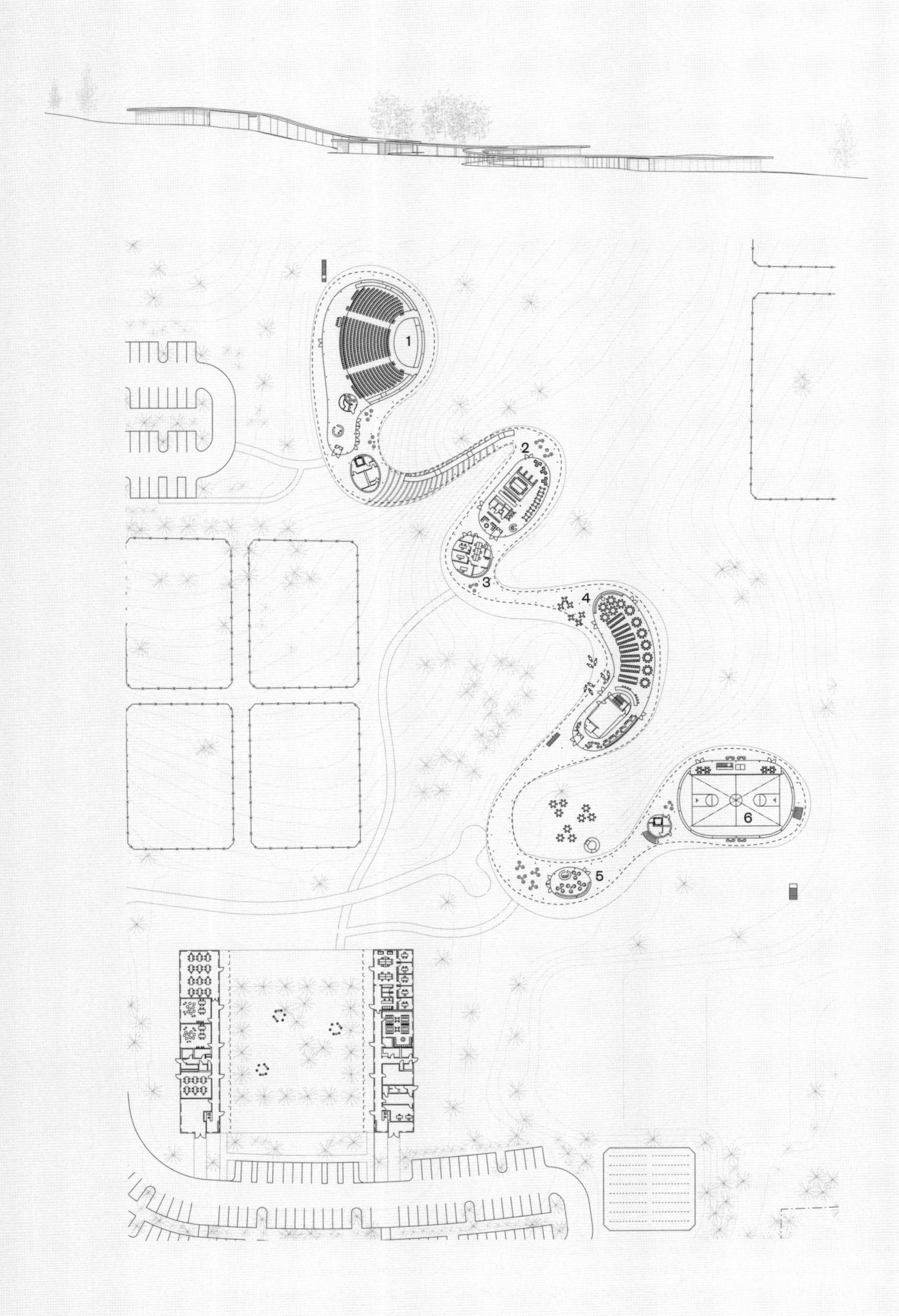

SANAA

Grace Farms
New Canaan, Connecticut

2012–15

From top: South elevation. Plan with sanctuary (1), library (2), office (3), living and dining rooms (4), foyer (5), and gymnasium (6)

Sheathed in a diaphanous expanded metal mesh with the fluid qualities of a fabric, this proposal combines a nearly 377,000-square-foot (35,000-square-meter) public library and a 290,625-square-foot (27,000-square-meter) art museum in ten stacked and intersecting volumes. Located in downtown Taichung on the site of the former Shuinan Airport and its related military command center, which were established during the Japanese colonial period in the 1930s, Taichung City Cultural Center is part of a master plan to transform the square mile (254 hectares) of defunct runways and military installations into a cultural park. SANAA's loose cluster of volumes opens plazas and park access within the voids

SANAA

Taichung City Cultural Center
Taichung, Taiwan
2013–ongoing

of the composition. At ground level, the rectilinear lobbies of the museum and library are playfully turned on a diagonal from one another, creating separate entrances. As the building rises, additional volumes are introduced to span the two institutions and form garden terraces. Vast, airy, glass-enclosed double- and triple-height atriums, bridged by catwalks, merge exhibition and project rooms with the elements of a garden conservatory. The design embodies what Nishizawa describes as a "'chemical' architecture," a loose arrangement of individual forms that is transfigured through its adjacencies: "It's a bit like water (H_2O), in which you can't see the hydrogen and the oxygen separately."[1] —PS

Previous spread from left: Aerial view of the model. Detail at special exhibition gallery
Above: Model detail at sculpture garden

1. "A Conversation with Kazuyo Sejima and Ryue Nishizawa," trans. Jamie Benyai, Liliana C. Obal, and Albert Fuentes, in "Sistemas deContinuidad/Continuity Systems: SANAA 2011–2015," special issue, *El Croquis* 179/180: 15.

134

SANAA

Taichung City Cultural Center
Taichung, Taiwan
2013–ongoing

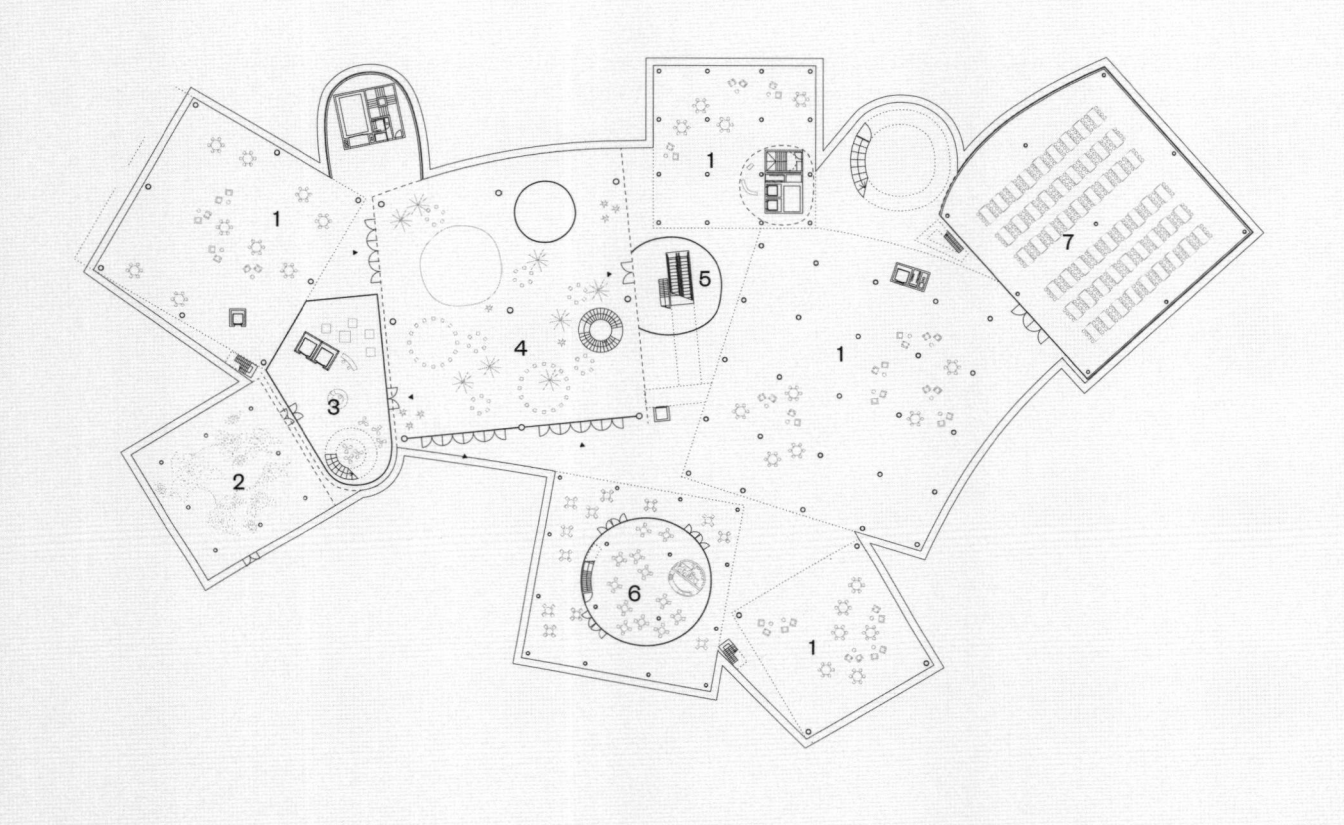

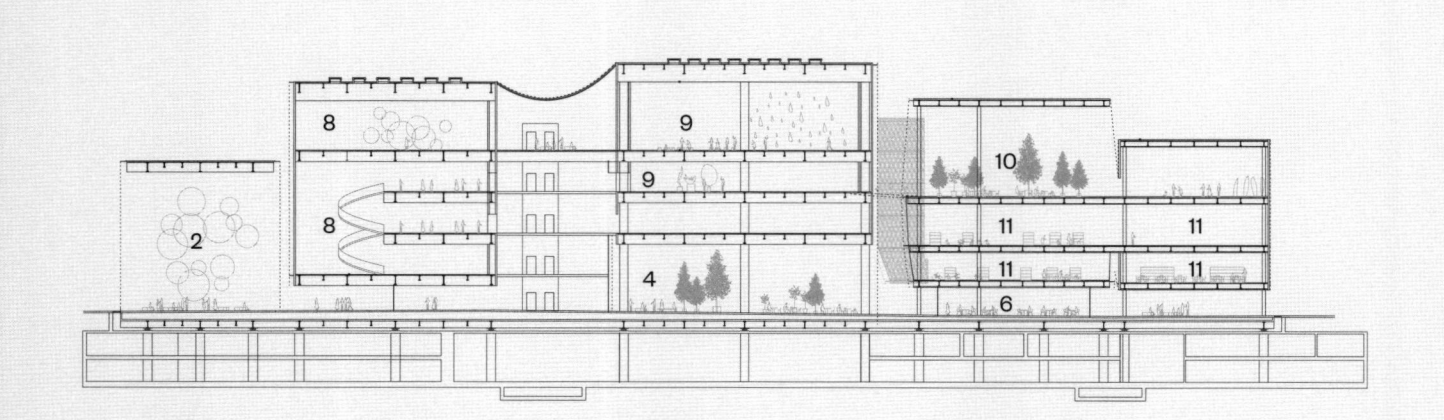

135

From top: Ground-floor plan with shaded plaza (1), project room (2), museum lobby (3), main entrance (4), library lobby (5), café (6), and self-study area (7). Section with special-exhibition gallery (8), permanent-exhibition gallery (9), garden (10), and reading area (11)

The Social Landscape of Architecture

Architecture has very broad repercussions. It is not only a private issue but also a social one. People walk along the street and see buildings every day. This is one of the more important things to happen in a city: architecture creates a landscape and an atmosphere for people, for life. Architecture's forms and roles have evolved in correspondence with social values and will continue doing so. Thinking about a new architecture approximates thinking about new social values; people use architecture variously in different places and times. A "home" in one country or region is not necessarily the same as a "home" in another. Yet even when it is made for an individual, architecture is also part of a collective experience. For example, a building generally has a longer lifespan than a person. A person might live between fifty and eighty years, while a building could last for centuries. Given the significance of architectural space to everyday life, the schematic of space is of grave importance for me.*

Ryue Nishizawa

Commissioned by the Japanese actor Yasuo Moriyama, this house with six rental units sits on a double lot in suburban Tokyo, creating its own microneighborhood. Composed of lightweight prefab-steel elements with extraordinarily thin load-bearing walls, the house is notable for fragmenting the typically compact envelope of the private house into volumes linked by communal external spaces, each room a separate building. Dispersed across the site, eleven units labeled "A" through "J" range in size from a free-standing bath to a three-story living space. Paths and courtyards are interspersed among the living units. On two sides, the complex opens directly to the city street, making it continuous with the urban

Ryue Nishizawa Moriyama House Tokyo 2002–05

fabric and accessible to passersby. The design proposes a mode of living characterized by the flexible rearrangement of domestic quarters; built into the plan is the structure's potential to evolve to accommodate future uses and a varied number of occupants. By combining the Japanese tradition of the pavilion house with contemporary needs, the scheme allows the owner to reconfigure the use of the different spaces and to extend and reimagine the life of the building. —PS

Previous spread: East facade
From top: Roof terrace of unit G. Kitchen of unit E

* Excerpts from "A Conversation with Kazuyo Sejima and Ryue Nishizawa," trans. Jamie Benyei, in "SANAA (Sejima + Nishizawa) 2004–2008," special issue, *El Croquis* 139; and "Architecture in Exhibition: Ryue Nishizawa," in *Art It Asia*, September 1, 2010, http://www.art-it.asia. Reprinted with modifications and permission by the architects.

142

Ryue Nishizawa   Moriyama House   Tokyo   2002–05

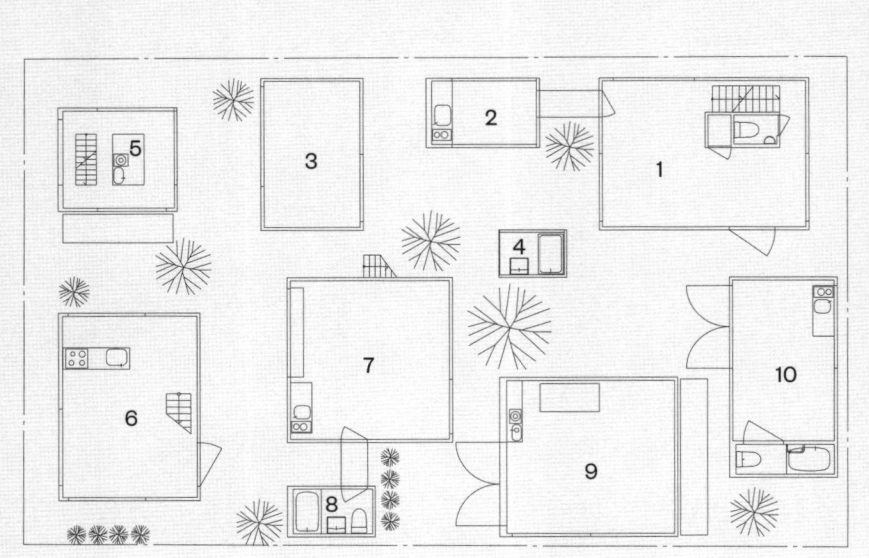

143

From top: North and east elevations. Ground- and second-floor plans with units A living room (1), B dining room (2), C annex (3), D bathroom (4), E kitchen (5), F living-dining area (6), G living room (7), H bathroom (8), I living room (9), and J bedroom (10). Site plan

The sixteen individual exhibition spaces of Towada Art Center are dispersed across an elongated site, alternately facing and angled away from the city's main axis of government offices. The design introduces urban space at the scale of architecture by interlinking multiple small buildings on a single plot of land. A glass corridor loops between the enclosures, providing a seamless visual connection to the city. The spaces, ranging in size from a small room to a gallery, were commissioned to hold specific works from the museum's permanent collection, along with a small selection of rotating exhibitions. By conceiving the galleries as freestanding structures, the architects were able to tailor the details, proportions, and

Ryue Nishizawa Towada Art Center
Towada, Japan
2005–08

lighting of each to work by contemporary artists including Jim Lambie, Yoko Ono, Ron Mueck, and Choi Jeong Hwa. Imagining the Towada Art Center as an agent to help revitalize the prefect's downtown, Nishizawa uses a fragmented form to invert the closed spaces typical of museums and introduces community-oriented elements like an art library and public-meeting room. Outside, the interstices of the structures double as sites for open-air displays and cultural events, setting the museum in direct relationship to the street.—PS

Previous spread: Aerial view along Kanchogai-dori
Above: Art library interior with Michael Lin's *Untitled*, 2008, emulsion on floor, 42' 11/16" × 29' 1/4" (1,300 × 892 cm)

Ryue Nishizawa   Towada Art Center
Towada, Japan   2005–08

From top: View from the northeast with Choi Jeong Hwa's outdoor sculpture *Flower Horse*, 2009. View from the southwest

From top: Aerial view of the art library. Detail of south facade with Jim Lambie's floor installation, *Zobop*, 1999, vinyl tape, dimensions variable

Ryue Nishizawa Towada Art Center
Towada, Japan
2005–08

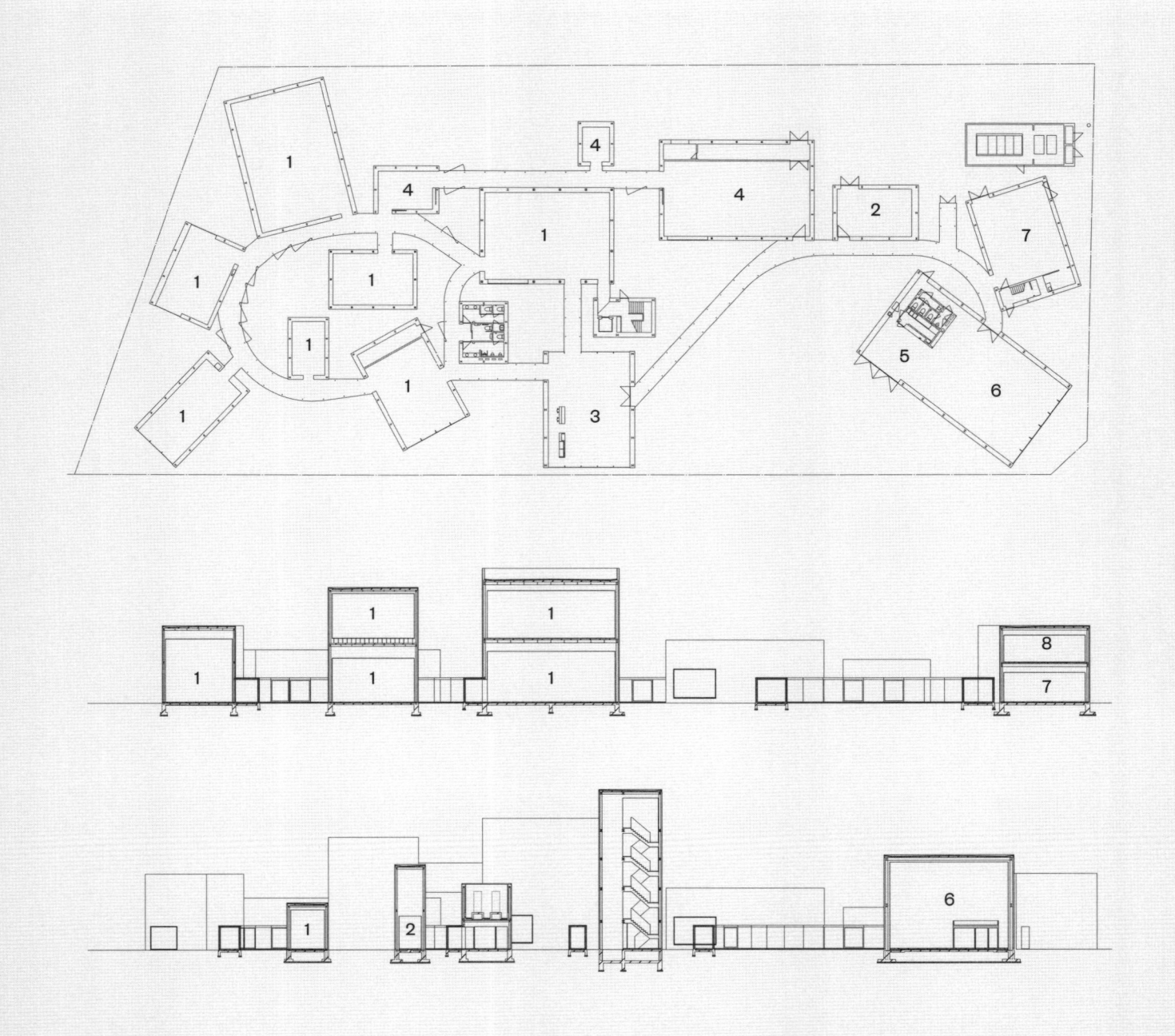

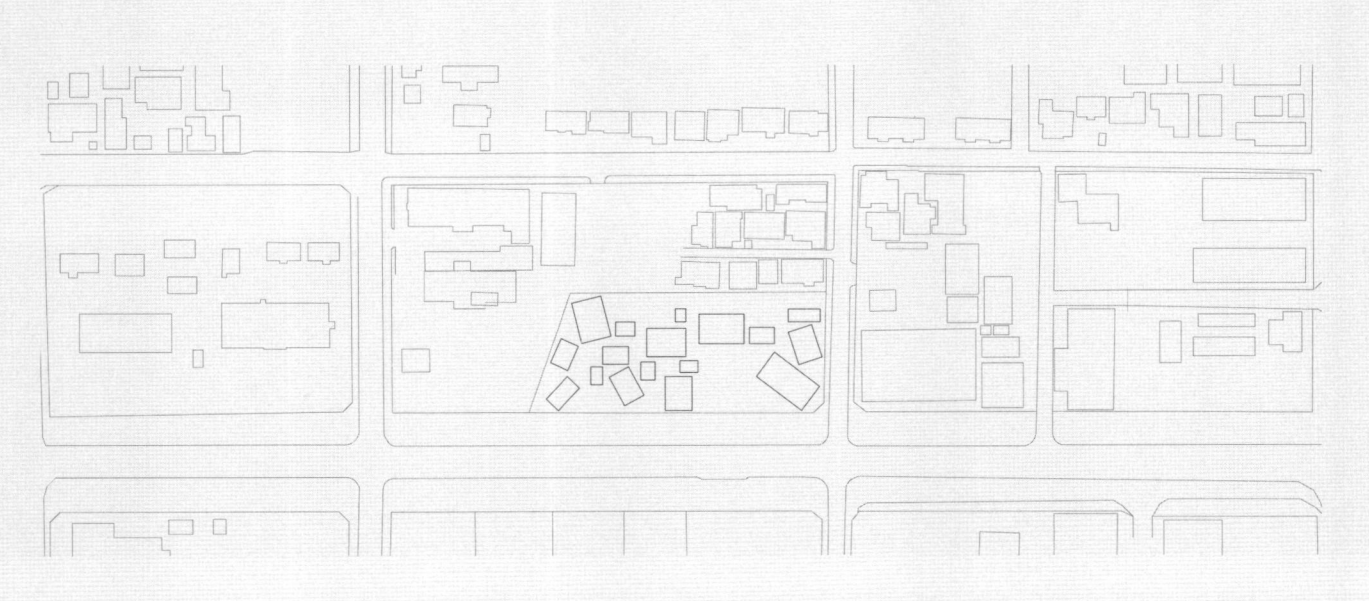

149

From top: Ground-floor plan with artwork space (1), backyard (2), entrance hall (3), gallery (4), café (5), art library (6), public-meeting room (7), and office (8). Sections. Site plan

Completing the curve of the existing topography, the waterdrop-shaped Teshima Art Museum sits at the apex of a hill overlooking the Seto Inland Sea. The museum is one in a series of contemporary art and architecture projects funded by the Fukutake Foundation and Benesse Holdings that also spans the neighboring islands of Inujima and Naoshima. The initiative was meant to spur Teshima's cultural and economic revitalization following the decline of its historic industries and a recent history of illegal industrial-waste disposal. Nishizawa's design offers a single crescent-shaped chamber holding an installation of pooled ground- and rainwater by the artist Rei Naito (Japanese, born 1961). A winding path

Ryue Nishizawa   Teshima Art Museum   Teshima, Japan   2004–10

leads to the structure, its narrow entry channel opening onto a vast space with only two large openings. Exposed to the elements, these openings frame views of the sky and provide orientation in the austere, edgeless interior. A 9 7/8-inch-thick (25-centimeter-thick) shell structure simulating the hill's irregular curvature creates the clear-span space of 197 by 141 feet (60 by 43 meters). To achieve this effect, Nishizawa used a mold of sculpted earth covered with mortar. Once the concrete had set over it, the earth was excavated, leaving behind an evanescent merging of art, light, and landscape. —PS

Previous spread: Interior view with *Matrix*, 2010, by Rei Naito
From top: Shop and café pavilion and museum from the west. Aerial view with Seto Inland Sea

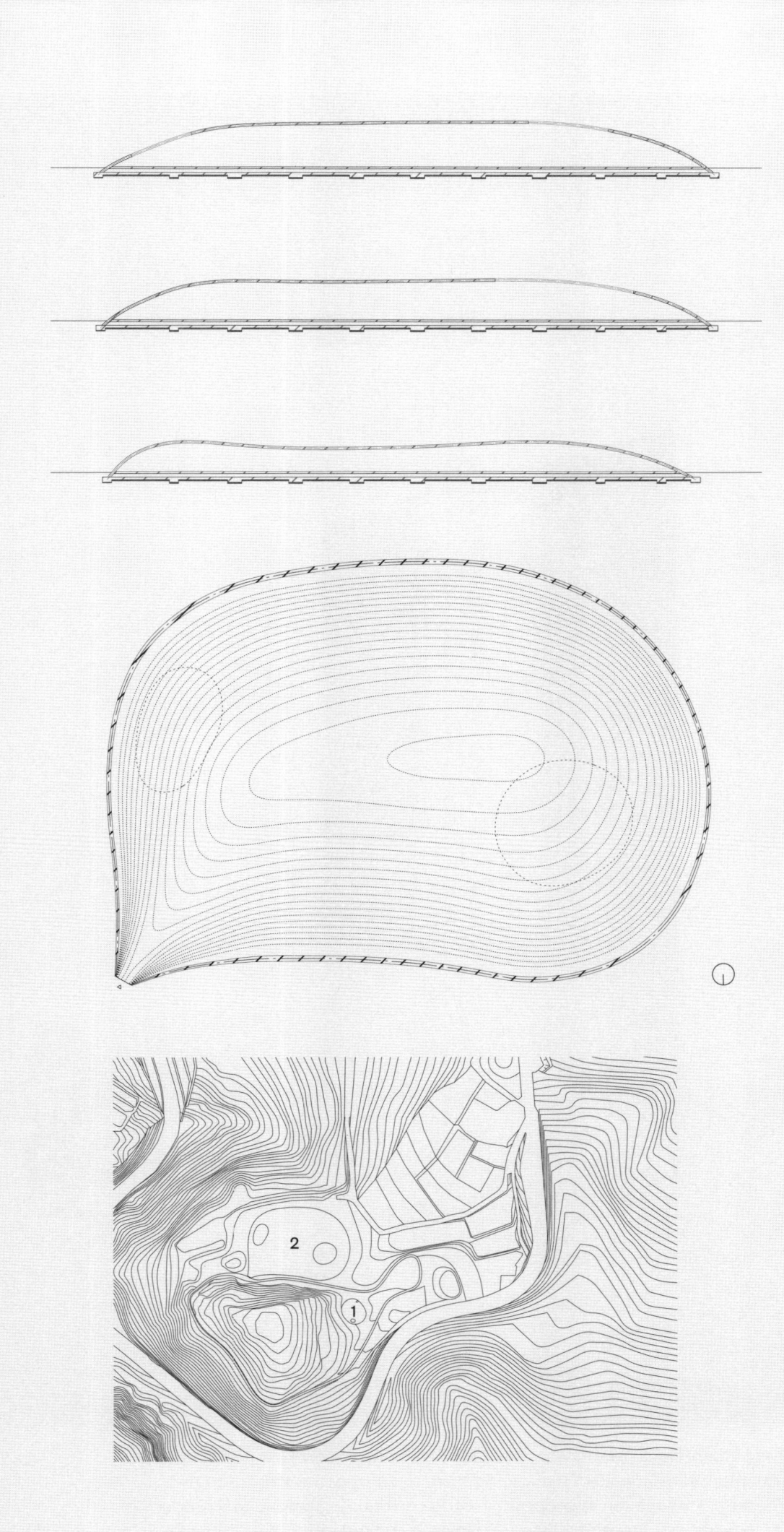

Ryue Nishizawa   Teshima Art Museum
Teshima, Japan   2004–10   153

From top: Sections through the concrete shell. Plan with contours of roof curvature. Site plan with shop and café pavilion (1) and museum (2)

Designed to house the work of Hiroshi Senju (Japanese, born 1958), a contemporary Nihonga-style painter known for his gestural depictions of waterfalls that capture the surge of water through poured paint, this museum incorporates—even appropriates—the surrounding landscape, rendering it inseparable from the act of viewing art. The single-story building is tucked into the middle of a garden whose plant varieties change seasonally; glass walls and bubble-shaped internal courtyards frame panoramic views of the garden. Senju's paintings, arranged chronologically, are dispersed throughout the space on freestanding concrete partitions, which display works individually or in pairs.

Ryue Nishizawa

Hiroshi Senju Museum

Karuizawa, Japan

2007–10

Each carefully proportioned partition is angled to set the artist's evocations of the natural forces visually adjacent to the exterior landscape, establishing a rhythm between inside and out. The splayed plan varies in proximity to the exterior as visitors move between the paintings, while the gentle slope of the museum floor introduces the site's topography. Long, curved benches align to the site's contours. At the artist's request, natural light, filtered by UV-cut glass and controlled by deep eaves, illuminates the museum.—PS

Previous spread: Interior view with work by Hiroshi Senju
From top: Aerial view with Color Leaf Garden. Interior

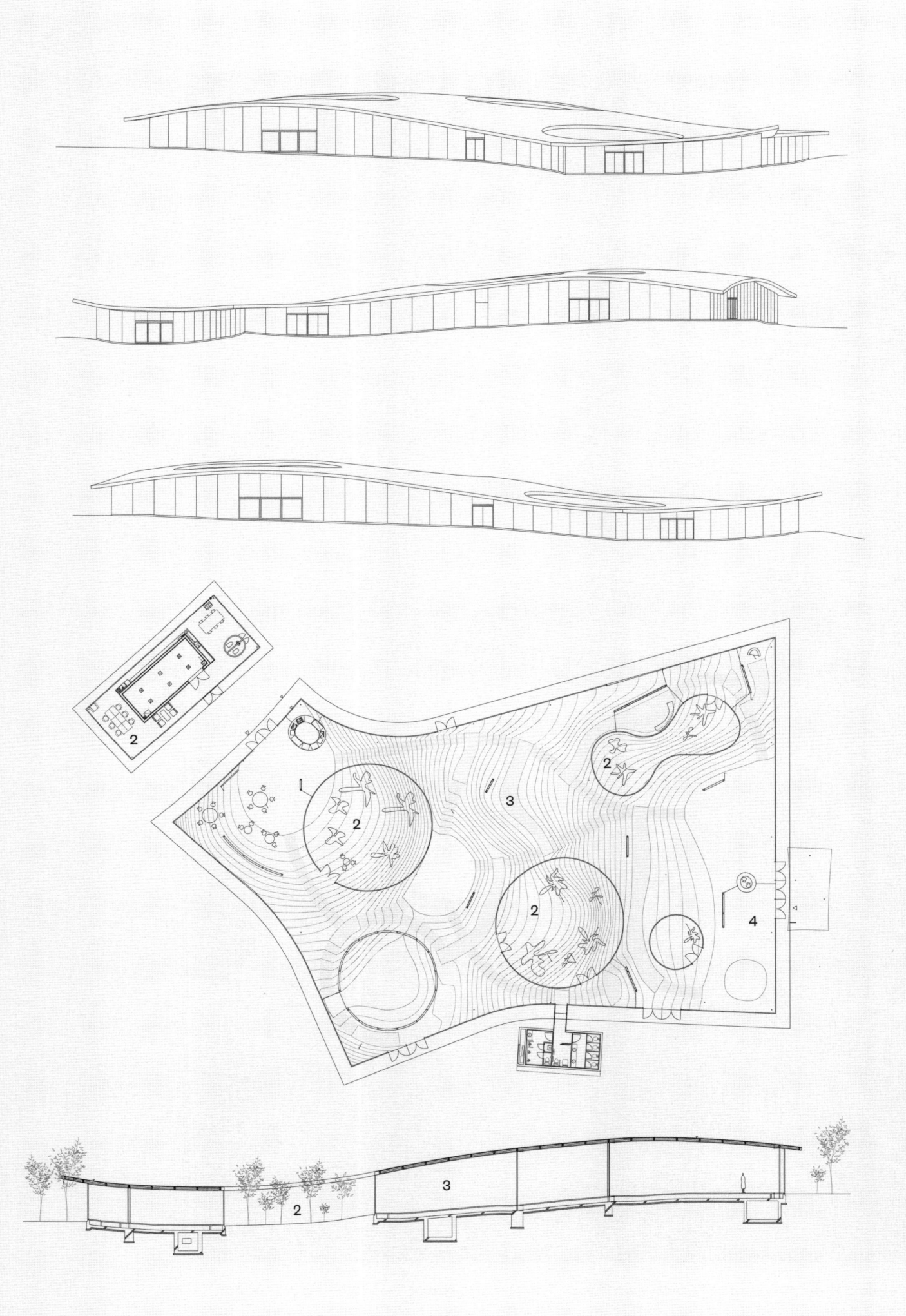

Ryue Nishizawa Hiroshi Senju Museum Karuizawa, Japan 2007–10 157

From top: Southwest, east, and west elevations. Plan with offices and storage (1), courtyard (2), gallery (3), and reception (4).
Section through courtyard and galleries

Located in a dense commercial area of downtown Tokyo, Garden and House occupies a sliver of land between two much taller residential towers. Only thirteen feet (four meters) wide, the house's four floors compose a permeable, vertically stacked garden that intersperses vegetation with a dining room, a kitchen, offices, and bedrooms for two professionals. Diminutive and with minimal structural needs, the design's details play with the threshold between interior and exterior. Interior walls are omitted to maximize the flow of light and air and to allow for the free arrangement of rooms and gardens with only curtains and windows as dividers. Concrete benches and planters double as parapets. A curtain on

Ryue Nishizawa Garden and House Tokyo 2006–11

an oval track is a reversible, soft enclosure that when unfurled forms an elliptical room. A layer of earth finishes an upper floor, introducing nature as a constructive element in the house. This compact yet airy domestic space retains references to modern architecture through its use of floating concrete floor slabs, while establishing a unique relationship both to the garden and the urban context. Underscoring the design's inherently ephemeral and contingent aspects, this garden plus house presents a revised mode of living in a metropolis.—PS

Previous spread: Fourth-floor office. View from the street
Clockwise from top: Aerial view. View upward through the oculus at the fourth floor. Spiral staircase at the second-floor bedroom

Ryue Nishizawa Garden and House Tokyo 2006–11

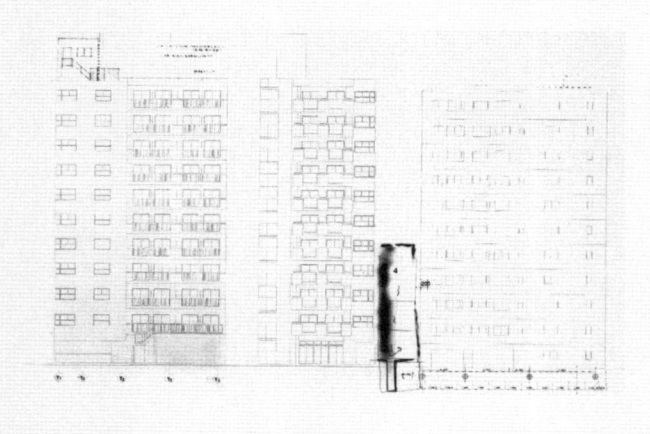

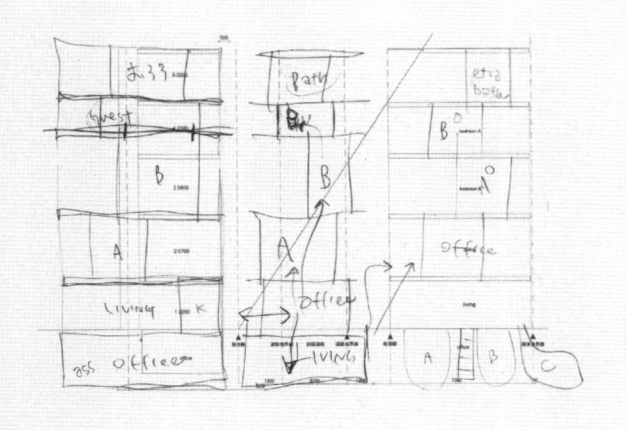

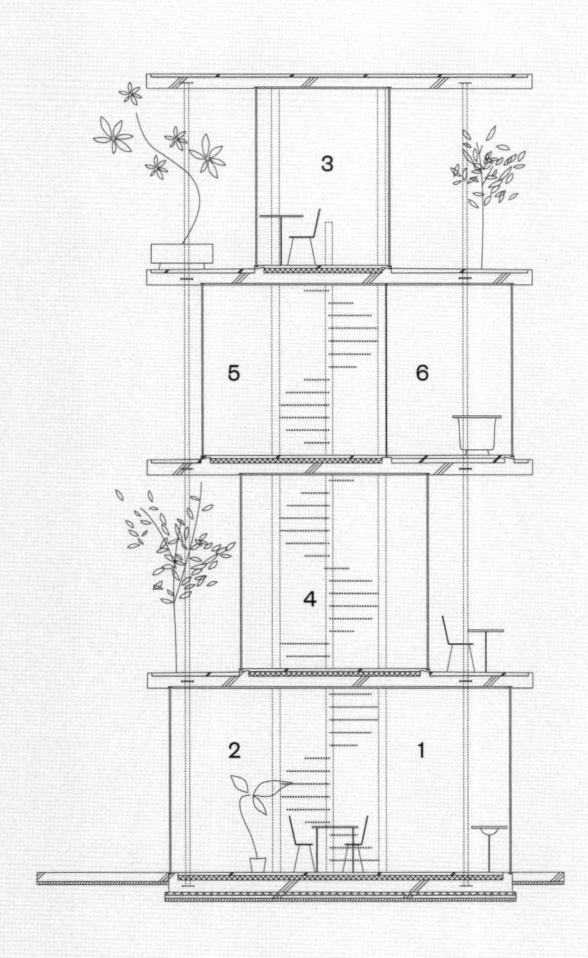

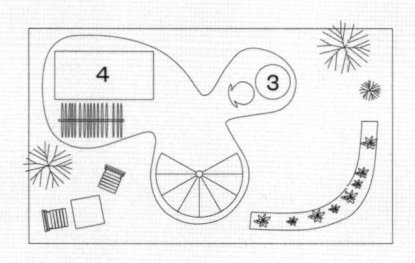

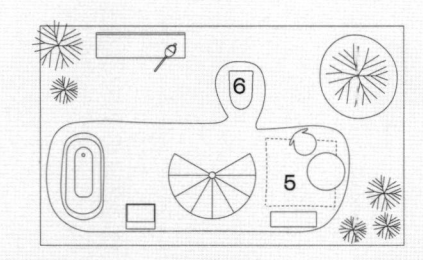

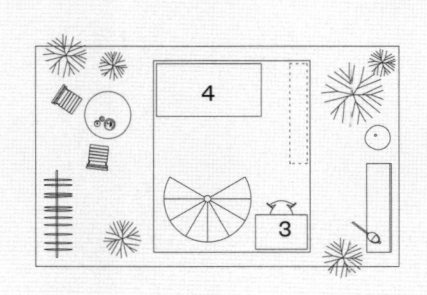

Top, clockwise from left: Elevation with the city block. Photocollage of the facade. Section studies.
Bottom, left to right: Section with kitchen (1), living and dining (2), office (3), bedroom (4), utility (5), and bath (6). Second-, third-, and fourth-floor plans

161

Notes on the Architecture to Come

Perhaps the architecture to come will hover between what is natural and what is human-made. Myriads of gradation will exist between interior and exterior. In this future, entities at various scales, from bodies to buildings to cities to landscapes, will resonate with one another. Architecture will transcend functionalism and diversify, whereupon new uses for it will be discovered. As in a forest, transparency and opaqueness will coexist. Various components will depend on and relate to one another, while at the same time remaining distinct. Architecture will exist where, like a cloud, the boundary between inside and outside grows ambiguous. People will freely find places to make their own; possess private space amid what is private space to the next as public space. Architecture will usher in opportunities, freedom, and connections among people. It will rouse people, inspire them to act. This future would be something primitive.

Sou Fujimoto

Located in a neighborhood of Oita, a city on Japan's southern island of Kyushu, this white, two-story house nests three boxes on a small plot. Built for a couple, the house was to replace the conventional home they had lived in for three decades. The largest box follows the perimeter of the plot and contains a garden and deck. Two smaller boxes, offset from the first, contain respectively a sleeping and studying area with tatami mats and a living and dining space. Toward the center of the house, where spaces hold more intimate activities, the ceiling heights decrease proportionally, from 25 to 16 to 10 feet (7.5 meters to 4.75 to 3.1 meters). The walls and roof are of equal thickness with a uniform surface that elimi-

Sou Fujimoto

House N
Oita, Japan

2006–08

nates extraneous detail to heighten the expression of the house's platonic geometry. A pattern of rectangular cutouts opens views between the spaces to reveal trees, a glimpse of an interior, and squares of sky. The plan's concentric layering of rooms makes each an antechamber to the next, establishing an intricately enmeshed mode of living. The rectangular openings—glazed only at the middle box—introduce a level of transparency through kaleidoscopic views that connect the inner domestic sanctum to the public street.—PS

Previous spread: East facade from the street
Above: Garden at the outermost box

Sou Fujimoto House N Oita, Japan 2006–08

From top: Southeast corner. View of the south facade with entrance

From top: Dining area at the innermost box. Approach from the east

Sou Fujimoto   House N   Oita, Japan   2006–08

From top: South elevation. Section with kitchen (1), dining room (2), and garden (3). Plan with bedroom (4), tatami room (5), and bath (6)

Conceived as a single, spiraling bookshelf, Musashino Art University Museum and Library is Fujimoto's first large-scale institutional building, built to replace the university's 1962 modernist structure by Yoshinobu Ashihara. The conceit of the spiral is evident from the exterior, in which a wall nearly thirty-three feet (ten meters) high unfurls from the building to form an entrance colonnade. At the interior, a grand staircase, composed in part of tiered shelves that double as informal seating, leads to a second-floor reading room. The reading room's 16-foot- (4.8-meter-) high walls, arranged concentrically and lined from floor to ceiling with bookshelves, continue the library's centripetal organization. The timber-

Sou Fujimoto Musashino Art University Museum and Library Tokyo 2007–10

frame walls, concealing the building's steel frame, transform the bookshelf into a structural element, suggesting, with the shelf's seemingly limitless spans, a utopic vision for the library. Fujimoto transposes two layers of experience in Musashino: a meandering course along the full length of the spiraling plan and, to address the library's functional requirements, a series of shortcuts, in which openings within the walls directly link different sections. The library continues his investigation of a "forest-like" architectural environment offering "a multilayered feeling that a number of rooms and countless different worlds are adjacent and interrelated."[1] —PS

Previous spread: Stairs leading to the second-floor open-shelf reading room
From top: Northeast corner. Reading room

1. Sou Fujimoto quoted in Yukio Futagawa, *Sou Fujimoto: Recent Projects* (Tokyo: A.D.A Edita, 2013), 81.

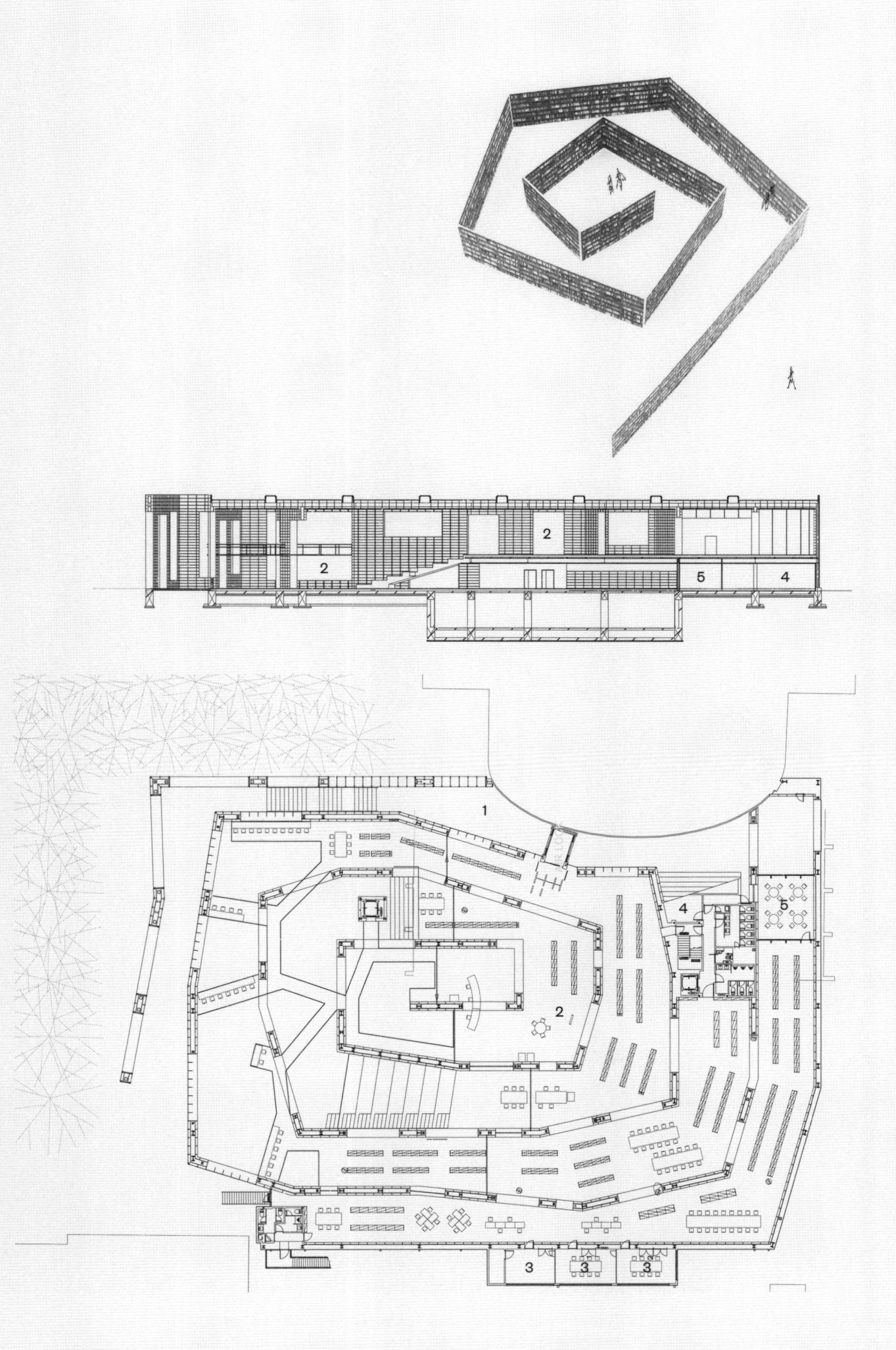

Sou Fujimoto Musashino Art University Museum and Library Tokyo 2007–10 175

From top: Diagram of a spiral bookshelf. South-north section. Second-floor plan with entrance area (1), open-stack reading room (2), study rooms (3), office (4), and south reading room (5)

House NA is located within a dense, low-rise residential neighborhood of Tokyo. Unlike the two- and three-story houses to either side, this dwelling is a continuous sequence of many platforms. Similar to an earlier conceptual project, the Primitive Future House, of 2001, House NA relies on a cascade of stepped podiums that replace traditional walls and floors. The design maximizes the small site by fragmenting each room and extending it across multiple levels. Stairs, ladders, and movable wooden steps connect twenty-one horizontal platforms. A wall at the rear of the house, which doubles as lateral bracing, hides the plumbing and HVAC, while lightweight concrete panels fitted within two-by-two-inch

Sou Fujimoto House NA Tokyo 2007–11

(fifty-by-fifty-millimeter) structural frames provide additional support along the side elevations. Freed of interior walls, the activity on one platform is visible and within arm's reach of the activity two levels down; conversations carry throughout. The conventional image of domestic space as a static enclosure is reenvisioned as a kinetic, open-ended progression of living spaces. Conceived in early sketches as the diagram of a tree, the house is described by Fujimoto as having "many branches," which, unlike separate "hermetically isolated rooms, [are] connected and continually redefining each-other."[1] —PS

Previous spread: Interior view east toward kitchen, dining, and library platforms
From top: Detail of west facade. South facade from the street

1. Sou Fujimoto, *Sou Fujimoto: Primitive Future* (Tokyo: LIXIL Publishing, 2008), 67.

Sou Fujimoto   House NA   Tokyo   2007–11

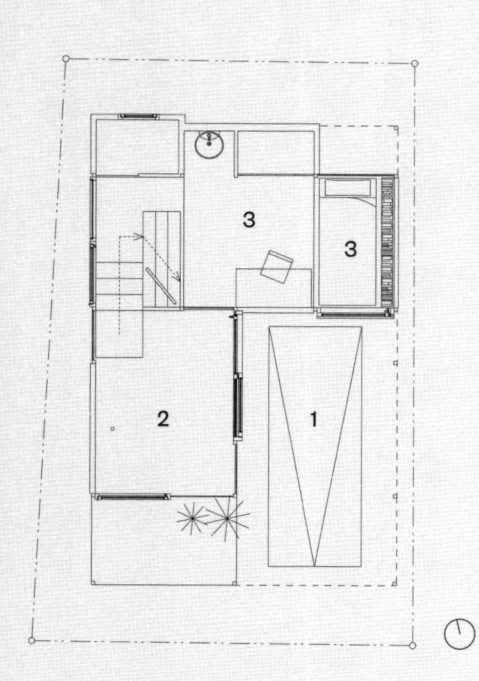

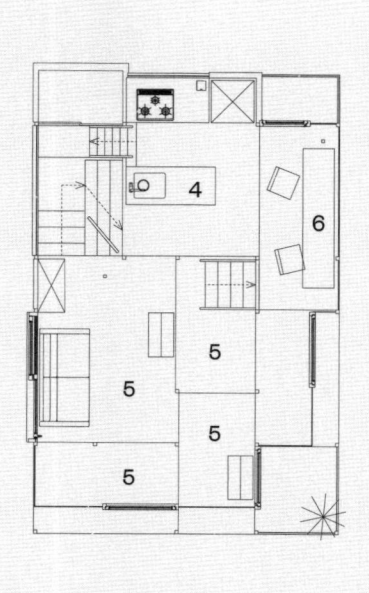

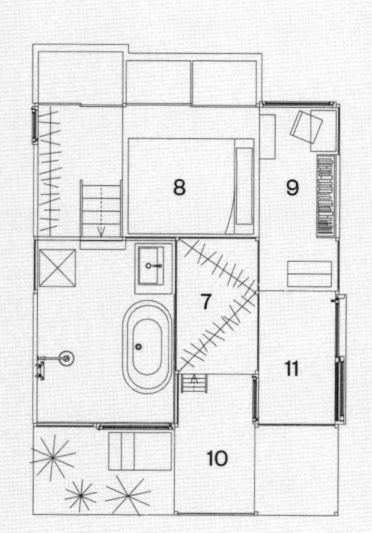

Clockwise from top left: South and east elevations. East-west section. Third-, second-, and ground-floor plans with car (1), entrance (2), guest room (3), kitchen (4), landing (5), dining (6), laundry (7), bedroom (8), library (9), terrace (10) and sunroom (11).

Perched on the edge of the Sava River, which together with the Danube frames Belgrade, this looping structure is one of the winning proposals in an international competition that called for a recreational and commercial center to link the historic city to the industrial waterfront. Located at the base of Kalemegdan Park, which contains fragments of the city's oldest settlements—including a fortress dating back to the Roman Empire—the site is the locus of several of the city's transportation arteries, including a public tramline, rail- and roadways, and the commercial waterway of the river itself. Fujimoto's proposal takes this activity as its starting point, ordering these confluences into a helical bundle of ramps. The curved

Sou Fujimoto   Beton Hala Waterfront Center   Belgrade, Serbia. Project   2011–12

ramps, not strictly concentric, overlap to provide enlarged spaces for cafés, chess tables, galleries, and retail spaces. A vast atrium at the center casts vertiginous views upward, framing a cross section of the layered, radial activity. At several points, strands of the circular plan pull out as a descending channel to link directly to the water or rise aqueduct-like on piers to bridge the adjacent road and lift pedestrians into the park. Proposing a visionary structure for Belgrade, Beton Hala offers a cinematic perspective on the city animated through the building's looping collection of promenades. —PS

Previous spread: Perspective from ramps
Clockwise from top: Perspective from within the central plaza. Aerial perspective of the port and Sava river from the northwest. Interior

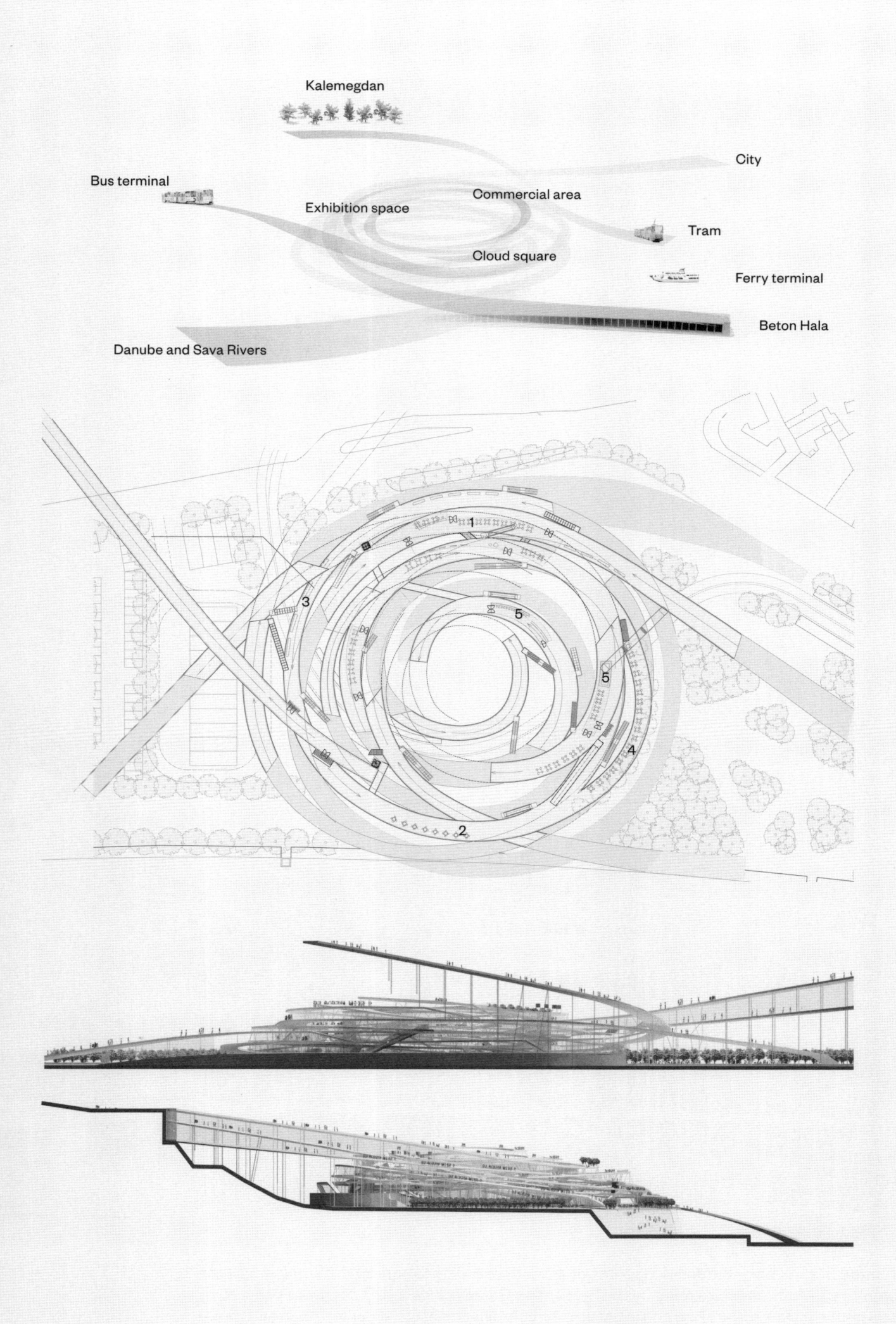

Sou Fujimoto Beton Hala Waterfront Center Belgrade, Serbia. Project 2011–12

Kalemegdan

City

Bus terminal

Exhibition space

Commercial area

Tram

Cloud square

Ferry terminal

Beton Hala

Danube and Sava Rivers

From top: Conceptual diagram of the ramps linking the city. Plan with art café (1), chess tables (2), street market (3), terrace (4), and café (5). Elevations

183

This latticed structure of steel bars thirteen-sixteenths of an inch (twenty millimeters) thick, one in a series of temporary summer pavilions commissioned by the Serpentine Gallery since 2000, creates a delicate, expansive grid across the gallery's lawn. The grid is based on a combination of increments fifteen and three-quarter feet (forty centimeters) and thirty-one and a half (eighty centimeters) in length, which vary the density of the structure, creating differing degrees of openness and a perceptual parallax. At the center, the thicket of latticework hollows to provide a multipurpose space, which is accessed from two points and provides an area for events and socializing. The grid divisions were selected for their close proportion to

Sou Fujimoto
Serpentine Gallery Pavilion
London — 2013

the human body; at the interior, these steel frames are fitted with glass panels to create tiered levels for seating and steps, transforming the pavilion into a navigable terrain for visitors to climb. Adjacent to the neoclassical portico of the gallery building, the pavilion, despite the precise order of its orthogonal grid, has an almost cloud-like, amorphous appearance that avoids any clear contour. It might be linked more closely to an idea of landscape; the openness and extreme thinness of the pavilion's structural elements, as though sketched in the air, create "soft territories and soft articulations, gradually changing atmospheres and functions that emerge through experience or through the behaviours of individuals."[1]—PS

Previous spread: View from within the steel-tube lattice
From top: East elevation. Café at center of pavilion

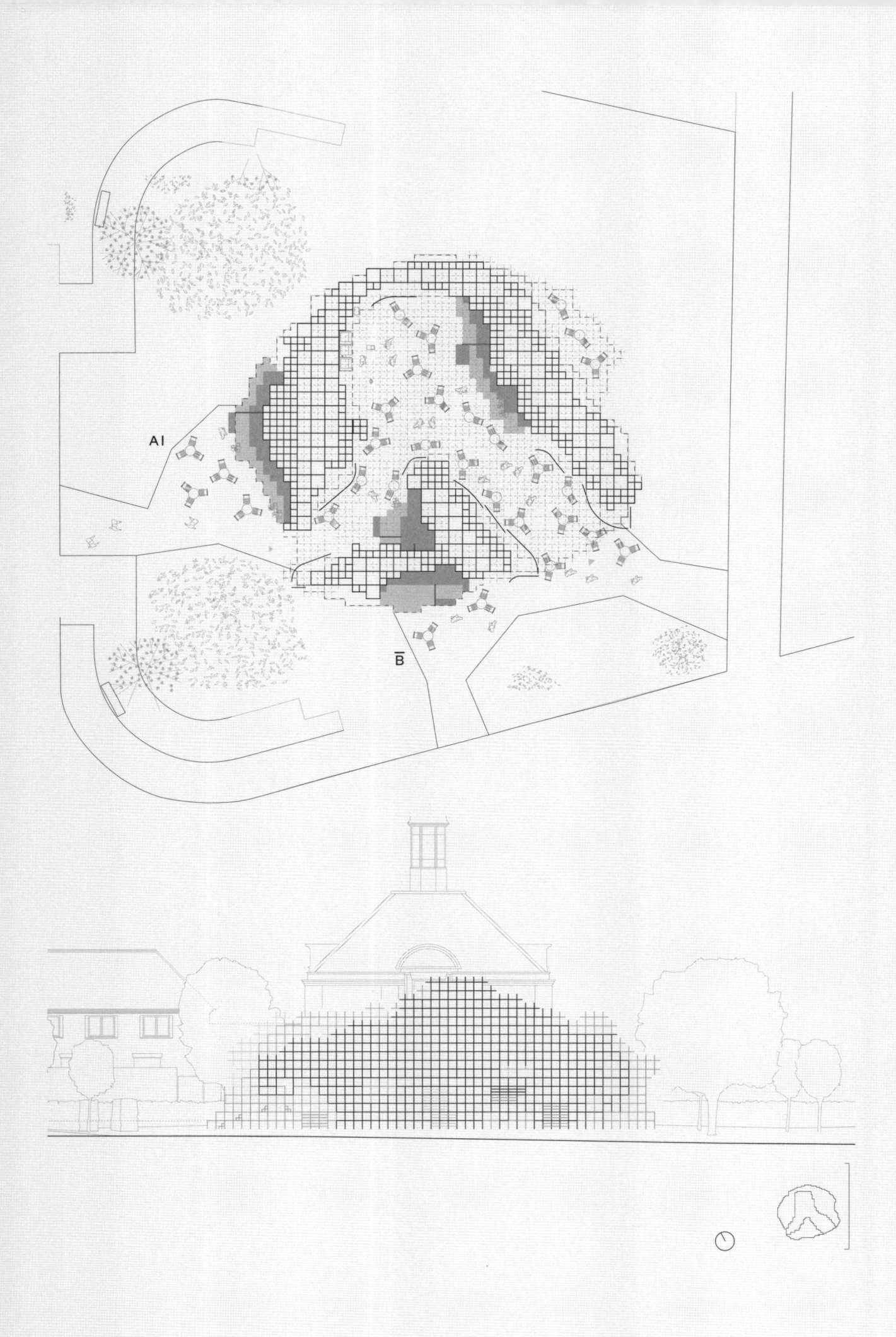

Sou Fujimoto   Serpentine Gallery Pavilion   London   2013

187

From top: Plan with café and event space. East elevation

Three People Who Shaped Postwar Japanese Architecture

The leading figure in the world of Japanese architecture today is, arguably, Toyo Ito. First, let us consider Ito the architect. After completing Sendai Mediatheque (p. 22) in 2001, which Ito describes as the Maison Dom-Ino of the information era, he did not settle into any singular style, but rather continued his search for new structural possibilities in a series of highly acclaimed projects. His efforts culminated in the radical spatial forms of the National Taichung Theater (p. 68), whose construction began in 2005 and is still underway.

Second, Ito the mentor has nurtured several young talents, each of whom emerged from his tutelage a unique, remarkable architect: Kazuyo Sejima, Akihisa Hirata, Toshiaki Ishida, Mitsuhiko Sato, Makoto Yokomizo, Hideyuki Nakayama, and Hirokazu Suemitsu, as well as members of Mikan and Klein Dytham Architecture (KDa), may be counted among them. Moreover, some of Ito's descendants became mentors in their own right: Ryue Nishizawa and Junya Ishigami, for instance, came out of Sejima's practice.

Third, there is Ito the educator. In this role, he has proactively engaged with students, especially since 2011, when he founded Ito Juku, a small, private architectural school to foster young talent. The school, whose inauguration coincided with the Great East Japan Earthquake, directed many of its activities toward recovery in disaster-stricken areas. He also advocates on behalf of the next generation of young architects. For example, Ito has no direct mentor-pupil relationship with Sou Fujimoto, yet he has consistently supported the younger architect, steering Fujimoto toward success. In 2005, for instance, Ito, as commissioner of Kumamoto Artpolis, selected Fujimoto's Final Wooden House in a competition for an all-timber structure; a few years later, in 2008, he invited Fujimoto to design a house for the future as part of the Tokyo Gas–sponsored Sumika project, one of four selected architects.

An analysis of the history of postwar Japanese architecture reveals that Kenzo Tange was the nation's first leading architect. Tange's work overlapped with Japan's efforts to rebuild itself in the wake of the atomic bomb; beginning with the Hiroshima Peace Memorial Museum, in 1955, Tange designed several state-level projects, including the stadium complex for the 1964 Tokyo Olympics, and the master plan and main event plaza for the 1970 World Exposition in Osaka. While promoting modernism as the appropriate form of architecture for Japan's postwar democracy—as evident in the 1958 Kagawa Prefectural Government Office, later replicated for other prefectural headquarters—he simultaneously engaged what was called *dento ronso* (the debate on tradition), contributing to monographs on the seventeenth-century Katsura Imperial Villa in the suburbs of Kyoto and on the Ise Grand Shrine in central Honshu. Tange's ability to navigate both the traditional and contemporary, and his penchant for monumental forms, installed him as a state architect.

The nature of Japanese architecture is such that one can depict a genealogy of talent by diagramming the mentor-pupil relationships established through various universities and studio practices, and Tange's own lineage is no exception. From the architect's laboratory and practice would emerge the likes of Fumihiko Maki, Arata Isozaki, Kisho Kurokawa, Sachio Otani, Reiko Tomita, and Yoshio Taniguchi, all of whom are today highly acclaimed architects in their own right.[1,2]

The star architect to follow Tange directly is his pupil Arata Isozaki. Whereas Tange devoted his practice to state architecture and government facilities, in turn shaping Tokyo and other important cityscapes, the younger Isozaki focused on the museums and cultural facilities concentrated in regional cities, such as the 1966 Oita Prefectural Library (fig. 1) and the 1974 Museum of Modern Art, Gunma. Moreover, compared with Tange, who raised the status of Japanese modernism internationally, Isozaki created an international network of architects by cultivating relationships with designers of the same generation, such as the Austrian Hans Hollein and the Briton Peter Cook. Isozaki is especially noteworthy for his contributions to the development of semiotic postmodern architecture in Japan; the 1983 Tsukuba Center Building and the 1990 Art Tower Mito are two representative examples. His extensive cross-disciplinary knowledge and profound understanding of the architectural history of Japan, and of the world, was immensely impressive. When I was an undergraduate student in the late 1980s Claude-Nicholas Ledoux and Michelangelo appeared on design curricula as a matter of course, such was the influence of Isozaki, who would frequently reference the works of the great historical architects.

fig. 1

fig. 2

Toyo Ito: The Division Line

Unlike those of previous generations, contemporary Japanese architects—especially those who are young or still in school—lack interest in the discipline's history. This may well be a global trend after postmodernism; but another reason might be that popular architects such as Ito, Sejima, and Ishigami never mention Western architectural history. In a 1998 interview,[3] I asked Ito about his favorite historical architecture. He responded that he was interested in nomadic tents more than he was in great cathedrals. Tange, recognizing within his historical moment an epic narrative of rebirth and nationhood, brought monumentality to modernism. Isozaki, for his part, remained cosmopolitan; he emphasized "Architecture with a capital 'A'"—a phrase he used often in the 1980s and 1990s to refer to Palladian and neoclassical styles—and wrote prodigiously on metaphysical theory. Compared to his forerunners, Ito is an architect after "history." He debuted in the 1970s, a decade plagued by the oil crisis. His contemporaries, most of whom were born in the first half of the 1940s, were Tadao Ando, Kiko Mozuna, Kijo Rokkaku, Osamu Ishiyama, Takefumi Aida, Itsuko Hasegawa, Kazuhiro Ishii, and Kazunari Sakamoto. Maki called them *nobushi*, or masterless samurais. This group, lacking opportunities for public-works commissions, began their respective careers by designing small houses typical of Japanese private commissions.

Early in his career, Ito's most important work was his 1976 White U (fig. 2), notable for its inverted U-shape. The interior space was extremely private, devoid of any relationship to nationhood or to history. However, the 1980s marked a turning point in Ito's style; increasingly, his structures opened themselves to the city, as is evident in his 1984 Tokyo-based private house, Silver Hut, whose roof appears continuous and light, and in his 1986 restaurant, Nomad, which, inspired by nomadic tents, captured the floating sensation of fabric fluttering in the wind. (The restaurant was demolished in 1989.) While the act of citing Western architectural history would reach its peak in the 1980s, Ito had already shifted his attention to the vernacularism of nomadic tents. This particular interest can be attributed to the influence of Sejima, who was on Ito's staff during this period, and is said to have been dubbed a "convenience-store girl" for her then radically new lifestyle.

As Japanese businesses recovered, the asset-price bubble economy expanded, grossly inflating real estate and stock prices, and enveloping Tokyo in a bizarre euphoria. In the 1980s, Ito pursued spatial qualities that corresponded to this newfound corporeality, which he emphasized by designing architectural skins, and created light and open spaces distinct from the solidity of Tange's structures or the "historical" operations of Isozaki's. Ito then passed on these traits to successive generations.

During the bubble era, Ito wrote "A New Architecture Is Possible Only in the Sea of Consumption,"[4] in which he criticizes the emergence of an unprecedented consumer society and postulates how one might adapt rather than succumb to it, all the while seeking out the possibilities of a new architecture. Ito managed to swim in the sea of consumerism and reach the opposite side of the shore without drowning. Inherent to his character are the agility and flexibility required to move with ease through the tides of time.

After the Great East Japan Earthquake, Ito's office quickly repaired the partially damaged Sendai Mediatheque—not without commendable effort—and from then on the architect was actively involved in restoring the disaster-stricken regions. Together with Kengo Kuma and Sejima, he founded *Kishin no kai*, a loosely affiliated group of architects that called on younger designers to help with the recovery process, including the Home-for-All initiative, which designed and built gathering spaces within the temporary complexes housing the survivors. The group's members questioned the egoism of design, seeking instead to reestablish the relationship between architecture and society.

Sensibility and Structural Design

Incidentally, Tange, Isozaki, and Ito are all graduates of the University of Tokyo, Japan's preeminent educational institution. Influencing Tange's career path were the close connections he would forge with a number of important politicians. Isozaki, meanwhile, maintained friendships with numerous artists, musicians, writers, and other cultural figures, which shaped his own unique position in the architectural discipline. Ito, for his part, set off on a third and altogether different path, working first for leading Metabolist architect Kiyonori Kikutake, a Waseda University graduate whom the 1960s Japanese architectural circle deemed poised to rival and overthrow Tange's monopoly on state architecture. From Kikutake's practice emerged architects Hiroshi Naito, Shozo Uchii, Mitsuru Senda, and Tadasu Ohe. Ito also spent time with Kazuo Shinohara and his coterie (now known as the "Shinohara School") at the Tokyo Institute of Technology. In other words, Ito chose to cross-pollinate his training at the University of Tokyo, whose architectural geneaology is known especially for logical thinking, with the sophisticated sensibility of Kikutake and the symbolism of Shinohara.

I speculate that the proclivity for avant-garde sensibility and structure can be traced through the genealogy of Kikutake, Ito, SANAA, the firm founded by Sejima and Nishizawa, and Ishigami. Common among these architects is their desire to maximize structural engineering technologies to create new spatial qualities, each to different effect. Kikutake developed acrobatic structures, identifiably robust and dynamic, such as the 1966 Miyakonojo Civic Center (fig. 3) and the 1967 Sado Grand Hotel.

Although Ito collaborates increasingly with structural engineers, his edifices often use simple geometrical rules that dictate the building's form. This can be seen in the 2002 Brugge Pavilion (p. 28) and the 2004 Tod's Omotesando Building (p. 36). SANAA, while rigorously pursuing the lightness, openness, and transparency pioneered by Ito, creates spaces nearly devoid of structural presence, belying the magnificent engineering technologies required in the construction. Their design is more graceful and delicate than Kikutake's.

Ishigami, for his part, has arrived at an extreme form of architecture that nearly transcends materiality in its evocation of invisibility and lightness. Yet, on account of his great skill, very few people realize how exceptional are his structural systems. His ultrathin Table, of 2005, a thirty-two foot (nine-and-one-half-meter) span of steel measuring little more than one-eighth of an inch (three millimeters) thick, serves as an example (fig. 4). I witnessed many visitors overlooking its astounding, gravity-defying proportions, precisely because of its status as an otherwise mundane, everyday object. In 2008, as commissioner for the Japanese Pavilion in the eleventh International Architecture Exhibition, La Biennale di Venezia, I tapped Ishigami to reimagine the building. Outside the pavilion, he built a delicate greenhouse that complemented rather than overwhelmed the surrounding trees, blending with its environment. In his exhibition *Architecture as Air: Study for Château la Coste* for the 2010 architecture biennial, superthin carbon columns with a diameter of two-fifths of an inch (0.9 millimeters) formed an enfilade nearly invisible to the eye.

Furthermore, Studio Velocity, founded by Miho Iwatsuki and Kentaro Kunhura, and Motosuke Mandai Architects, the next generation of young Japanese avant-garde designers, are each made up of architects who emerged from Ishigami's office. Both worked on Ishigami's 2008 Kanagawa Institute of Technology Workshop (p. 222) and his Table, inheriting his style, and can be considered the fifth generation in the Kikutake line. It is important to note that Ito's circle was liberated from the shackles of university inbreeding, with Ito undertaking mentees based on talent regardless of institutional pedigree: Sejima (Japan Women's University), Nishizawa (Yokohama National University), Ishigami (Tokyo University of the Arts), and Hirata (Kyoto University) are among them.

Inventing New Architectural Principles

When I curated the 2014–15 exhibition *Architecture since 3.11* at the 21st Century Museum of Contemporary Art, Kanazawa (p. 106), I showcased Ito's Home-for-All project—whose participants also included SANAA, the firm founded by Hirata, and Sou Fujimototo, to name a few—in a prominent display, signaling the country's period of transformation. What binds this group of designers is a desire to invent new architectural principles by dismantling established formal hierarchies and replacing them with architectural forms appropriate for the twenty-first century. For example, SANAA's forms may appear at first to consist of the kind of simple geometries intrinsic to modernism, as in the 21st Century Museum, a simple circle inset by rectangles. And yet, the design generated spaces previously unimaginable. SANAA does this very elegantly as if in pursuit of potentialities left unfinished by modern architecture. For this reason, we might call it "alternative modernism," a form of modernism that could have been. If postmodernism can be considered a rhetorical transgression against modernism, then alternative modernism is the reformation of the modernist linguistic system itself. That is to say, rather than merely changing the permutational combination of words, the very definition of each word is reevaluated and reformulated, much as Sendai Mediatheque questioned the meaning of columns and walls at a fundamental level. Alternative modernism exists within the framework of modernism for its contemporaneous use of building materials that epitomize the modern period, such as steel, concrete, and glass. However, the difference lies in alternative modernism's integration of computer technologies into design, enabling the exploration of altogether distinct potentialities previously underdeveloped by modernism.[5] One can recognize the traits of alternative modernism in the work of SANAA, Hirata, Fujimoto, and Ishigami. Although undoubtedly other architects since the 1990s have explored the same issues, the architects from Ito's school seem to be the most successful at engendering new spatial phenomena and experiences.

SANAA returns to the glass spaces often favored by modernism, but surpasses pure transparency by manipulating translucencies, reflections, and geometric patterns in a manner reminiscent of optical art. More recently, SANAA has generated curvilinearity unlike any in architectural history, their forms unregulated by theories of structural mechanics or by geometrical systems based on circles and ellipses. SANAA deploys these subtle curves not as novel forms but rather as fresh spatial experiences. Notably, Sejima speculated on the meaning of Le Corbusier's use of multifarious curves for her undergraduate thesis; now she is leading the realm of curvilinear design.

Hirata and Fujimoto, both of whom were born in 1971, are friends and belong to the same generation as Ishigami. The generation of architects that preceded them, those born in the 1960s, and who formed loose associations that foregrounded the work of the collective over any individual in it, looked to urbanity to construct a set of architectural principles to be applied universally, rather than responding to a structure's particular site and environmental conditions. Atelier Bow-Wow and Mikan are two such examples. But both Hirata and Fujimoto adopted approaches that deviate from those of their peers only a few years their senior. Hirata, whose interests lie in natural forms, has sought new architectural possibilities in convoluted structures and twisted spatial topologies. It was Hirata, who, while working in Ito's office, came up with the foundational idea for the National Taichung Theater. Fujimoto, by contrast, creates incredibly original architecture without reference to difficult philosophical ideas or to contemporary art, and through operations so simple they conjure the apocryphal egg of Columbus. As if to restart the history of architecture from its origins, Fujimoto is reconstituting the coordinate field on which all geometries are established.

If we may generalize that geometry gives order to architecture through perpendicular angles and parallel lines, then a new geometry for architecture might be simple at the same time that it is capable of rendering complex and multifaceted spaces. This idea of a new geometry is one of the characteristics of alternative modernism. Here, too, Ito is a trailblazer. He proffers as new architectural principles the transformation of abstraction and a shift from pure geometry to generative geometry. For example, his 2002 Serpentine Gallery Pavilion appears to be a complex design but in fact it was composed with a simple system: a palimpsest of superimposed lines, created by a repetitive operation, designated the aperture pattern.

We recognize now that the advancements in computing in the 1990s signaled the advent of a virtual architecture with formal complexity, albeit on a screen. However, perhaps because many of these renditions were conceived ultimately never to be built, the outputs were complex for complexity's sake and the respective systems tended to be excessively elaborate. These young recipients of Ito's tutelage embrace computational technology while forgoing the complexity it enables, and, in doing so, are beginning to form their own respective histories for a new architecture of the twenty-first century.

fig. 4

Notes

1. Teijiro Muramatsu, *Nihon kenchikuka sanmyaku* (Tokyo: Kajima Shuppankai, 2005).
2. Shozo Baba, *Nihon no kenchiku sukuru* (Matsudo: Okokusha, 2002).
3. Toyo Ito, interview by Taro Igarashi, "Toyo Ito Interview," 1998, ICC Interview Series 19, Hive Intercommunication Center, http://hive.ntticc.or.jp/contents/interview/ito.
4. Toyo Ito, "A New Architecture Is Possible Only in the Sea of Consumption," in *From Postwar to Postmodern, Art in Japan 1945–1989: Primary Documents*, ed. Doryun Chong, Michio Hayashi, Kenji Kajiya, and Fumihiko Sumitomo, trans. Maiko Behr (New York: Museum of Modern Art, 2012). Essay first published in 1989 as "Shôni no umi ni hitarazu shite atarashii kenchiku wa nai," in *Shinkenchiku* 64, no. 11 (November 1989): 201–4.
5. Taro Igarashi, Yasuaki Onoda, Mitsuhiro Kanada, and Takeshi Goto, *The Alternative Modern* (Tokyo: TN Probe, 2005).

Tangling

I want to create an architecture that is ecological in the purest sense of the word. "Tangling" is the term I prefer for it. The living world we inhabit, from the microlevel—a protein, say—to the macrolevel—a jungle, perhaps—is an interwoven or entangled mesh of order. From an incipient cause, one living thing becomes entangled with another, and then another thing tangles with the previous, and so on. Such reciprocation results in an order of refined coexistence. Needless to say, human beings are, as biological forms, part of this order. And architecture, as a human activity, is also part of this interwoven mesh. When seen from a slightly different perspective, the cities created by humans can also be understood as ground-surface expansion, or even as ground fermentation. The human species is a kind of micro-organism fermenting ground surfaces by means of agriculture and architecture. This view leads us to the following definition of architecture: *Architecture is the potential for tangling*. This is to propose a new architecture linked to the nature of living systems. I believe this idea has the potential to be expanded by others, beyond my own work.

Akihisa Hirata

This showroom for agricultural equipment in Niigata, on the northwest coast of Japan's main island, arrays shiny machines—tractors, rotary tillers, and seeders—among angled concrete walls. One of Hirata's first built projects, the design selected through a competition on a website, Showroom H is notable for its structural clarity. Based on an oblique grid of sixteen-and-a-half-foot (five-meter) increments, the showroom features bays formed by walls sliced diagonally to terminate in reduced, almost diminutive, anchor points at the floor. The excised portions of the walls open views across the showroom. The skewed grid and unfinished concrete lend the showroom a dramatic, cave-like tectonic, creating a display

Akihisa Hirata   Showroom H Masuya   Niigata, Japan   2006–07

that is an unusual, atmospheric advertisement for its products. Showroom H evinces Hirata's interest in patterns in which the repetition of simple operations—dividing, folding, pleating—transfigures regular forms into complex, experientially surprising architecture. The diagonal walls of the showroom, generated through formal rules and construction conventions, create an altogether different space when experienced physically. In the architect's words, the room becomes an "animated topography"; moving in and about it has the effect of "touching both intellect and instinct."[1] —PS

Previous spread: Street facade
Clockwise from top: Exterior detail of triangular concrete panels. Facade. Showroom interior with tractors and snow blowers

1. Akihisa Hirata, "Toward an Animated Architecture," in "Now in Japan: New Geometry and Decoration," special issue, Space 479: 41.

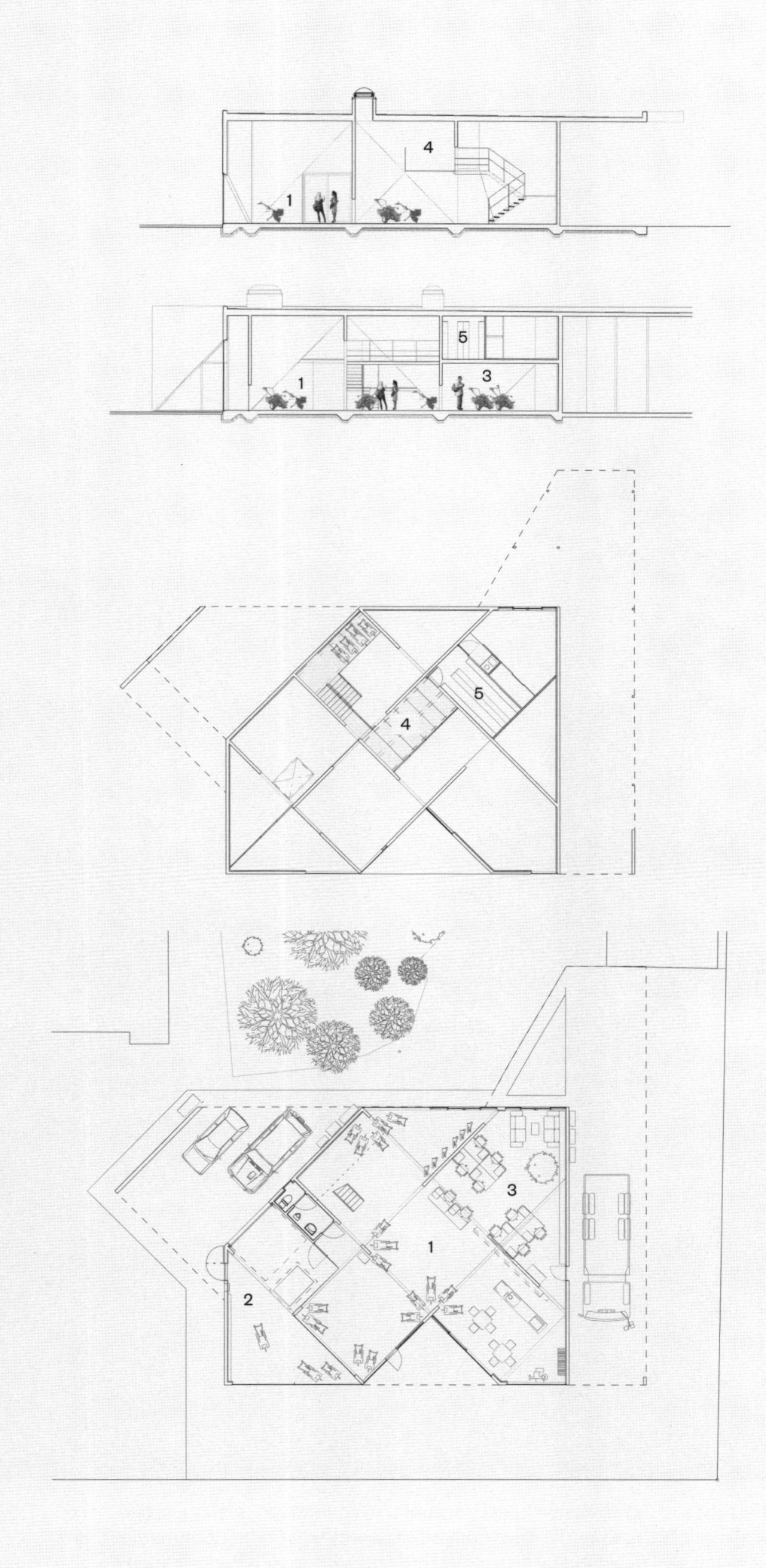

Akihisa Hirata   Showroom H Masuya   Niigata, Japan   2006–07

From top: Sections. Second- and ground-floor plans with showroom (1), workspaces (2), offices (3), loft (4), and warehouse (5)

Located in the verdant, hilly landscape of Taiwan's northeastern coast, Architecture Farm is a single-family house proposed for Next Gene 20, a residential development of twenty villas commissioned during the country's recent real estate boom and designed by a group of international architects for parklike plots within the scenic site. Hirata's proposal began with the idea of a collection of homes he describes as a "farm," both in the spirit of the architecture's organic vocabulary and in the sense of an experimental field in which to "grow" topological design ideas. The house proposed for Next Gene pleats a single surface into reticulated, ribbonlike walls that weave together the private and public spaces of the house.

Akihisa Hirata Architecture Farm Aodi, Taiwan 2007–08

Bedrooms as well as living and dining rooms are located within the furrows. The curves of the walls both provide structural support and define enclosures, creating an arrangement of domestic spaces in a reciprocal relationship: the bedroom's softly curving walls become the bowed kitchen ceiling. Hirata generates adjacent spaces through a process he calls "tangling," likening the variability of the rooms to the "persuasive power" possessed by trees and other growing forms that "exist within a certain range" and "[do] not prescribe one specific final form."[1]—PS

Previous spread: Aerial perspective of the outdoor spa
From top: Perspective of the north facade. Entrance at the west facade

1. Akihisa Hirata, Google Doc shared with the author, January 31, 2015

Akihisa Hirata Architecture Farm
Aodi, Taiwan 2007–08

Pleats gene

Floor 3

Floor 2

Ground floor

Clockwise from top right: North-south section. Third-, second-, and ground-floor plans with foyer (1), living room (2), outdoor spa (3), kitchen (4), dining room (5), bedroom (6), game room (7), gym (8), and family room (9). Sketch pleating together the private and public areas of the house. Diagrams showing the degrees of pleating and generation of geometric forms

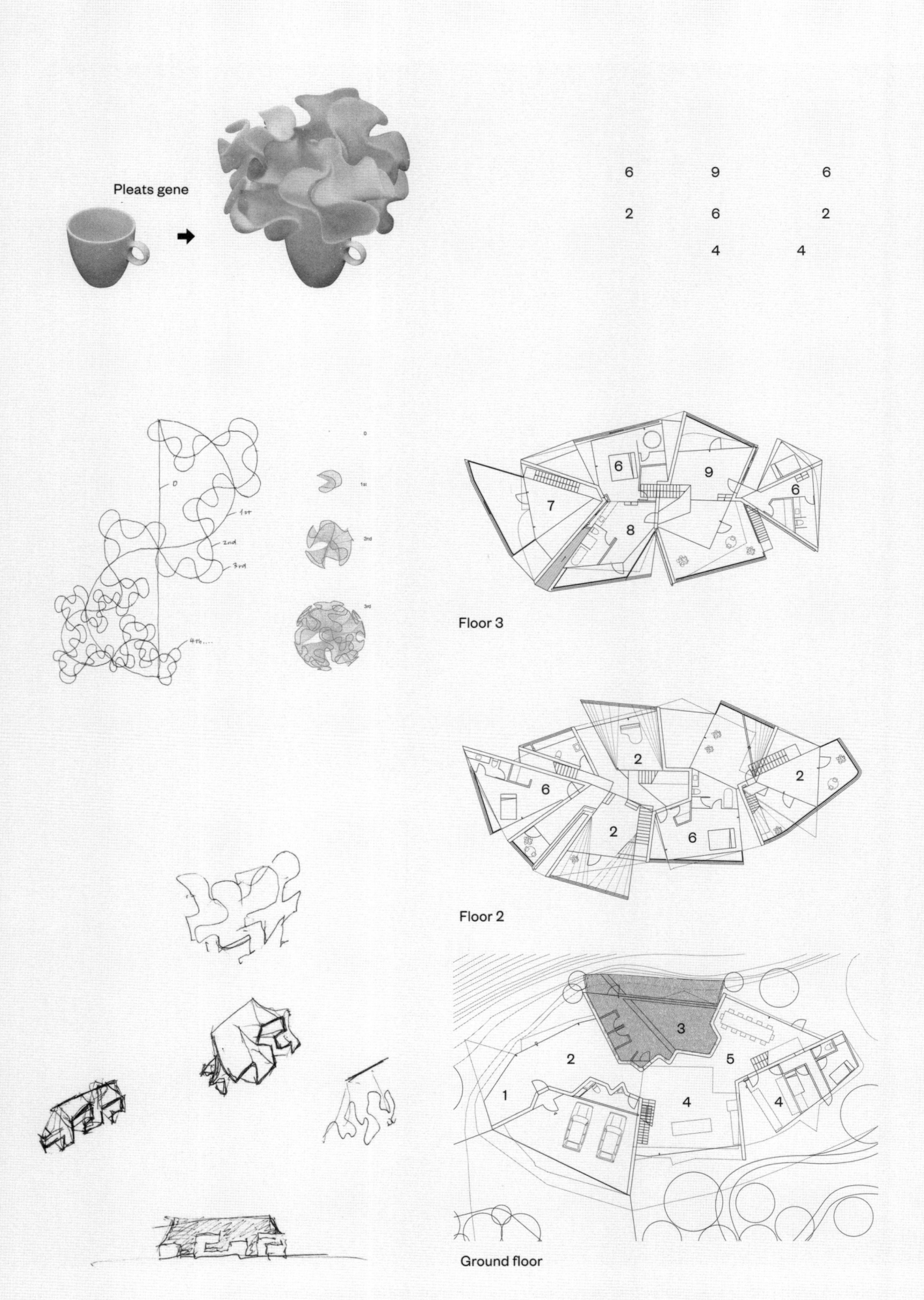

Resembling an intricately folded paper sculpture, this temporary pavilion was installed adjacent to the entrance to the Museum of Contemporary Art Tokyo, where it provided a space for exhibitions and performances by younger artists. Three walls create a semi-enclosed gallery based on a triangular plan. At its uppermost edges, the gallery's tidy silhouette erupts into a voluminous cluster of pleated triangular planes that spill over the sides to form an arrangement of overhangs and spaces to shelter. Fabricated out of thin steel plate painted white, the folds of the planes follow a mathematical formula for a hyplane, a polyhedron made by combining isosceles triangles. Hirata explores the use of geometry and open-ended, algorithmic form-finding at different scales throughout his work. The recursive nature of these rule-based patterns preserves the idea that each design can be adapted or added to indefinitely. Bloomberg Pavilion adapts this folding geometry to the needs of the gallery: refracting natural light through the roof and framing interior views in ornate abstraction. The angled surfaces, regulated by the geometry, catch different gradations of light and shadow, exaggerating the lightweight structure's dimensionality and appearance of cascading disorder.—PS

Akihisa Hirata Bloomberg Pavilion, Museum of Contemporary Art Tokyo 2010–11

Previous spread: View upward through pleated roof
Clockwise from top: Interior exhibition space. Pavilion on the terrace at the Museum of Contemporary Art Tokyo. Night view

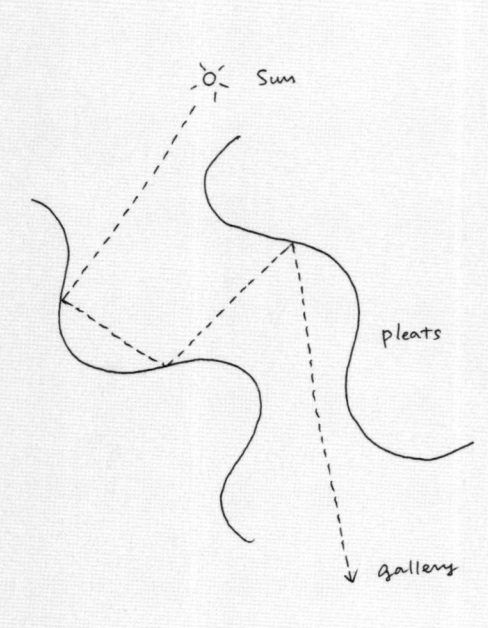

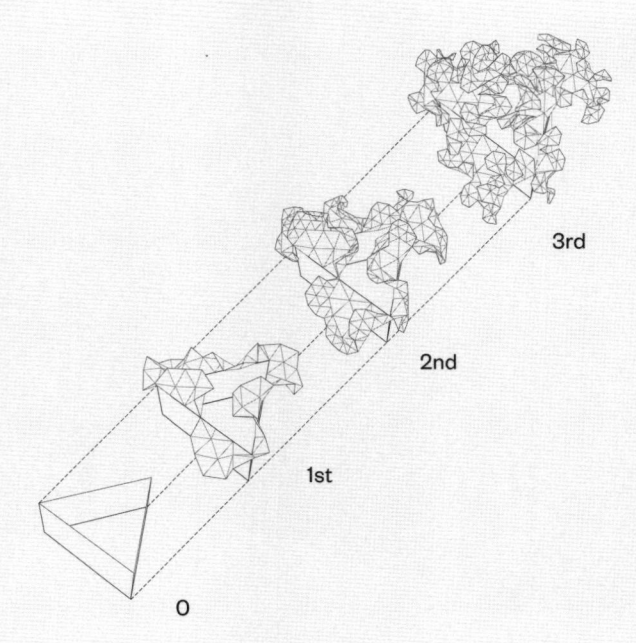

Clockwise from top left: Elevations. Section. Axonometric diagram of the bending of isometric triangles to create pleats. Diagram of the refraction of sunlight. Plan with pleats and steel and plywood structure

Foam Form reimagines the harbor of Kaohsiung, a city on the southern coast of Taiwan, as a four-tiered landscape created out of a porous, branching structure that doubles as a promenade and vertical park. The site, a large international port that has played a significant role in the city's economic development since the early twentieth century, was the subject of an international competition that asked for proposals to combine the port's administrative and industrial functions with a revitalized, recreational waterfront. Foam Form's extended, spongelike structural lattice distributes the port's amenities—music auditoriums, exhibition areas, and retail spaces, both old and new—across the 6-acre (2.46-hectare)

site, becoming a bridge as it crosses Love River, a canal leading into the city. Inspired by aggregations of soap bubbles—a spatial phenomenon that has historically fascinated architects for its potential to create enclosures with minimal surface areas—the design adapts this cellular pattern to the multiple scales of landscape, its apparent disorder enhancing the parklike ambiance. Designed as twenty-eight individual steel units to be fabricated offsite and brought by boat downriver for onsite welding, Foam Form proposes an economy of scale to realize a fairly complex architecture. —PS

Previous spread: Perspective of the landscape bridge spanning Kaohsiung Harbor
Above: Promenades along the branching structure

Akihisa Hirata Foam Form Kaohsiung, Taiwan. Project 2011

From top: Pop-music center. Auditorium interior

Aerial perspectives of the harbor

Akihisa Hirata Foam Form
Kaohsiung, Taiwan. Project 2011

From top: Steel structure inspired by soap-bubble pattern. Site plan with auditorium (1), landscape bridge (2), maritime exhibition area (3), pop-music center (4), and industrial area (5). Plan of pop-music center with workspace (6), recording studio (7), multimedia studio (8), shop (9), and restaurant (10).

Located on a relatively narrow plot in northwestern Tokyo, Hirata conceived this garden residential complex as a collection of loosely stacked boxes, each containing a single room and offset to create multiple small internal courtyards scattered throughout the structure. One or more corners of each box fold into a pleated opening that lets onto a planted terrace. The geometry of the pleats creates a series of idiosyncratic ledges and overhangs that accommodate small shrubs and blooming vegetation. The openings, which vary in orientation, frame views across the building's landscape of jumbled volumes and link the interiors with gardens. Attentive to the close proximity between neighboring units

Akihisa Hirata Tree-ness House Tokyo 2009–ongoing

necessitated by apartment dwelling, Tree-ness House weaves together several scales of relationship—between domestic interiors and their planted terraces, for example, and between different inhabitants. The pleated corners fold outward to provide a double-height view while establishing a screen of privacy between adjacent units. In renderings and sketches, the project has an implied urban scale: the geometric pleats provide an architectural means to fold green spaces into living quarters, one that could be expanded to stitch nature into the "complex ecosystem" of the city.[1] —PS

Previous spread: Perspective of "tree-ness city"
Clockwise from top: Aerial perspective. View from dining room to adjacent terraces. View upward through atrium

- Plants
- Pleats
- Box

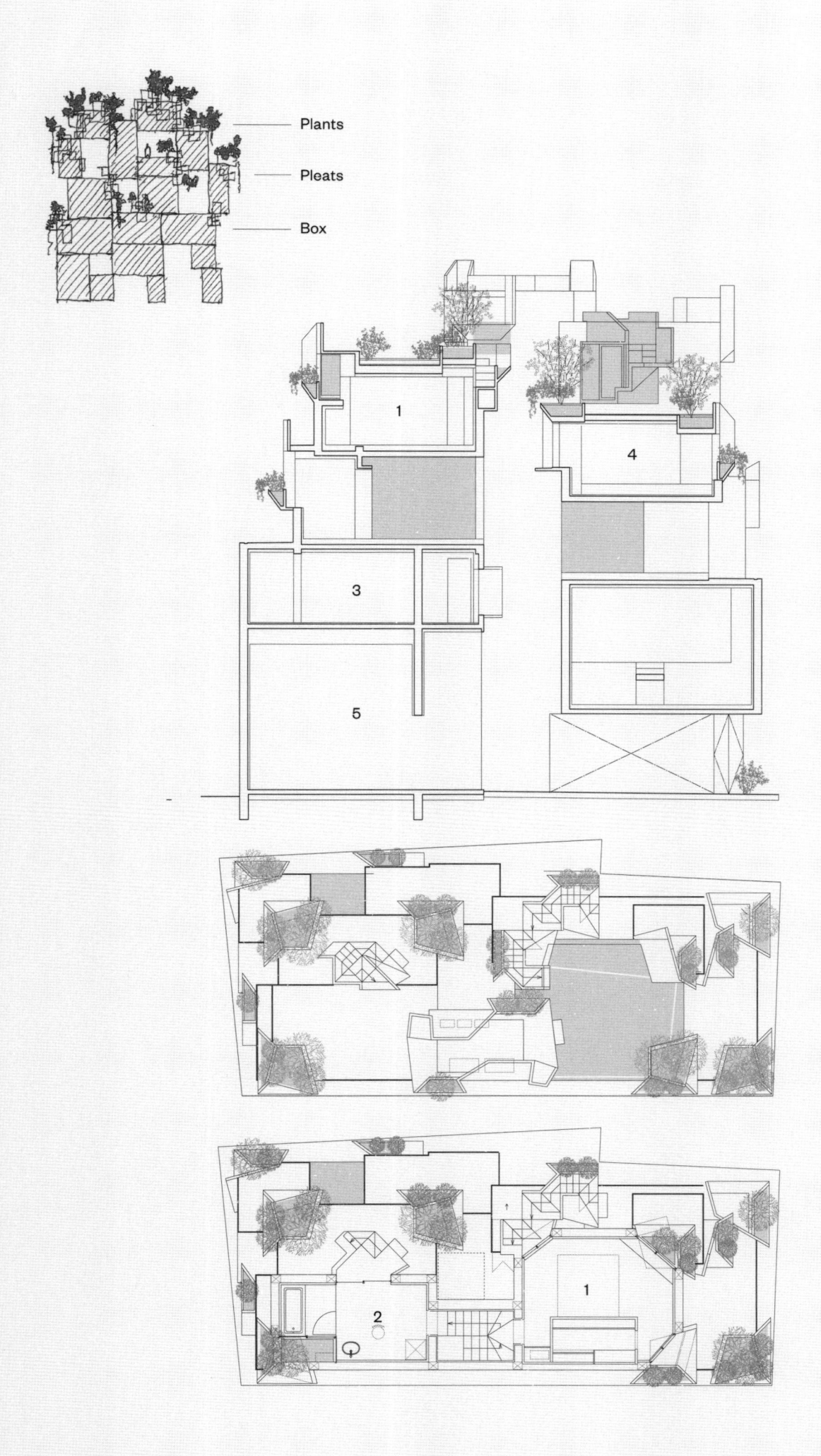

From top: Diagram of components: plants, pleats, and box. Section. Roof and fifth-floor plans with master bedroom (1), bath (2), living room (3), children's room (4), and gallery (5)

Akihisa Hirata   Tree-ness House   Tokyo   2009–ongoing

Freeness in Architecture

I wish to think about architecture freely; to expand my perspective on architecture as flexibly, broadly, and subtly as possible, beyond the stereotypes of what architecture is considered to be. The society that we live in is gradually changing, accepting an array of values more diverse than ever before. It is becoming increasingly difficult for preconceived building types and/or functions to respond to our current circumstances. As architects we need to listen with care and humbleness to the voices of all the people on this earth who are in need of architecture. Perhaps we might set aside the generalities of architecture—the common practices, categories, and styles—and reconsider architecture afresh, as if constructing buildings in a world where all concepts of architecture are nonexistent. To think about architecture freely does not mean creating building forms that indulge the architect's self-expression. Rather it means to consider and confront, sincerely and candidly, the roles of architecture sought after and needed. We should consider what it means to think freely, and whether architecture should incorporate past customs and conventions. We should ask ourselves who is architecture for? Is it for everyone or for a specific individual? Is it for humans or for all animate beings? It may be necessary to think about architecture in a context where all elements are considered with equal importance. I wish to think about architecture freely. I anticipate a future where new roles and conditions for architecture materialize that have never previously been imagined.
Junya Ishigami

This glass-enclosed, single-story workshop on the campus of the Kanagawa Institute of Technology consists of a 21,500-square-foot (2000-square-meter) open room filled with 305 slender rectilinear columns made of steel plate. The columns, which vary in size and orientation, measure a mere five-eighths of an inch (sixteen millimeters) at their thinnest; arranged in organic clusters, they harbor a series of open-ended activities that includes pottery, model-plane construction, and metal casting. Ishigami described the process of composing the space as akin to conceiving "a building as if planning a forest."[1] The design was realized over two years using hand drawing and a CAD software specially developed

Junya Ishigami
Kanagawa Institute of Technology (KAIT) Workshop
Atsugi, Japan 2005–08

to make small adjustments to the positions and dimensions of the columns. The resulting field of columns transforms subtly as the visitor moves through them, altering spatial perceptions. The workshop's creative take on building contingencies, such as the choice of freestanding HVAC units to allow for its extremely thin steel-deck roof, and its everyday appropriation by students and faculty—setting up workstations, shifting furniture, arranging plants—makes the completed building a meditation on constructed and organic states of equilibrium.—PS

Previous spread: Interior at the southeast corner
Above: Rectilinear steel columns at the interior

1. Junya Ishigami, *Another Scale of Architecture* (Kyoto: Seigensha Art Publishing, 2010), 51.

Junya Ishigami Kanagawa Institute of Technology (KAIT) Workshop
Atsugi, Japan
2005–08

From top: East facade. Interior

From top: Multipurpose work spaces at the interior. Southwest corner

Junya Ishigami Kanagawa Institute of Technology (KAIT) Workshop
Atsugi, Japan
2005–08

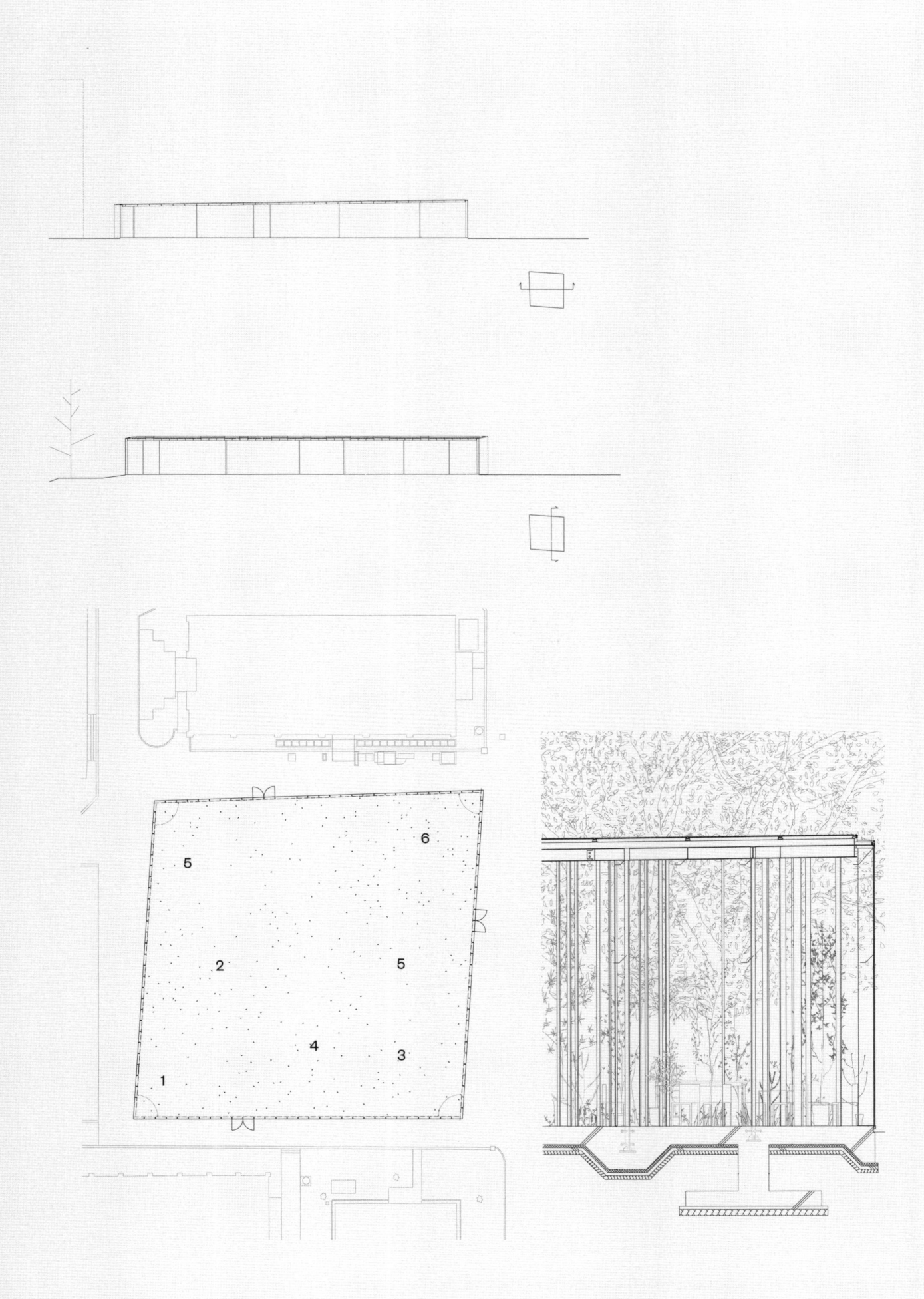

Clockwise from right: Section detail of the roof girders and columns. Plan showing orientation of 305 columns with entrance (1), woodworking space (2), casting space (3), machine-tool space (4), working space (5), computer and administration spaces (6). North-south and west-east sections

Multipurpose Plaza, designed for a site adjacent to Ishigami's Workshop at the Kanagawa Institute of Technology, is a vast, column-free space bound by a ceiling and floor that curve gently inward toward the middle of the building. The architectural brief requested a cafeteria, indoor recreational space, lounge, and multipurpose area. Components requiring specific amenities, such as the cafeteria, were placed along the perimeter in order to free a central area of nearly fifty-four thousand square feet (five thousand square meters). The low ceiling curves in parallel with the floor so that from within the space the two planes appear to coincide, obscuring the view of the perimeter walls. This artificial horizon plays

Junya Ishigami
Kanagawa Institute of Technology Multipurpose Plaza
Atsugi, Japan
2009–ongoing

with actual and perceived scale and offers a richly ambiguous perceptual experience. Following the site's topography, the floor sits below ground level and is covered with a layer of topsoil and vegetation that modulates the internal temperature. A steel roof three-eighths of an inch (nine millimeters) thick and punctuated by unglazed openings casts light onto the gardens below, the interior exceeding the dimensions of conventional architecture to approach something closer to landscape. Ishigami expressed his intent to make the students "feel as if they have traveled to some faraway place."[1] —PS

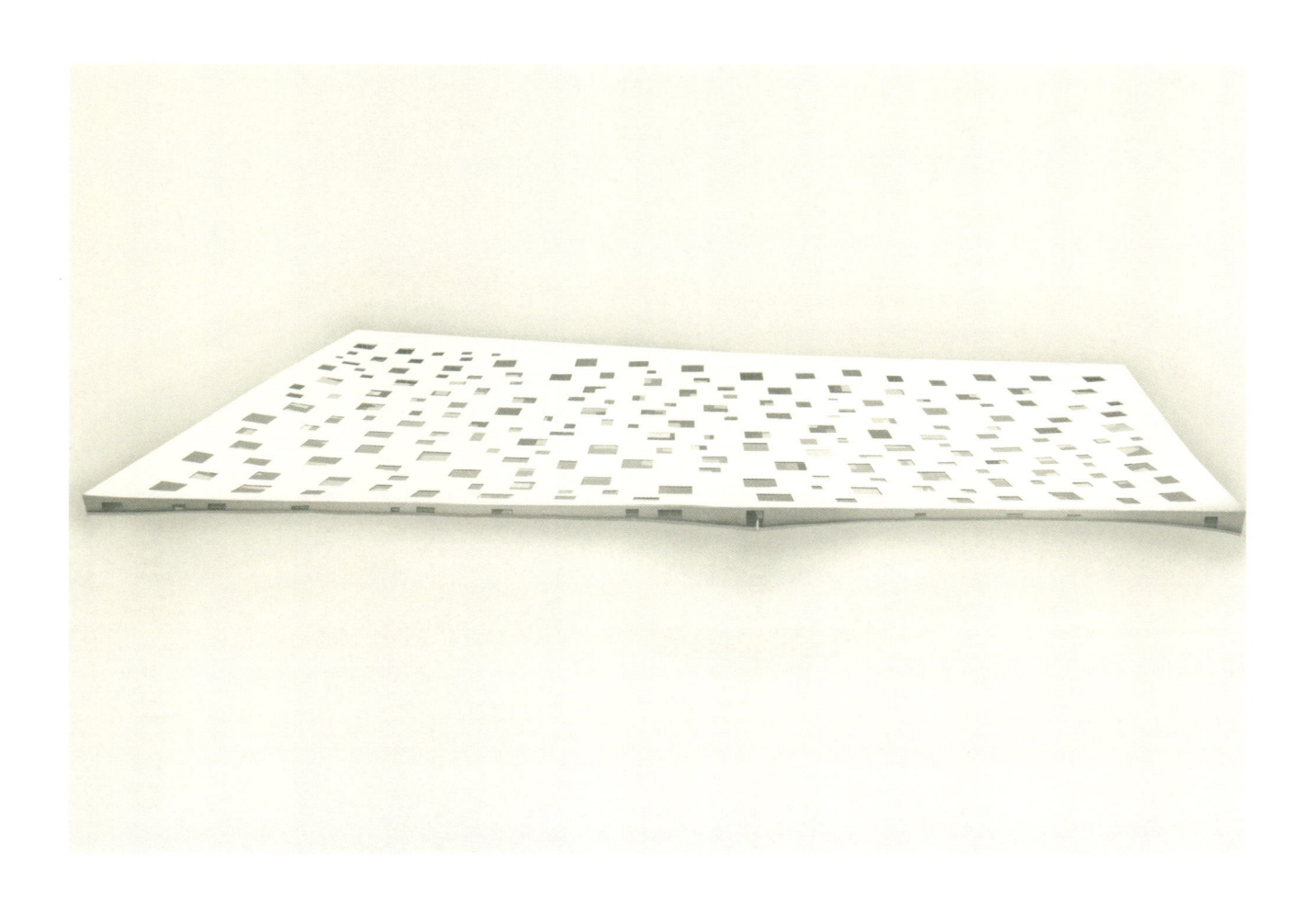

Previous spread: Interior view of the model
Clockwise from top: Aerial view of the model with west facade. A paper model in construction. Detail of the openings at the roof with planted gardens below

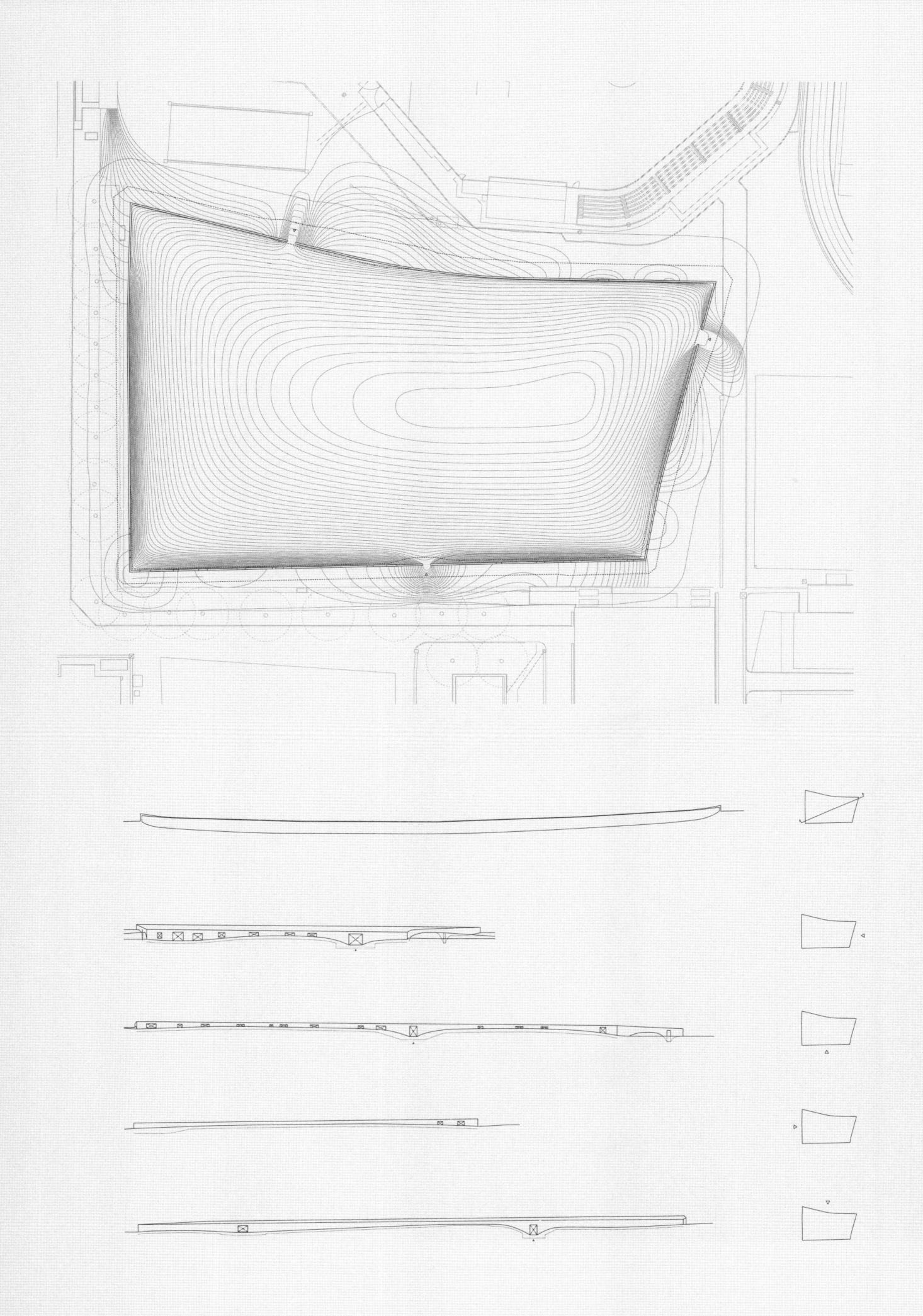

Junya Ishigami   Kanagawa Institute of Technology Multipurpose Plaza   Atsugi, Japan   2009–ongoing

From top: Plan indicating ground-level contours. Southwest-northwest section. South, west, north, and east elevations

Located in a quiet suburb, this small house for a couple began with a conceptual exercise: Ishigami laid out everyday furnishings, from chairs to bookshelves, next to plant varieties likely to live in the yard, equating the living and growing elements of the house with its built components. This reciprocity between the vegetal and the inanimate determined a design that encloses the entire plot in lightweight exterior walls to create an expansive, open interior that is both a garden and a house. The double-height space hosts a small, freestanding kitchen unit with stove and sink, a dining set, and a small bedroom, all of which are arranged independently of the exterior walls. An undulating line of soil interweaves trees and

Junya Ishigami   House with Plants   Japan   2009–12

flowering shrubs with floorboards. A second-story terrace accessed by a ladder provides all of the comforts of a conventional living room while floating amid the treetops of a domestic forest. The house's simple construction method—a steel frame inset with structural plywood—and flexible interior spaces accommodate the unconventional needs of maintaining a living, growing interior. Hidden behind an understated exterior is a complete world in miniature. —PS

Previous spread from left: Interior garden. Dining area
Clockwise from top: Interior garden viewed from the living room. Southwest facade from the street. Interior garden

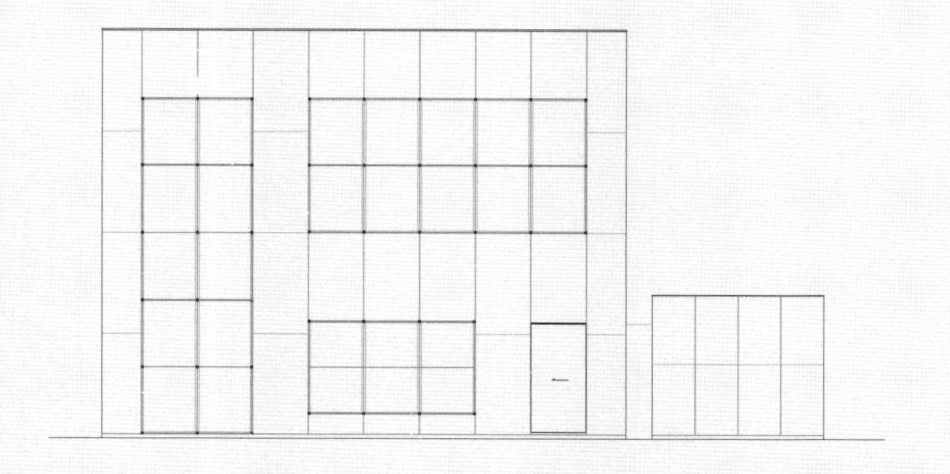

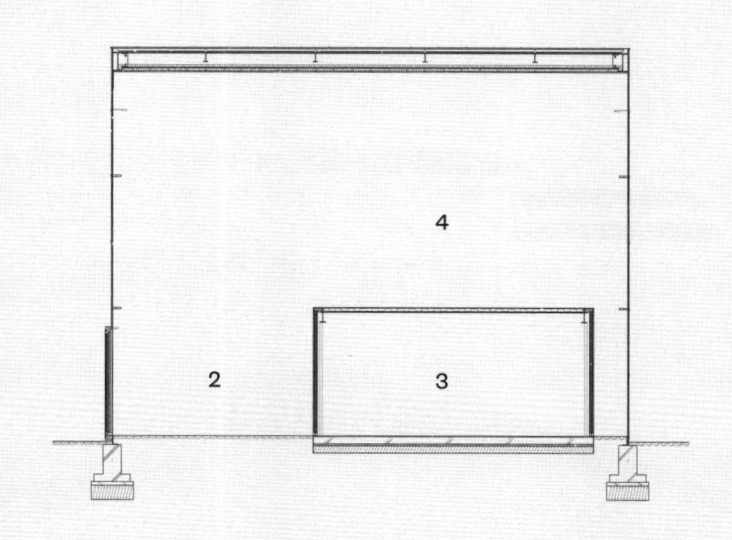

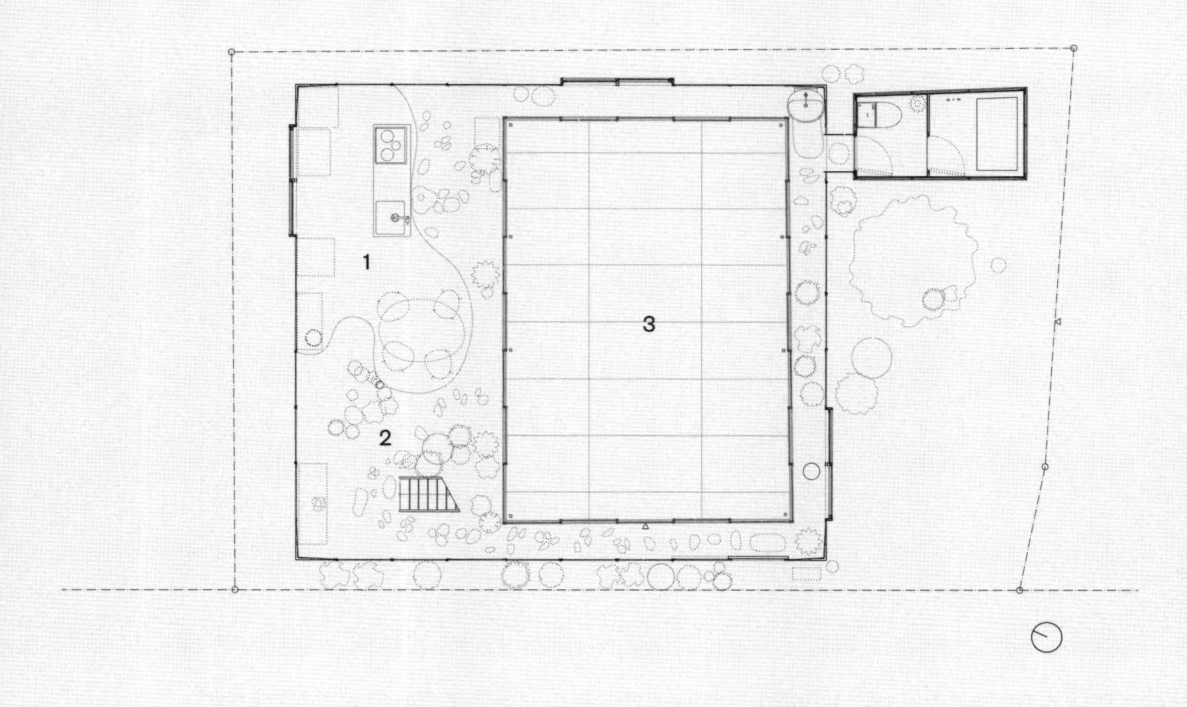

Junya Ishigami — House with Plants — Japan — 235 — 2009–12

From top: Southwest elevation. Section. Ground-floor plan with dining area (1), garden (2), living room (3), and terrace (4)

The seaside Port of Kinmen Passenger Service Center subtly shifts between landform and landmark: at a distance, the building appears continuous with the region's mountainous geography; closer in, it becomes an active port. Kinmen, an archipelago in Taiwanese territory just off the coast of China's Fujian province, has been marked since 1949 by military disputes between the two states, its coastal landscape still littered with military bunkers and tunnels. Since 2000, the Taiwanese government has attempted to reinvent this relationship by opening trade and tourism between the two states. The Passenger Service Center project is emblematic of this effort. Spanning nearly 1640 feet (500 meters),

Junya Ishigami
Port of Kinmen Passenger Service Center
Kinmen, Taiwan
2014–ongoing

its four levels include retail shops, tourist information kiosks, customs offices, arrival and departure lobbies, and observation decks—all interspersed with parkland. In cross section, gabled trusses evoking the island's traditional Fujian-style swallow-tail roofs form the landscape's structural armature. The deep eaves created by the trusses circulate sea air throughout. The project's integration of landscape and architecture extends contemporary reinterpretations of the waterfront, in which soft infrastructure and attentiveness to ecology counteract the typically hard-edged civil-engineering projects that were standard in the twentieth century.—PS

Previous spread: Perspective toward Taiwan Strait
From top: Park spaces below the eaves of the roof. Arrival hall

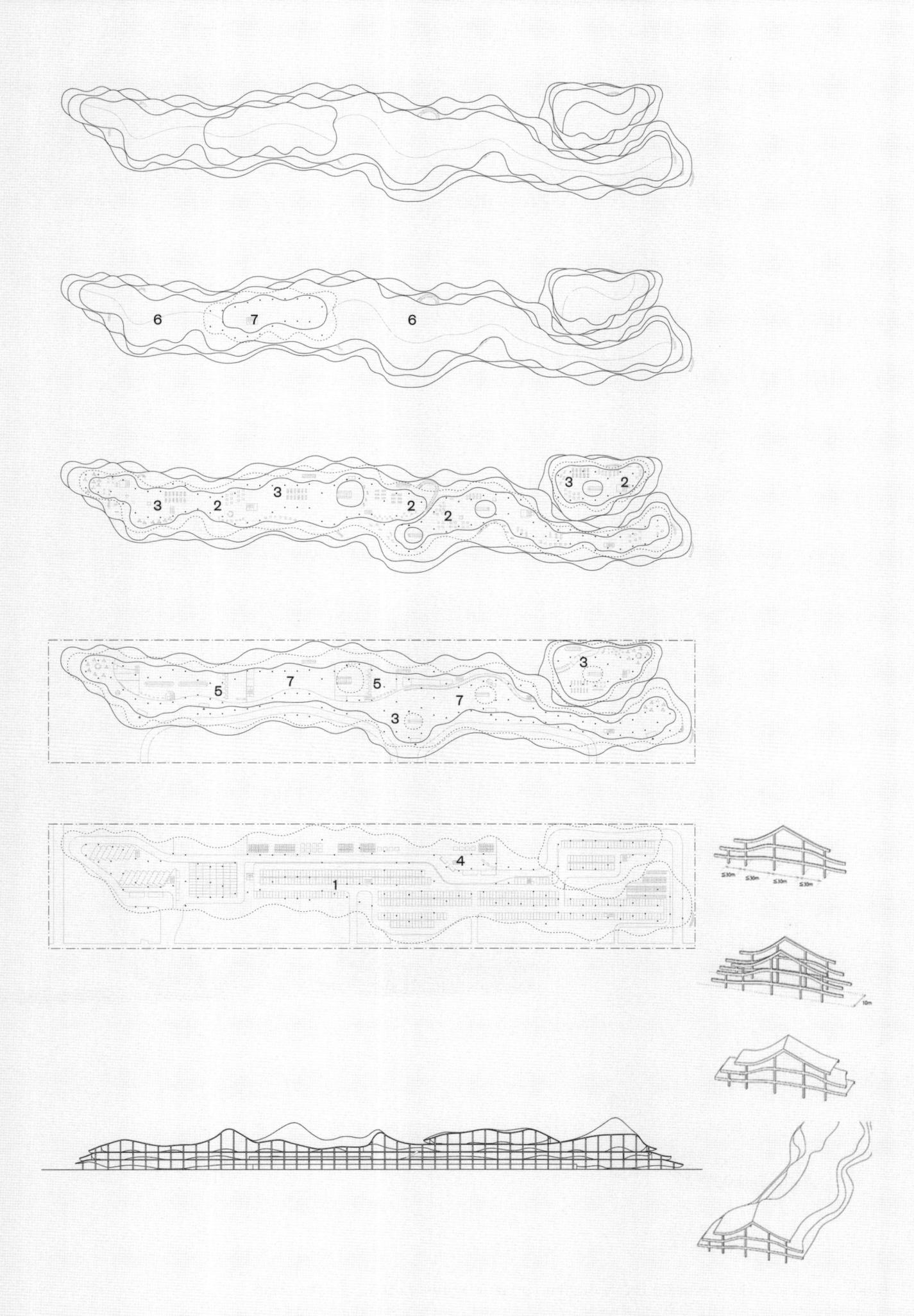

Junya Ishigami Port of Kinmen Passenger Service Center Kinmen, Taiwan 2014–ongoing

From top: Plans of roof, levels two through four, and ground level with parking lot (1), retail spaces (2), departure and arrival halls (3), drop-off area (4), passport control (5), observation deck (6), and administrative offices (7). Section. Axonometric diagram of the structural system

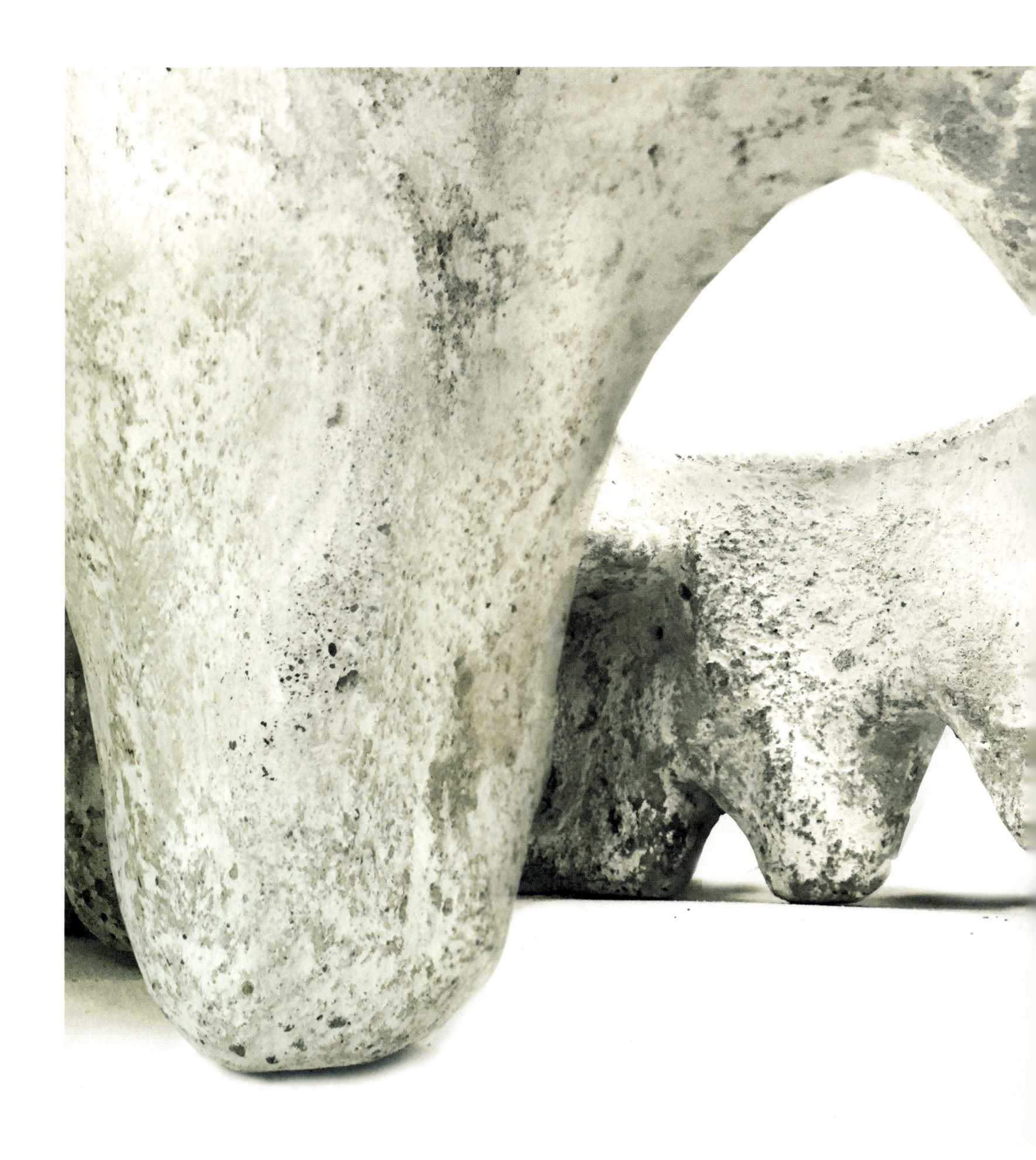

This design combines a residence with a restaurant through an unusual subterranean construction process. The structure is to be created by digging a series of holes, arrayed organically across the site and filled with concrete. Excavating the soil around the poured concrete defines stalactite-like structural piers of a sculptural interior, while glass fitted to the resulting structure provides enclosure. Spaces for dining, sleeping, and entertaining weave throughout. In line with Ishigami's ongoing search for a "new nature"[1]—an architecture that mediates the increasingly ambiguous distinctions between natural and artificial environments—the project's use of raw soil and a process embracing accidents and

Junya Ishigami   House and Restaurant   Japan   2013–ongoing

irregularities frees the resulting architectural form from inherently rationalizing systems of construction and contemporary digital technologies. In exploring a material uncommon to building—soil and its active microscopic world—Ishigami sought "to identify means for simultaneously portraying such parallel environments.... To portray the human environment and what is outside of it as equal, simultaneous, and parallel."[2] House and Restaurant's exploration of negative and positive space occupies architecture's liminal edge.—PS

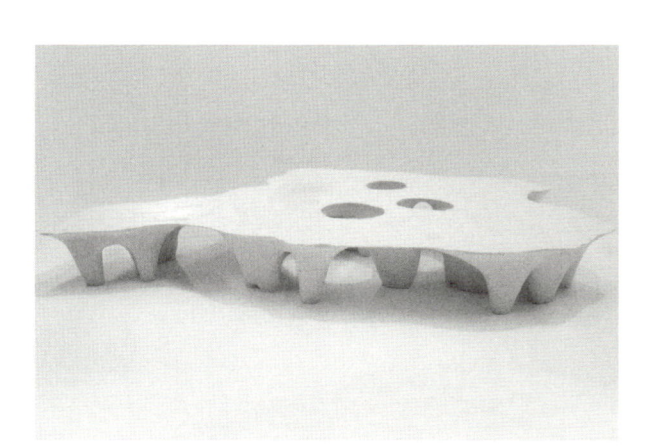

Previous page: Detail of the concrete piers in the model
Clockwise from top: Detail of the living spaces. Model of the structural piers. Detail of the model

Junya Ishigami   House and Restaurant   Japan   2013–ongoing

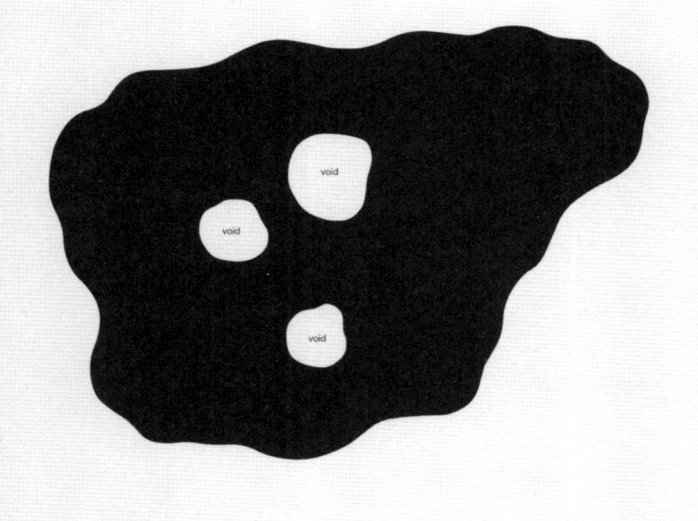

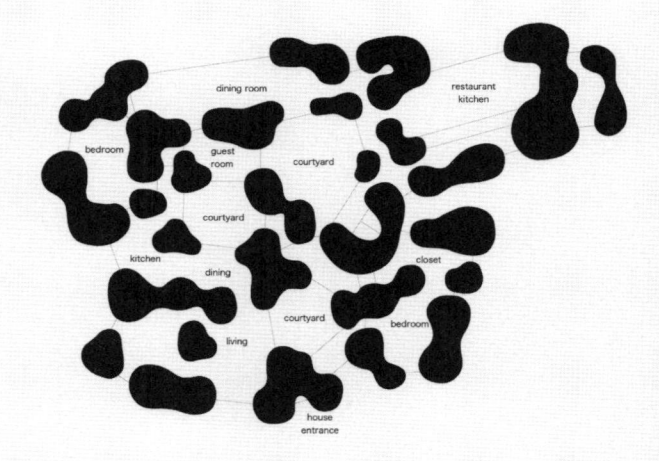

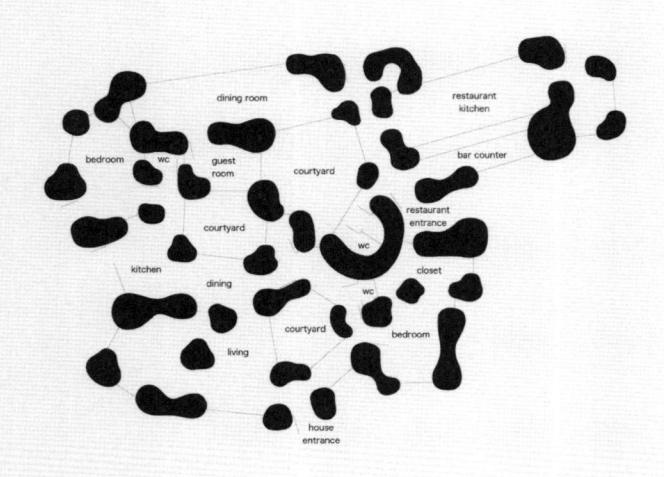

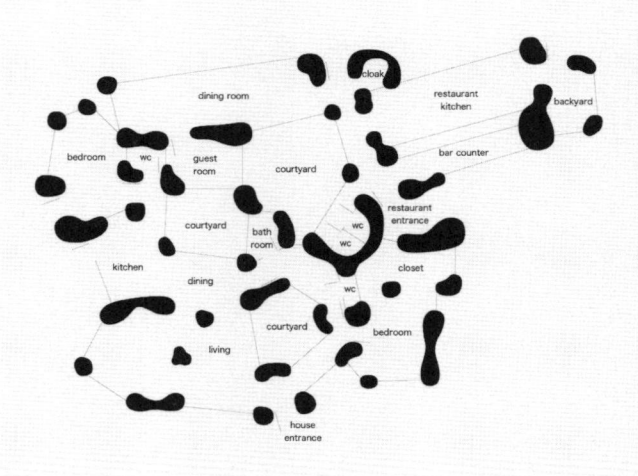

From top: Roof and ground plan with voids for living and dining spaces. Cross sections showing excavated spaces

Distant Stars

When in 1960 a group of young Japanese architects calling themselves "Metabolists" arrived on the world stage with panache and authority, Japan's architectural scene emerged as an essential reference point for contemporary architecture; in 2016, more than half a century later, it continues to endure in this role. A cursory survey of the architectural history of the intervening decades reveals an extraordinary diversity of questing work and vigorous talent. Yet, despite the wide-ranging artistic trajectories and discursive positions among these particular architects, observers beyond Japan have tended to blur their distinguishing characteristics, fusing individual careers into a luminous, globular mass, a cluster of bright things orbiting a powerful but inscrutable meaning, like heavenly bodies in a distant galaxy circling a black hole. We call this black hole "Japan."

The architects participating in this exhibition compose one particularly bright constellation: Toyo Ito, Kazuyo Sejima, Ryue Nishizawa, Sou Fujimoto, Akihisa Hirata, and Junya Ishigami. This essay proposes to map the territories they share, while also preserving their marks of distinction. Maps of architectural scenes in Japan tend to be plotted along genealogical lines, at least initially. The present group is linked by a line of descent: Sejima and Hirata worked for Ito; Nishizawa and Ishigami worked with and for Sejima—these are the two basic groupings. Only Fujimoto stands outside the system of apprenticeship and patronage that remains so essential to securing advancement in the Japanese architectural world. Despite Fujimoto's "aloofness,"[1] Ito's backing has been crucial in bringing the younger architect to public attention and in furnishing him early on with opportunities to experiment.

The line of descent spans three generations and encompasses the sweep of Japanese postwar history: Ito, the "father" of the group, was born in Keijo (Japanese-occupied Seoul) in 1941 at the height of the war years, and came of age during the cultural and political turbulence of the 1960s. Of the architects considered here, Ito's approach most fully embodies the critical, socially engaged perspective forged in that decade. The second generation is represented by Sejima, who, born in 1956, bypassed the rigors of reconstruction and growth. Sejima joined Ito's office in a different age, an era in which production had given way to consumption, spawning the formation of the so-called *shinjinrui* (new humans), whose identity was defined less by what they did than by what they bought. Nishizawa, separated from Sejima by a decade, was the first to taste the uncertainties brought about by the collapse of the asset-price bubble in 1991, along with the transformations to space and to communication enabled by the Internet and the mobile phone. By the time Fujimoto, Hirata, and Ishigami established their offices in the early 2000s, this combination of precarity and possibility formed the basic parameters of existence in Japan, which the Great East Japan Earthquake of March 2011 only underlined.

While the above genealogy charts affiliation and obligation, and offers a rough historical context, it is silent on the intellectual and artistic concerns that animate the works of these figures. To trace these conceptual interests, I will weave an analytical net using four key terms that characterize the contemporary discourse of architecture in Japan: nature, publicness, lightness, and abstraction. In what follows, I will elaborate these terms as linked pairs before condensing them into a formulation that I suggest grasps the unity of the constellation, which I shall term "field minimalism."

Nature + Publicness

Discussions of Japanese architecture inevitably reference nature. Accounts by external observers are replete with such allusions, as are the discipline's native discourses.[2] The term "nature," however, has no singular meaning.

Ito, the constellation's origin and its center of gravity, conceives nature in terms of material presence and dynamic structural forces, a view that crystallized during the construction of the Sendai Mediatheque (p. 22) at the turn of the millennium. This constituted the occasion of a Damascene conversion for Ito. In the 1980s and 1990s, responding to the instability and artificiality of cities in constant flux and the increasing penetration of daily life by mediated imagery and simulated experience, Ito had emerged as an eloquent apostle for a poetics of the virtual, revealing through his work the invisible pneuma of an urban environment suffused with electronic media. As vividly expressed by Thomas Daniell, Ito's translator and closest reader, architecture was "a kind of 'spray' that coats and thereby reveals the spectral outlines of the informational field, like water droplets modelling air turbulence or metal filings tracing a magnetic field."[3] The Sendai Mediatheque, with its pellucid volume penetrated by steel mesh tubes "conceived as structures that sway and dance like seaweed in the water,"[4] was to be the definitive architectural representation of this vision. However, during the grueling process of construction, the brute physicality of the massive steel elements his design so airily deployed overwhelmed Ito. Since then, nature has for Ito come to serve as a touchstone for the "real," the realm of material substance and dynamic structural forces elaborated initially in small projects such as the 2002 Serpentine Gallery Pavilion, in London (p. 32), and which climaxed in the ongoing, decade-long creation of National Taichung Theater (p. 68).[5] He has explicitly promoted this interpretation of nature as a corrective to what he regards as the pallid insubstantiality of the work of the younger generations of Japanese architects (the chief standard-bearers being Ito's own "children" in the present exhibition).

In contrast to Ito, Fujimoto's conception of nature is less about substance and more about patterns. He sees in nature rich ordering patterns and emergent complexity, but also finds inspiration in landscape archetypes such as mountains, forests, trees, and clouds—metaphorical resources carrying spatial and architectural potential. "A garden is the initial state of Architecture," Fujimoto writes of an archetype of spatial ambiguity he pursues in his work (fig. 1).[6] The garden here represents the innumerable interrelations between elements in a continuous state of change, a coruscating kaleidoscope that transcends the distinctions between the natural and the artificial. For Fujimoto, "Architecture is a garden with a roof; Garden is architecture without a roof."[7]

In Hirata's work, references to nature tend toward the "organic" as a principle of generative development and unfolding. Where Fujimoto is content to translate emblems of nature into architecture through metaphor and analogy, Hirata would prefer to develop precise mathematical descriptions of what he calls the "tangles" and "pleats" that nature tenders through its generative processes.[8] The "fermented geometries" that result from this pursuit, characterized by recursive foldings and involutions, can be felt in works such as the architect's 2011 Bloomberg Pavilion (p. 204).[9] "We want to create a 'tangled order,'" writes Hirata, "an entire world that is shaped by an organic unity of various things related to architecture."[10]

As with his contemporaries, nature is fundamental to Ishigami's thinking. Here, however, nature operates as neither spatial metaphor nor generative principle, but as a kind of horizon of radical possibility, whose latent potential for magic and surprise is veiled by convention and habit. Even facets as quotidian as the weather harbor this potential: "Some days it hails in the middle of a sunny day. They are surprising, but such days occur, and they are part of nature. I would like the things I create to have something of that combination of reality and surprise."[11] Ishigami's architecture is an instrument that both harnesses and unleashes this capacity. In his 2008 Kanagawa Institute of Technology Workshop (or KAIT, fig. 2), Ishigami created a forest of 305 columns, each with a unique rectangular profile and orientation—a field of fluctuating, interpenetrating spaces of ambiguity. Invoking a term used by Ito, but with antithetical results, Ishigami describes his works as devices to "reveal reality as it is, rather than as we would wish it to be."[12]

In the work of Sejima and Nishizawa, individually as well as in collaboration, the concept of nature merges with notions of "environment" and "landscape," terms that are less about ecology than they are an idea of publicness—the organization and qualities of spaces of interpersonal encounter and interaction. The question of publicness is the second major conceptual hub around which contemporary Japanese architectural discourse orbits. Publicness relates to access, use, and occupation (in the sense of occupying space); it conveys openness and spontaneity. In Japan, the etymology of the term "public" (kōkyō) and the history of its associations have freighted the concept with affiliations to state power and nation building—this is the "public" of the Metabolist architects of the 1960s. "Publicness" (kōkyōsei) on the other hand (and for want of a better term) connotes bottom-up rather than top-down decision-making processes; popular rather than official affiliations; and an emphasis on freedom rather than control. The term thus carries a critical charge tinged with the traces of a radical politics.[13]

In spatial terms, these ideas manifest in the architects' careful attention to the boundaries and gradations between public and private spaces, and their concern with the patterns of human occupation and interaction in built space. In the Sejima/Nishizawa/SANAA oeuvre, these ideas are mobilized using architectural strategies inspired by the openness and loose spatial structure of landscape. The transparent lobby of the 2004 21st Century Museum of Contemporary Art, Kanazawa (p. 106), for instance, serves as a publicly accessible interstitial zone between the surrounding urban environment and the museum. In the 2010 Rolex Learning Center (p. 124), at the École polytechnique fédérale de Lausanne, in Switzerland, the undulating gradations of enclosure and openness, and the building's continuously shifting horizon line, act as spatial devices that "tune" degrees of separation and connection between building occupants. Sejima and Nishizawa explore these same ideas in their smaller-scale buildings (fig. 3), too, as seen in the dissolved perimeters and dispersed occupancies of Nishizawa's 2005 Moriyama House (p. 140), in Tokyo; and in the clustered, interlocking dwellings interleaved by garden courtyards in Sejima's 2014 Nishinoyama House, in Kyoto. Both houses reconfigure the relation of publicness and privacy in the contemporary dwelling. Ito's archi-

Fig. 1: Sou Fujimoto (Japanese, born 1971). Primitive Future House. Project. 2001. Scale model 1:50. Acrylic, 19 11/16 × 19 11/16 × 19 11/16" (50 × 50 × 50 cm). Collection the architect. Fig. 2: Junya Ishigami (Japanese, born 1974). Kanagawa Institute of Technology Workshop, Japan. 2005–08. Interior view. Fig. 3: Ryue Nishizawa (Japanese, born 1966). Garden and House, Tokyo. 2006–11. View from the street. Fig. 4: Sou Fujimoto (Japanese, born 1971), Akihisa Hirata (Japanese, born 1971), Kumiko Inui (Japanese, born 1969), and Toyo Ito (Japanese, born 1941). Home-for-All, Rikuzentakata, Japan. 2012

fig. 1

fig. 2

tectural thinking and activism have also explicitly engaged with publicness, his Home-for-All initiative (fig. 4) for communities devastated by the 2011 Japan Great East Earthquake, a prominent case in point.[14] The interaction of bodies and spaces animates Ito's thinking. The practitioner frequently calls for an architecture that releases *iki-iki* (vitality) in its occupants; the modernist grid, with its blank standardization and repetition, is the deadening villain in this narrative. Since building Sendai Mediatheque, Ito has focused on ways to evade or transcend modernism's "cage of rationality."[15] Whereas in the work of Sejima and Nishizawa, publicness manifests in open terrains shaped by subtly manipulated boundaries, in Ito's work it appears as extensive three-dimensional spatial explorations, and achieves full expression in the "emerging grid"[16] that generates the spongey, fluid matrix of National Taichung Theater. Publicness is for Ito more tactile and embodied than for SANAA; the bodies that populate Ito's spaces contain flesh and blood and mass, whereas those of his protégés appear ever more virtual.

Taken together, these two terms, nature and publicness, intimate a third concept: the field. The term "field" captures the range of approaches within the constellation, most of which entail design development from the bottom-up, where smaller units or relationships are aggregated without first imposing, top-down, a macro-level organization. In its sense derived from physics, as a spatially extensive area of influence, "field" encapsulates something of Fujimoto's cloud-like clusters of elements, of Hirata's unfolding surfaces, and of Ito's spacio-structural matrices. The term "field" also exists within the lexicon of landscape metaphors and horizontally unfolding spaces that register Sejima, Nishizawa, and Ishigami's particular fascination with the everexpanding single-story domain, as in Sejima's Multipurpose Facility, in Onishi (p. 84), of 2005, Nishizawa's 2010 Hiroshi Senju Museum (p. 154), in Karuizawa, and Ishigami's KAIT Workshop.

The notion of the field proposed here resonates with the language of "field conditions," a statement of theoretical architectural principles launched into circulation in the late 1990s by American architect and theorist Stan Allen; to this day, it continues to have currency within English-language architectural and landscape discourses.[17] Allen uses the term to describe "any formal or spatial matrix capable of unifying diverse elements while respecting the identity of each,"[18] a relationship between part and whole that transcends principles of formal and spatial composition in both classical and modernist modes. Compositions generated under field conditions are concerned with local relations between elements and remain relatively indifferent to overall form. They express repetition, porosity, and interconnection, and contain something of the organizational characteristics of flocks, swarms, and crowds. They facilitate change, accident, and improvisation.

Many of the principles of formal organization and design logic Allen describes are evident in the work of Ito and his descenants. Although any vector of influence would have been reflected and refracted through various translations and second- or third-hand encounters, the point is that the ideas animating the work of this group of architects are not insulated in a hermetically sealed package made in Japan and disconnected from the wider conversation in architecture; they are, in fact, very much a part of it.

Lightness + Abstraction

The second pairing brings together the ideas of "lightness" and "abstraction," which I provisionally bundle into the term "minimalism."[19] For the broader audience or casual observer, minimalism perhaps captures this work's most overt stylistic characteristics: its apparent purity of architectural intent; its clearly expressed spatial ideas that appear neither thickened with the accretions of history and use, nor blurred by pragmatic compromises with structure and material. Whereas the terms "nature" and "publicness" relate to the sources and goals of architectural invention, "lightness" and "abstraction" relate to aesthetic effects and conceptual methodology.

Lightness has long been evident in the work of Sejima and Nishizawa. Ito once said that Sejima's buildings had the quality of line diagrams directly translated into buildings "with the utmost brevity," without acquiring material thickness along the way.[20] Ishigami takes this tendency toward weightlessness even further, most spectacularly with two early works, his 2006 Table, an impossibly slender table thirty-two feet (nine and one-half meters) long and eight and one-half (two and one-half meters) wide but only one-eighth of an inch (three millimeters) thick; and his 2008 Balloon, a five-story, helium-filled metallic cuboid volume levitating above an art museum floor. But lightness also refers to the limpid space found in the works of these architects, the kind of luminousness that suffuses Ishigami's KAIT Workshop or Nishizawa's Hiroshi Senju Museum.

fig. 3

fig. 4

To be sure, Ito has strongly criticized this interest in lightness among those who descended from Sejima's lineage as "bloodless," charging them with having generated architecture designed for "androids in a space where neither body heat, perspiration, nor smell exist."[21] In his own recent work he has explicitly sought out material density, presence, and mass, qualities that underscore the real or the primal. According to Ito, such characteristics serve as an essential ballast in a society ever more attached to the digital and the mediated. But it was precisely Ito who, with his 1984 Silver Hut and his readings of the consumer landscapes of bubble-economy Tokyo, opened the door to the exploration of the virtual and the ephemeral. As the author Italo Calvino suggested around the same time in his *Six Memos for the Next Millennium*, lightness captures something essential about experience in our networked, mobile, urbanized era—its weightlessness, its velocity, its airy detachment from historical place, physical materiality, or weighty consequence.[22] It is the same quality found in the atmospheres of the novels of Haruki Murakami or photographs of Takashi Homma; it feels at once very Japanese (or more accurately, very Tokyo), and yet thoroughly contemporary and meaningful for those outside Japan.

Lightness manifests somewhat differently in the work of Fujimoto and Hirata, whose work tends more toward abstraction. It is most obviously expressed in the structures' "whiteness," or optical lightness. The use of white as the default color with which to elaborate architectural ideas recalls the whiteness of the works of early modernists such as Le Corbusier and Walter Gropius, and signals (whether consciously or not) an alignment with the modernist methodology of exploring formal and spatial concepts abstracted from their material supports.[23]

Abstraction relates to a number of methodological approaches and formal maneuvers found across this constellation of architects, and emerges when the formal, conceptual, and intellectual agendas are prioritized over constructional, material, and programmatic ones. A number of Fujimoto's early projects (notably the Children's Centre for Psychiatric Rehabilitation in Hokkaido, his homeland) manipulated basic geometrical elements, typically cubes, to explore systematically—almost scientifically—how to finely tune spatial relations between architectural elements. Ito's investigation of the relationship between structure and skin across his oeuvre, from the Brugge Pavilion (p. 28) to the Serpentine Gallery Pavilion, from Tod's Omotesando Building (p. 36) to the Mikimoto Ginza 2, of 2005, in Tokyo, is so methodical and rigorous that it's as if he is unfolding a mathematical theory. In Sejima, Nishizawa, and Ishigami's work, we can also find abstraction in the reduction and purification of ever more direct, unelaborated modes, as with SANAA's Glass Pavilion at the Toledo Museum of Art (p. 112) or Ishigami's projects at KAIT.

The combination of lightness and abstraction is salient to Japanese minimalism. An emphasis on simplicity, reduction, and focused attention has been an enduring feature of the tradition of the Japanese tea ceremony since the time of the great tea master Sen no Rikyu (1522–1591) and the associated aesthetic philosophy of *wabi-sabi*, which finds beauty and value in subtlety, imperfection, and austerity.[24] This suite of characteristics forms the primary qualities associated with Japanese minimalism. After the architectural excesses of the bubble economy of the 1980s, Japan post-growth has seen qualities of restraint and directness across a wide spectrum of contemporary Japanese architecture. When realized as an aesthetic principle, this economy of means becomes minimalist. Daniell has divided these minimalist tendencies into "visceral" and "ephemeral" streams, the former emphasizing architecture's corporeal properties, the latter exploring its perceptual effects.[25] The lightness and abstraction of the work of the architects in this exhibition may be positioned in the latter category.

Such minimalism, however, has little connection to the developments in North American art during the 1960s, as exemplified by figures such as Donald Judd, Tony Smith, and Robert Smithson, whose works were originally described as "literalism," but were later classified as Minimalism.[26] The material attenuations and spatial purifications in the work of Sejima and Nishizawa (fig. 5) arise from carefully manipulated spatial boundaries rather than from any focus on objecthood or presence, such as with the impassively set objects characteristic of the sculptural work of American minimalist artists. In the field of architecture, however, Japanese minimalism may have come to displace the original American referent, and through SANAA's rampant success in defining an architectural language for the exhibition of contemporary art, it has effectively become the default backdrop for a sense of the contemporary itself.

fig. 5

Fig. 5: Walter Niedermayr (Italian, born 1952). *Bildraum S 240*, 2010. Digital pigment print, three panels, installation dimensions. 40 15/16" x 13' 11/16" (104 x 399 cm). Courtesy the artist and Galerie Nordenhake Berlin / Stockholm. © Walter Niedermayr.

Conclusion: Opening the Field

If the work of the present constellation is considered the elaboration through architecture of a set of ideas relating to nature, publicness, lightness, and abstraction, and encoded in the formulation "field minimalism"—what could be its contemporary significance? To do full justice to the question would require significantly more space than available here; however, I can begin to outline how this approach might open fresh territories of thought that would resonate far beyond the local contexts of architectural discourse in Japan.

A first opening lies in the desiccated well of minimalism. The dissipation of the conceptual and formal strategies of postmodernism in the 1990s led to the reemergence of a neomodernist architectural vocabulary—clean, flat, rectilinear structures uninflected with overt symbolic content or ornamental flourish that have routinely been labelled "minimalist" in the popular design media. Such minimalism is efficient insofar as its material consistency and formal simplicity is relatively cheap to produce. But its intellectual sheen and evocations of a rarefied elite world render it irresistibly appealing to a wealthy professional class, making for a particularly profitable marketing strategy. Such commercial ends have drained minimalism of any of the resistant qualities that once motivated its strategies of reduction and presence.

The abstraction and lightness found in the work of the present constellation, however, holds the potential to reinvigorate the architectural discourse of minimalism through its concern with revealing relations, forces, and effects. The way Ishigami's work uncovers latent properties of magic and illusion embedded in material reality; or the slender gridded armature of Fujimoto's Serpentine Gallery Pavilion traces a subtle matrix against which relations between bodies and environment can be disclosed; or the exquisite economy by which Nishizawa's 2010 Teshima Art Museum (p. 150), in Kagawa, evokes invisible flows of life and energy—these are architectural experiences of extraordinary force and richness.

The more consequential opening, however, perhaps lies not in this architecture's specific principles and methods but in its posture. These architects combine an habitual disciplinary rigor and depth with openness and curiosity to the world. This is an attitude to contemporary modernity—with its artificiality and consumerism, its technology and media, its speed and flux and lack of depth—that is neither defensive nor celebratory, alienated nor ardent. Rather the position is one of detached curiosity, the kind of focused reserve scientists take on in studying natural phenomena. Architecture becomes an instrument to map and measure this world, employing its own methods and codes, and deepening its disciplinary resources. Such an architecture is autonomous from the world yet engaged with it; reflects the world yet is critical of it. Such an architecture is at once intimate and remote, near and far. It is this conjunction of proximity and distance that constitutes the depth of this constellation's field.

Notes

1. "Alone and aloof" was how Ito described Fujimoto in the second round of the 2000 competition for the Aomori Museum of Art, in which Ito was a judge. This competition first brought Fujimoto to attention within Japan's architectural world. See Toyo Ito, "Casting Off Weak Architecture," *Sou Fujimoto: Primitive Future* (Tokyo: INAX Publishing, 2008), 9.
2. For more than a century, each successive generation of Western architects that has sought inspiration in Japan—including Frank Lloyd Wright, Bruno Taut, and Walter Gropius—has ascribed to the culture a peculiar native sensitivity toward nature and sought to interpret its architectural traditions in light of this.
3. Thomas Daniell, "The Fugitive," in Toyo Ito, *Tarzans in the Media Forest & Other Essays*, Architecture Words 8 (London: Architectural Association Publications, 2011), 13.
4. Toyo Ito, "Tarzans in the Media Forest," in Toyo Ito, *Tarzans in the Media Forest & Other Essays*, Architecture Words 8 (London: Architectural Association Publications, 2011), 118.
5. This emphasis on the "real" in Ito's work since Sendai Mediatheque was addressed in the exhibition *Toyo Ito: The New "Real" in Architecture*, at the Tokyo Opera City Art Gallery, October 7 through December 24, 2006.
6. Sou Fujimoto, "Garden," *Primitive Future*, 101.
7. Ibid.
8. Akihisa Hirata, "Fermented Geometry," in *Tangling* (Tokyo: INAX Publishing, 2011), 78–123.
9. Ibid.
10. Ibid., 83.
11. Ishigami in conversation with the author, quoted in Worrall, "Junya Ishigami," *Icon* 62 (August 2008): 61.
12. Ibid., 63.
13. For a more detailed account of the etymology and various resonances of the term "public" in Japan, see Worrall, "Nature, Publicness, Place—Towards a Relational Architecture in Japan," in *Eastern Promises: Contemporary Architecture and Spatial Practices in East Asia*, ed. Christoph Thun-Hohenstein, Andreas Fogarasi, Christian Teckert (Ostfildern, Denmark: Hatje Cantz, 2013), 93–99. Published in conjunction with the exhibition of the same name at MAK: Austrian Museum of Applied Arts/Contemporary Art in Vienna.
14. This project, initiated by Ito, engages architects to build small community spaces for residents displaced after the 2011 Great East Japan Earthquake and was exhibited at the Venice Architecture Biennale of 2012, winning the Golden Lion award.
15. The "cage of rationality" is a term I use in an earlier discussion of Ito to describe his objections to the modernist grid. See Worrall, "Base and Superstructure in Toyo Ito," in *Toyo Ito: Forces of Nature*, ed. Jessie Turnbull (New York: Princeton Architectural Press, 2012), 122. The term is a nod to Max Weber's "iron cage of rationality" from *The Protestant Ethic and the Spirit of Capitalism*, first published in German in 1905. Ito's views on the impoverishments of modernism recall Weber's analysis of bureaucratic rationality.
16. Ito uses the term "emerging grid" (which also appears as "emergent grid" in various articles in English) to depict a generative methodology for transcending the Cartesian grid of modern architecture. Ito introduced the term in the 2006 exhibition *Toyo Ito: The New "Real" in Architecture* at the Tokyo Opera City Art Gallery and achieves its most developed representation the "spongey fluid matrix" of National Taichung Theater. The term describes the formation of a field of interconnected, nonuniform spaces starting with a uniform grid; each space, accommodating programmatic or structural forces, influences its neighbors in three dimensions.
17. Stan Allen, "From Object to Field: Field Conditions in Architecture and Urbanism," in *Points + Lines: Diagrams and Projects for the City* (New York: Princeton Architectural Press, 1999), 90–103.
18. Ibid., 90.
19. My tentativeness in deploying the term "minimalism" arises both from the overexposure of the term in application to Japanese architecture, and the specificity of its meanings in American art-historical discourses. However, a better term that avoids these problems but can still denote the relevant qualities of abstraction and lightness has yet to be found.
20. See Toyo Ito, "Diagram Architecture," in *El Croquis* 77, no. 1: 18–24.
21. Ibid., 20.
22. Italo Calvino, *Six Memos for the Next Millennium* (Boston: Harvard University Press, 1988).
23. Under Terunobu Fujimori's classification of the Japanese architectural scene into the "Red School" and the "White School" everyone in the present constellation would be filed under White School. Further discussion of this classification can be found in this volume; see, Fujimori, "Magical Spatial Inversion" p. 73. See also Dana Buntrock, *Materials and Meaning in Contemporary Japanese Architecture* (New York: Routledge, 2010). Parenthetically, in the historical survey *Japan Architects 1945–2010*, a 2014 exhibition at the 21st Century Museum of Contemporary Art in Kanazawa, organized jointly with the Centre Pompidou in Paris, curator Frédéric Migayrou's chromatic historical schema declared "white" the color of the contemporary period.
24. These three aesthetic qualities are elaborated in Haga Koshiro, "The Wabi Aesthetic through the Ages," in *Japanese Aesthetics and Culture: A Reader*, ed. Nancy G. Hume (Albany: State University of New York Press, 1995), 245–78.
25. Thomas Daniell, "The Visceral and the Ephemeral," in *After the Crash: Architecture in Post-Bubble Japan* (New York: Princeton Architectural Press, 2008), 37–44.
26. For a critical history of these terminological distinctions, see Mark Linder, *Nothing Less than Literal: Architecture after Minimalism* (Cambridge, Mass.: MIT Press, 2004).

Toyo Ito (born Keijo, 1941)
Toyo Ito & Associates, Architects
(established Tokyo, 1971)

Toyo Ito studied architecture at University of Tokyo before working at the offices of Kiyonori Kikutake from 1965 to 1969. He opened his own studio in Tokyo, known initially as Urban Robot (Urbot), in 1971, before establishing Toyo Ito & Associates, Architects, in 1979. His earliest projects were individual residences, including Aluminum House (1971), in Kanagawa, and White U (1976), in Tokyo. His practice gained international prominence following his critically acclaimed, technically innovative Sendai Mediatheque (1995–2001). Recent projects by Toyo Ito & Associates, Architects, include Minna no Mori Media Cosmos (2011–15), in Gifu, Japan, and National Taichung Theater, currently under construction. Following the Great East Japan Earthquake in 2011, Ito started Home-for-All, a reconstruction initiative to provide buildings for impacted communities. Ito has been a visiting professor at Harvard Graduate School of Design, University of Tokyo, Columbia University, University of California, Los Angeles, Kyoto University, and Tama Art University. His writings have been widely published and his work broadly exhibited, including in *Toyo Ito: Generative Order* (2008) at the Taipei Fine Arts Museum. Ito has received numerous international awards including the 2013 Pritzker Architecture Prize, the Golden Lion for Lifetime Achievement at the eighth International Architecture Exhibition, La Biennale di Venezia, the 2010 Praemium Imperiale, and the Royal Gold Medal from the Royal Institute of British Architects in 2006.

Kazuyo Sejima (born Ibaraki, 1956)
Kazuyo Sejima & Associates
(established Tokyo, 1987)
SANAA (established Tokyo, 1995)

Kazuyo Sejima studied architecture at Japan Women's University before working in the offices of Toyo Ito. Sejima established her own studio, Kazuyo Sejima & Associates, in Tokyo in 1987. Her significant early projects include Saishunkan Seiyaku Women's Dormitory (1990–91), in Kumamoto, Villa in the Forest (1992–94), in Chino, and Police Box (1994), in Tokyo. With Ryue Nishizawa, Sejima founded SANAA (Sejima and Nishizawa and Associates) in 1995. SANAA's recent projects include Grace Farms, in New Canaan, Connecticut, and Okayama University Café, in Japan, both completed in 2015. Both Sejima and Nishizawa maintain individual practices parallel to SANAA, which have achieved international recognition and are often sites of intensely experimental work. Sejima's recent work includes Inujima Art House Project (2008–10) and Nakamachi Terrace Community Center and Library (2010–14). She has taught at Princeton University and École polytechnique fédérale de Lausanne, and is currently a visiting professor at Tama Art University, Japan Women's University, Kanazawa College of Art, Okayama University, Keio University, and University of Applied Arts Vienna, Austria. In 2010, Sejima and Nishizawa were corecipients of the Pritzker Architecture Prize. They have also been awarded the Golden Lion award at the ninth International Architecture Exhibition, La Biennale di Venezia, in 2004, the Kunstpreis Berlin from the Berlin Academy of Arts, in 2007, and the Rolf Schock Visual Arts Prize, in 2008.

Ryue Nishizawa (born Kanagawa, 1966)
Office of Ryue Nishizawa
(established Tokyo, 1997)
SANAA (established Tokyo, 1995)

Ryue Nishizawa studied architecture at Yokohama National University while working in the offices of Toyo Ito & Associates, Architects. After graduation, he worked with Kazuyo Sejima at Kazuyo Sejima & Associates in Tokyo. With Sejima, Nishizawa founded SANAA (Sejima and Nishizawa and Associates) in 1995. In 1997, he founded Office of Ryue Nishizawa, maintaining this practice in parallel with SANAA. SANAA's proposal for Taichung City Cultural Center in Taiwan is currently in design and the firm has recently been selected to extend both the Art Gallery of New South Wales in Sydney, Australia, and the Shiga Museum of Art near Kyoto. Nishizawa's recent work includes Roof and Mushroom Pavilion, in Kyoto, completed in 2013, and Ikuta Church, in Kanagawa, completed in 2014. Nishizawa has taught at Princeton University, Harvard Graduate School of Design, and École polytechnique fédérale de Lausanne. He is currently a professor at Yokohama Graduate School of Architecture and a visiting professor at Kanazawa College of Art and Okayama University. In 2010, Nishizawa and Sejima were corecipients of the Pritzker Architecture Prize. They have also been awarded the Golden Lion award at the ninth International Architecture Exhibition, La Biennale di Venezi, in 2004, the Kunstpreis Berlin from the Berlin Academy of Arts, in 2007, and the Rolf Schock Visual Arts Prize, in 2008.

Biographies

Sou Fujimoto (born Hokkaido, 1971)
Sou Fujimoto Architects
(established Tokyo, 2000)

Sou Fujimoto studied architecture at University of Tokyo before establishing his own studio, Sou Fujimoto Architects, in 2000. His projects include Children's Centre for Psychiatric Rehabilitation (2003), in Hokkaido, Final Wooden House (2006–08), in Kuma-gun, Musashino Art University Museum and Library (2007–10), and the 2013 Serpentine Gallery Pavilion, in London. Fujimoto's recent work includes winning competition designs for École Polytechnique at Université Paris-Saclay and House of Hungarian Music in Budapest. Fujimoto has taught at Tokyo University of Science, University of Tokyo, Kyoto University, Keio University, and University of Wisconsin-Milwaukee, and was a judge at the World Architecture Festival in 2015. His writings have been published widely and his work exhibited internationally, most recently in *Sou Fujimoto: Futures of the Future* (2015), held at Toto Gallery and Shanghai Museum of Contemporary Art. He was awarded a Royal Institute of British Architects International Fellowship in 2012, and received the 2014 WSJ Magazine Architecture Innovator Award, 2013 Marcus Prize, and 2008 Private House award from the World Architecture Festival for Final Wooden House. He was corecipient of the Golden Lion at the thirteenth International Architecture Exhibition, La Biennale di Venezi, in 2012. In 2008, Fujimoto published *Primitive Future* (INAX, Tokyo), which became the year's bestselling architecture book.

Akihisa Hirata (born Osaka, 1971)
Akihisa Hirata Architecture Office
(established Tokyo, 2005)

Akihisa Hirata studied architecture at University of Tokyo and completed postgraduate studies at Kyoto University Graduate School of Engineering. He worked for Toyo Ito & Associates, Architects, from 1997 until 2005, when he founded Akihisa Hirata Architecture Office in Tokyo. Hirata's recent work includes the Higashi Totsuka Church (2015), in Yokohama, and Kotoriku Meguroku Collective Housing (2012–14), in Tokyo. He has lectured at Harvard Graduate School of Design, Bauhaus Dessau, and the Bartlett School of Architecture at University College, London. He is currently a part-time lecturer at Tohoku University, Kyoto University, University of Tokyo, and Tama Art University. In 2015, his work was shown at the Museum of Contemporary Art in Krakow and at the Triennale di Milano. An exhibition of his work, *Akihisa Hirata: Tangling*, was held at London's Architecture Foundation Project Space, in 2012, and at Grand Hornu Images, in Hornu, Belgium, in 2013. Hirata was a corecipient of the Golden Lion at the thirteenth International Architecture Exhibition, La Biennale di Venezi, in 2012, and has also been awarded the 2015 Colored Concrete Works Award, the 2012 Elita Design Award, ELLE DECO's Young Japanese Design Talent Award, in 2009, and the Japan Institute of Architects' 2008 New Face Award.

Junya Ishigami (born Kanagawa, 1974)
Junya.Ishigami + Associates
(established Tokyo, 2004)

Junya Ishigami studied architecture at Tokyo University of the Arts, receiving an MFA in 2000, before working at Kazuyo Sejima & Associates from 2000 to 2004. In 2004, he established Junya.Ishigami + Associates. Ishigami's acclaimed first building, Kanagawa Institute of Technology Workshop, received the 2009 Architectural Institute of Japan Prize. Recent work includes a commission for a public sculpture in Sydney, Cloud Arch, and a winning competition proposal for House of Peace (2014), a structure for Copenhagen's Nordhavn harbor. His work has been the subject of multiple publications and exhibitions including, most recently, the monograph *Junya Ishigami: How Small? How Vast? How Architecture Grows* (Hatje Cantz, 2014). Ishigami is currently an associate professor at Tohoku University in Sendai. In 2015, he taught at Princeton University School of Architecture, and in 2014, at Harvard Graduate School of Design. Ishigami's installation work includes Balloon (2007) at the Museum of Contemporary Art in Tokyo, and Architecture as Air: Study for Château la Coste (2010) at the twelfth International Architecture Exhibition, La Biennale di Venezi, which was awarded the Golden Lion and the Global Award for Sustainable Architecture and was exhibited in 2011 at the Barbican's Curve, a gallery space in London.

Colophon

Published in conjunction with the exhibition *A Japanese Constellation: Toyo Ito, SANAA, and Beyond*, at The Museum of Modern Art, New York, March 13–July 4, 2016. Organized by Pedro Gadanho, Director, Museum of Art, Architecture and Technology, Lisbon, with Phoebe Springstubb, Curatorial Assistant, Department of Architecture and Design, The Museum of Modern Art.

Major support for the exhibition is provided by the E. Rhodes and Leona B. Carpenter Foundation, The Japan Foundation, and Chris A. Wachenheim.

Generous funding is provided by Obayashi Corporation, Kajima Corporation, Shimizu Corporation, Takenaka Corporation, the Graham Foundation for Advanced Studies in the Fine Arts, Kumagai Gumi, and The Obayashi Foundation.

Additional support is provided by the MoMA Annual Exhibition Fund.

Special thanks to Muji.

Support for this publication is provided by the Dale S. and Norman Mills Leff Publication Fund.

Produced by the Department of Publications The Museum of Modern Art, New York
Christopher Hudson, Publisher
Chul R. Kim, Associate Publisher
David Frankel, Editorial Director
Marc Sapir, Production Director

Edited by Sarah Resnick
Designed by Edwin van Gelder at Mainstudio, Amsterdam
Production by Marc Sapir
Printed and bound by Gorenjski Tisk Storitve, Slovenia

This book is typeset in Founders Grotesk
The paper is 120 gsm Munken Polar Rough

"Magical Spatial Inversion," by Terunobu Fujimori, was translated from the Japanese by Dana Buntrock, pp. 73–76.
"New Architecture after History," by Taro Igarashi, was translated from the Japanese by Terrance Lejete, pp. 189–92

Published by The Museum of Modern Art
11 West 53 Street, New York, New York
10019-5497. www.moma.org

© 2016 The Museum of Modern Art, New York

Copyright credits for certain illustrations appear on page 255
All rights reserved

Distributed in the United States and Canada by ARTBOOK | D.A.P.
155 Sixth Avenue, New York, New York, 10013
www.artbook.com

Distributed outside the United States and Canada by Thames & Hudson Ltd.
181A High Holborn, London, WC1V 7QX
www.thamesandhudson.com

Library of Congress Control Number: 2015956789
ISBN: 978-1-63-345009-7
Printed in Slovenia

Front cover: Toyo Ito. Sendai Mediatheque. 1995–2001. See p. 22; Sou Fujimoto. House N. 2006–08. See p. 166; Akihisa Hirata. Bloomberg Pavilion, Museum of Contemporary Art Tokyo. 2010–11. See p. 204
Back cover: Ryue Nishizawa. Garden and House. 2006–11. See p. 158; Toyo Ito. Brugge Pavilion. 2000–2002. See p. 28; Akihisa Hirata. Showroom H Masuya. 2006–07. See p. 196
Flaps: SANAA. New Museum of Contemporary Art. 2003–07. See p. 120; Ryue Nishizawa. Garden and House. 2006–11. See p. 158

Image Credits

In reproducing the images contained in this publication, the Museum obtained the permission of the rights holders whenever possible. Should the Museum have been unable to locate the rights holder, notwithstanding good-faith efforts, it requests that any contact information concerning such rights holders be forwarded so that they may be contacted for future editions.

Photographs

© Akihisa Hirata Architecture Office: 15, right
© 2016 Artists Rights Society: 73, left
© Benoit Pailley: 122, bottom
© Christian Richters: 118
© Daici Ano: front cover, bottom; 56–57; 58, top; 154–55, 172–73; 174, bottom;
© David Vintiner: 253, left
© Dean Kaufman/Trunk Archive: front-cover flap, left; 120, 121; 75, right
© Iwan Baan: back-cover flap, top; front cover, top right; 42, top and bottom left; 48–49; 50, bottom; 58, bottom left; 60–61; 62; 64–66; 68–69; 84–86; 92, bottom; 94–95, 98–99; 100; 109, top; 112, 113; 122, top; 124–25, 128–29; 130; 152, bottom; 156; 158–59; 160; 166–68; 169; 170; 174, top; 176–78; 184–86; 247
© Ishiguro Photographic Institute: 44–45; 46, bottom left and bottom right
© junya.ishigami + associates: 191, 222–26; 230, bottom left and top; 232–33; 234; 240–41; 242, bottom left and top; 246, right
© Hibino Katsuhiko, Collection 21st Century Museum of Contemporary Art, Kanazawa: 110, top
© Kazuyo Sejima & Associates: 82; 88–89; 90, top; 91, top; 92, top; 96, bottom right
© Kentaro Tsukuba: 190, right
© Koji Taki: 189, right
© Luca Gabino: 253, middle
© Nacása & Partners Inc.: back cover, right and bottom left; 28–29; 30, bottom; 32–33, 36–38; 196–98
© Naoya Hatakeyama: front cover, top left; 22–25; 26, top; 75, left
© Office of Ryue Nishizawa: 140–41; 142, bottom; 144–47; 148; 152, top
© Ryuji Miyamoto / Courtesy of Taka Ishii Gallery Photography / Film, Tokyo: 189, left
© SANAA: back cover; 106–8; 109, bottom; 110, bottom; 114; 126, top and bottom right; 132–34
© Scott Norsworthy: 73, right
© Sou Fujimoto: 246, left
© SS Osaka Co., Ltd: 58, bottom right
© Takashi Homma: 80–81, 96, top and bottom left; 142, top
© Takashi Okamoto: 252, middle and right
© Takumi Ota: front cover, bottom; 204–5; 206
© Tasuku Amada: 253, right
© Teshima Art Museum: Noboru Morikawa: 150–51
© Tomio Ohashi: 46, top; 74, right; 75, left
© Toyo Ito & Associates, Architects: 26, bottom; 30, top; 34; 40–41; 42, bottom right; 50, top left and top right; 70, 252, left
© Walter Niedermayr. Courtesy: the artist and Galerie Nordenhake Berlin/Stockholm: 116–17, 248
© Yasushi Ichikawa: 15, middle; 228–29; 230, bottom right.

The Museum of Modern Art, Department of Imaging and Visual Resources: 12; Thomas Griesel: 11, right; nakatubotaeko: 161.

Drawings and Diagrams

© Akihisa Hirata Architecture Office: 199, 203, 207, 213, 217
© 2016 Artists Rights Society: 75, right
© junya.ishigami + associates: 227, 231, 235, 239, 243
© Kazuyo Sejima & Associates: 83, 87, 93, 97, 101
© Office of Ryue Nishizawa: 143, 149, 153, 157
© SANAA: 111, 115, 119, 123, 127, 131, 135
© Sou Fujimoto: 171, 175, 179, 183, 187
© Toyo Ito & Associates, Architects: 27, 31, 35, 39, 43, 47, 51; 54, top; 55, 59, 63, 67, 71.

Renderings

© Akihisa Hirata Architecture Office: 200–202, 210; 211; 212, bottom; 214–16
© junya.ishigami + associates: 236–37; 238; 242, bottom right
© kuramochi + oguma and Akihisa Hirata Architecture Office: 208–9; 212, top; © kuramochi + oguma (CG imaging), Toyo Ito & Associates, Architects: 52–53; 54, bottom
© Moreau Kusunoki Architectes: 11, left
© Sou Fujimoto: 180–83.

Board of Trustees

David Rockefeller*
Honorary Chairman

Ronald S. Lauder
Honorary Chairman

Robert B. Menschel*
Chairman Emeritus

Agnes Gund*
President Emerita

Donald B. Marron
President Emeritus

Jerry I. Speyer
Chairman

Leon D. Black
Co-Chairman

Marie-Josée Kravis
President

Sid R. Bass
Mimi Haas
Richard E. Salomon
Vice Chairmen

Glenn D. Lowry
Director

Richard E. Salomon
Treasurer

James Gara
Assistant Treasurer

Patty Lipshutz
Secretary

Wallis Annenberg
Lin Arison**
Sid R. Bass
Lawrence B. Benenson
Leon D. Black
Eli Broad*
Clarissa Alcock Bronfman
Patricia Phelps de Cisneros
Mrs. Jan Cowles**
Douglas S. Cramer*
Paula Crown
Lewis B. Cullman**
David Dechman
Glenn Dubin
Joel S. Ehrenkranz*
John Elkann
Laurence D. Fink
H.R.H. Duke Franz of Bavaria**
Glenn Fuhrman
Kathleen Fuld
Gianluigi Gabetti*
Howard Gardner
Maurice R. Greenberg**
Anne Dias Griffin
Agnes Gund*
Mimi Haas
Alexandra A. Herzan
Marlene Hess
Ronnie Heyman
AC Hudgins
Barbara Jakobson*
Werner H. Kramarsky*
Jill Kraus

Marie-Josée Kravis
June Noble Larkin*
Ronald S. Lauder
Thomas H. Lee
Michael Lynne
Donald B. Marron*
Wynton Marsalis**
Robert B. Menschel*
Khalil Muhammad
Philip S. Niarchos
James G. Niven
Peter Norton
Daniel S. Och
Maja Oeri
Richard E. Oldenburg**
Michael S. Ovitz
Ronald O. Perelman
Peter G. Peterson*
Emily Rauh Pulitzer*
David Rockefeller*
David Rockefeller, Jr.
Sharon Percy Rockefeller
Lord Rogers of Riverside**
Richard E. Salomon
Marcus Samuelsson
Ted Sann**
Anna Marie Shapiro*
Gilbert Silverman**
Anna Deavere Smith
Jerry I. Speyer
Ricardo Steinbruch
Daniel Sundheim
Yoshio Taniguchi**
Eugene V. Thaw**
Jeanne C. Thayer*
Alice M. Tisch
Joan Tisch*
Edgar Wachenheim III*
Gary Winnick

Ex Officio

Glenn D. Lowry
Director

Agnes Gund*
Chairman of the Board of MoMA PS1

Sharon Percy Rockefeller
President of The International Council

Tom Osborne and Ann Schaffer
Co-Chairmen of The Contemporary Arts Council

Bill de Blasio
Mayor of the City of New York

Scott M. Stringer
Comptroller of the City of New York

Melissa Mark-Viverito
Speaker of the Council of the City of New York

*Life Trustee
**Honorary Trustee